ESCAPE FROM CAMBODIA

By

SEREY S. TEP

Based on the life story of a Cambodian refugee who escaped from the communist after American force withdrawal and later became a US marine

Copyright © 2011 by Serey S. Tep

All rights reserved. No part of this book shall be reproduced, stored in a retrieval system, or transmitted by any means, electronic, mechanical, photocopying, recording, or otherwise, without written permission from the publisher. No patent liability is assumed with respect to the use of the information contained herein. Although every precaution has been taken in the preparation of this book, the publisher and the author assume no responsibility for errors or omissions. Neither is any liability assumed for damages resulting from the use of information contained herein.

ISBN 978-0-9837406-1-2

Published by Serey S. Tep at CREATE SPACE

NOTE: This book is based on the life story of the author. All names, places and events, which involved in this book were changed or never mention.

Preface

At the beginning of this book, when I started I couldn't bring myself to describe about me without going through a lot of emotion. So, I had to describe it as a part of a Cambodian refugee life that he had live through times, dimensions and places on this planet Earth. There were good times, bad times and the miserable worst of times; in 1971 after he lost both of his parents in the war and in the Cambodian Army when he was captured by the communist and chained to the pig pen left to die. He thank to a Goddess Avatar who came to the rescue, gave him hope and a will to live, and eventually she helped him escape; he'd named that Avatar " Sparkle Eye ". In the best of times were the sublime memorable times that he'd described the most in this book; they were the time when he made love to the Goddess Avatars. Yes why not?, his miserable life were full of sadness and sorrow, so he does not want to dwell in them because if he think too often about them it just like reap open old wound; there were lives disappear into the unknown. Loves were separated by circumstance, fade away and lost through times. In the US Marines Corps, it gave him a new beginning and a new perspective about the United States. Through times and dimensions, he had gain some and loose a lots but that's life, all he could do was to overcome, adapt and improvise.

All names and some locations in the story are changed or never mention to protect everyone involved; through the years I live in the US, I always tell part of the story to friends and coworkers during breaks, barbeque and beer in the backyard, hunting or fishing trip, and any gathering or many of the Super bowl games. Many people told me to write it down before I lost my mind or kick the bucket and take it with me down to the unknown. So by the encouragement of some friends, I tell the story of what I had been through, what I had seen in the event and passage of time that I live through, and the way I felt at that moment and dimension.

I apologize beforehand for any mistake in the book, since this is not a literary work of Shakespeare, and because I hadn't learned to speak or read and write English until I was in my twenty. And following the word of wisdom of a great uncle, I also had to sacrifice myself to learn English with my...... Well, it's in the book.

I dedicate this book to Victoria who
Encourage me to write this story
She is always in my thought
I was telepathically touched deeply
By the shadow of
This Goddess Avatar from afar
And a beautiful feeling that will never
Realize or written.

Escape from Cambodia

Contents

1- A Trip to the Jungle	9
2- Make Love Class 101	27
2A- First Goddess Avatar	31
3- New Found Knowledge	49
3A- Lady M	50
4- Vietnam War Spilled into Cambodia	57
4A- Benchmark 13	60
5- In the Cambodian Army	67
6- A Break from the War	79
6A- Lady S	80
6B- How to connect Baby Arms and Legs	84
6C- The Princesses	89
6D- The Mamasan	98
7- On the Bank of the Mekong River	103
7A- Princess Devy	109
8- Return to the Battle field	115
8A- Song Krear Mear	123
9- Divine Celestial Dancer	133
9A- Unexpected Goddess Avatar	144
10- Chained to the Pig Pen	149
10A- Sparkle Eye	154
11- The turning Point	169
12- Exodus	189
12A- Journey for Wisdom Quest	204
13- A Thai Chompa Angel	213
14- A Goddess Avatar	245
15- Global Celestial Nymphs	267
15A- The Crusader	==
15B- The Missionary Chaperone	270

15C- The English Teacher	273
15D- Latina Nymphs	279
16-Celestial Nymphs Continue	289
16A- Russian Connection	==
16B- Black Beauties	295
17- In the United States Marine Corps	303
17A- It's not just a Job It's an Adventure	305
18- Tour of Duty	313
18A- Okinawa	==
18B- Japanese Cherry Blossom	318
18C- Feast with the Men of the Imperial Navy	322
18D- The Love Motel 328	

C1-A Trip to the Jungle

Looking through the bus windows, the gray mountain range blended in the horizon ahead. Alongside the national route toddy palm trees grown tall on the rice field dike, lakes, rivers and villages raced back as the bus moved forward toward the Northern Province. The excitement welled up in Virak's heart, he could not wait to set foot on those enchanted forest. Ever since he can remember, it was home where his heart belongs. In the capital city of Phnom Penh, the home where he lived with his parents, he considered it as a temporary lodging while he was going to school there.

Yesterday was the last school day before the long summer vacation; last night, as it's happened before almost every year Virak was so impatient waiting for the sunrise that he could not fall asleep. Today, now that he was on the northbound bus the excitement and the drowsiness make him feel like a dream. A few weeks before school closed, he received a wish list and some gold from his grandfather. Yes, then gold was a currency of choice anywhere. The year was 1969; even though he was already grownup his mother still think that he was too young to handle the gold and the wish list, so it was natural that his mother normally managed it every time it was brought there by his grandfather's servants. His mother sat high on a shiny hard wood platform, chewed a mouthful of beetle nut and spitted juice in a brass spittoon. She was instructing and pointing to her servants who sat around on the colorful reed mat covered floor. Every year, when she read the wish list, my mother always shook her head to express her disapproval.

"Your grandfather wants ten cases of Manat water (Banana extracted flavored carbonated water) And twenty boxes of imported cigar, ten cases of Neguita rum, ten cases of Hennessey cognac and twenty cases of Tiger beer" Then, she exclaimed "How in the world does he know about all these things, he never set foot outside that jungle" She sight and continued "And this Number Four want ten bundles of saffron color silk cloth with gold thread" She looked up at Virak and said.

"Is she become a Supreme Lady now"

"Yes mother, his third wife died last year" She shook her head.

"It just that she has a smidgen of the lost empire royal blood line she think that she still lives in a palace. And Number Five, Number Six, Number Seven, and Number Eight she wants what?!! Number Eight? One wife just dies so he has room to add another one?!!"

"I had asked him when I was there last year, and, he said that Number Eight was offered to him by the chief of the distant sub clan for peace, protection and harmony among relatives" She looked sharply at Virak and groaned.

"Oh Lord! He had polluted your mind! By the way, they are not Numbers, they are ladies, and they do have names. You need to tell him or whoever wrote this"

"Yes, mother, I will..." He replied, and started to walk out of the room.

"Wait a minute, get back here, and who is this on the list here and the name Sunthary Devy, who is she? She want five pairs of laced panty and bra, and they mentioned that you know her size, do you? And how do you know her bra and panty size?" Virak hesitated a moment and said.

"Oh! ... Sunthary, she is a widow left behind by a dead hunter-warrior, she stay at Grandfather's house and she's taking care of my place. I don't know her size; I never really pay much attention to her. They say, she is in mourning, and she always wrapped herself with a dark loose cape" His mother frowned.

"Why a widow, who always wear a loose dark cape want five pairs of laced bra and panty for in the jungle?" Virak tried to defend Sunthary.

"May be she want all these things to keep out bugs and geckos".

Everybody in the room broke out laughing except his mother, who looked at him with a stern face and pointed to the door. He just smiled and left the room. On the bus Virak put on a kaki jacket, leaned back and closed his eyes tried to get some sleep, but the road was getting bumpy that made the bus rocking like a boat. Virak did not think that he could get any sleep then suddenly, Sunthary appeared in his thought, a woman covered in loose dark cape, everybody said she was a very pretty woman, but he came to realized that he did not know what she was really look like. She looked a few years older than him and she kept to herself in the old nanny chamber beside his room. Most of the time, they were only exchanged a few words and he never really took a good look at her. He questioned himself, did he treated her like a servant? He didn't think so; he thought he gave her some space because she was in mourning. Besides, he was always busy from dawn to dust everyday in the jungle village. She was there taking care of his place because of his grandfather intervention. People said at the time when her husband died, many hunter-warriors fought among themselves trying to possess her because she was an unusual exceptional beauty and descended from the royal blood line of the old empire. His grandfather put a stop to it by brought her to live in his compound, and told everybody to back off because she was in mourning. He let her lived in the old nanny chamber next to his place because it's always empty most of the year. She took upon herself the responsibilities to keep up his place, and served him when he was there last year. His friends in the jungle told him that how lucky he was to have such a beauty lived nearby every day, he never said anything or gave them any notion about her, even though they kept asking him about her look, her curves and her smell. Oh, yes, her smell was unmistakably the "Wild Passion" orchid scent; it's one of many scents that people preserved in palm oil, because of its sublime smell, and it will be heighten and magnify if it smelled from a woman body. It will attract all the attention but yet it soothed and calms any soul; it created a good feeling, a sense of well being that the face almost smiles for no apparent reason. With a scent of a woman lingered in his mind, he closed his eyes and drifted away into the stratosphere. When he came to his sense, he felt the bus stop moving and everything were quiet. He slowly opened his eyes; saw the green surrounding with the dark trail under the tall canopies and the bamboo forest. He knew that he was at the point where the road end and the jungle begin. Vicheyear was one of Virak's grandfather most trusted assistant who woke him up and told him.

"Let us mount the elephant and get to the first overnight camp before nightfall"

Virak was eagerly stepping out of the bus, went toward his favorite elephant Rama. Next to the road, there were a dozen elephants came along side the bus where a group of worker loaded all the boxes, cases, and packages into the baskets and the platform on back of the elephant. After they finished loading everything and moved from the road a little distant; Vicheyear ordered the elephant Colum to stop on the trail and everyone including Virak took off all of their town clothes and put on the jungle garbs, it's just like they'd shed civilization and embraced the wild. They pulled out their weapons from the storage under the platform, and wore them proudly, Vicheyear handed Virak a short sword that he received it with a nod of acknowledgment.

Despite the weight on their back the elephants moved swiftly on the jungle floor through the dark trail toward the mountain; it just like they tried to move away from the civilization in a hurry into the jungle where they could feel safer and more at home. On the few front elephant, the hunters trained their crossbow at the jungle looking for some games which will appear on the menu tonight at the overnight camp. Their diet on the jungle trail consisted of the small games like midget deer, snake, bird, rabbit or monkey. The overnight camp was a strategic position that was chosen by Vicheyear; it's a small clearing on the river bank, at the back was lined with the impenetrable bamboo forest; it's only one way in and out where they set a huge bonfire to announce their present in the jungle. They unloaded some heavy pieces from the elephants back, and all hands help to set up camp. The men erected the temporary shelters, feed the elephants, and gathered firewood. The women took turn to cook and bath in the river. When the food were done, they sat around the camp fire, ate their meal and reminisced about the trip to town and many other subjects late into the night; they asked Virak about life in the city and the things were going on around the world, and he asked them about his grandfather and everything that happened in the jungle. They started to break up when it's getting late, some men and women went to sleep in the temporary shelter; some warriors and women, went up on the elephant to sleep on the platform. Virak laid quietly alone in the covered platform on Rama, looked at the stars in the dark night sky, listened to the call of the tiger and the women moaning on the elephants back.

Virak's first night in the jungle, he slept soundly devoid of dream. When he woke up in the morning, it was foggy and chilly; the elephants were already moving on the trail; the morning sky started to get out from the grip of the night by turning gray at the east. He sat up at the front edge of the platform, rolled the bamboo blind up; he could feel the chill air from the morning mist. He pulled a blanket to wrap it around his shoulder and moved his body back and forth, followed the movement of the elephant stride on their way to the next overnight camp. In late afternoon of the fourth day, they saw smoke rise about the forest canopies and were excited because they were close to their home. The warrior blew their horn to give the signal to the people in village.

The village was situated on a river bank where it was widened and looked just like a small lake; it fed by many tributaries from the higher plateau. At the center, there were a few tall long roofs, where they were served as a daily main meeting hall, a food processing and distributing center, and the main biggest roof was the ceremonial and reception hall. The road was branched out from the main center hall to many clusters of house that spread out into the jungle. The bamboo forest and tall old trees surrounded the house cluster throughout the village; in each cluster, people grove vegetable and fruit tree orchard, and raised some animal for food. There were clear open space between the main halls and the river bank; and at the river, there were many little coves of sandy beach in between the rocks and boulders.

The elephant Column moved slowly when it came near the center of the village, especially when it came near the food distribution center. At the ceremonial hall, Virak's grandfather and the rest of the clan who had their name on the wish list sat patiently watching the elephant column filed in and started to unload. Virak signaled Rama to kneel, grabbed a hold to his collar, stepped on his cocked foreleg, and slid down to the ground. When he looked up, the first person he saw was his grandfather who smiled broadly, stepped forward with his arm stretched out.

"Welcome! Welcome my grandson, the jungle spirit bless us all by bring you safely to us. How was your journey? Are you well?" Before Virak could answer him he turned to the Old Wise Men who chanted some Pali or Sanskrit verses that nobody could understand.

"Hey, Old Man remind me to make some Bujea to Lord Visnu you hear"

"Greeting, Grandfather, I am glad to see you in good health, and good spirit, with the blessing from the Lord Visnu may you live a long life" Virak put his hand together up to his forehead and bowed to him.

"Fine, now come, everyone eager to see you" Next Virak went to greet the Old Vise Man, and everyone in the hall last. Wife Number Four tried to distinguish herself from everybody else; she stopped Virak with her entourage in tow, rubbed the silk cloth with gold thread in her hand, and said out loud.

"Oh, my grandson, how can I thank you enough for your generosity that bless me with all these bundles, May our ancestor spirit of the ancient empire protected and nurtured you always" Virak's body turned half way already to take his leave; he smiled feebly and reminded her that she was not his grandmother.

"You are very welcome, wife Number four, enjoy your gift" She squinted her eyes, and quickly snapped.

"Grandma, is just fine"

"Ok, excuse me" With that note, Virak turned around, left the ceremonial hall while everybody was busy with their gift from the capital. At the entrance to the main hall of Grandfather compound, there stood Sunthary Devy, this time, Virak took a good look at her; he think, she look different from the last time he saw her in dark loose cape. She wore lacy bright color clothing, and greeted him with sparkle in her eyes and a soft smile on her face.

"Greeting, young master, how was your journey?" Virak was surprised.

"Hi Sunthary you never call me that before, why now?" She smiled softly, lowered her eyes, opened her rose petal lips, and spoke softly.

"Your grandfather protected me by put me to stay in the nanny chamber; I took upon myself to take care of your place because I need to do something to take my mind away from my miserable life. Later, after you return to the capital, I ask him to assign me my work and my place. He just told me to do what I am doing now, that is find. So, I think, I am your servant and, isn't that what they call you, master?

"Yes, which is what they call me and I don't like it at all. By the way, you are not my servant. He put you in the nanny chamber, maybe he think that I am still a little child, so now I don't need a nanny anymore, you can be a governess, a teacher, a caretaker; You can chose what you want to do but don't call me master anymore"

"Yes, master, I mean yes, I understand" Virak looked at her she just laughed playfully, he was glad that she was at ease with full of life. He didn't think she was in mourning anymore. He didn't ask her anything, he just enjoyed watching her being her own self. She carried herself with a dignify manner somewhat mature but she was fun to be with. Near the entrance to his area, the nanny chamber was secured with chain and padlock, they walked pass the chamber, she put her package on the floor, and proceed to come in his room to arrange it and he asked her.

"Why didn't you put your stuff in your chamber first? Before you set up mine?"

"This is not my room now; I don't have any key for that lock"

"I thought he let you stay in this room?"

"Yes, but after you returned to the capital, Supreme Lady told me to move to the servant quarter; she said since you were not here, so, I did not need to be in this room, I should be with the rest of the servant"

"Why didn't you ask Grandfather?"

"No, I did not want to bother him with just a small matter like this, and I accepted Supreme Lady's decision"

"Number Four, she should not have anything to do or say around my domain, whether I am here or not. Now, I want you to fetch all of your belonging and set yourself up in this place from now on"

"Yes, young master, but I don't have the key"

"Never mind about the key, didn't I told you not to call me that?"

"I am sorry, I cannot help because you order me, and act like a master would do"

"I am sorry, that I get carried away, I just want you to be comfortable in your chamber. Next time, please, remind me, or guide me ok"

She just smiled, said "Ok", and went toward the servant quarter. Virak went outside to look for an axe, he brought it back and swung at the lock, he kicked the door in and it swung open. Stepping inside the chamber, the room looked empty but he still could smell trace of the "Wild Passion" orchid scent. He was amazed and wondered of how long ago did she vacate this room? That her scent was still linger. He put the axe aside and walked into his area, her scent smelled much stronger in here than in the room outside, he guess, she spend more time in here. Virak felt tired but it's kind of relaxing, he lied down on the bed and tried to close his eyes. After finishing set up her belonging, she walked into his room; his mind was still half conscious, and his eyes was half close, he heard she said "Thank you", he acknowledged her by nodding his head , and drifted to sleep.

Virak thought he was sleeping but the sublime fragrance of her scent it's kind of captivated his attention. Virak turned his head and followed her movement, she kneeled by the pile of boxes and bags to arrange and sort them out; she wore a white short silk blouse and blue sky long silk skirt, under the mellow candle light, Virak looked at her long shiny black hair, her slender arms, her full breast, her small waist and her round rear end. Oh, Lord Siva, he felt like he was in a dream that an Apsara (The celestial dancer from heaven) came down from the bar relief wall of Angkor Wat, and drifted into his dimension in the flesh. Virak thought he paid too much attention to her in just a few short hours; he turned around and felt asleep with an erection that won't go away.

It's Virak's first morning in the jungle village, the sun shone so bright that mean he slept late. He stepped out of his bedroom after dressing up. Sunthary had already set up his morning meal, it consisted of a few oranges, and some baked wild potato, some spicy strips of broiled dry venison and a gourd full of water. It's a lot of food for one person.

"Come on, Sunthary have some of these, it's too much food for me alone"

"No thank you, I already ate, go ahead eat them, you are going to need it, because this is your first day back, it's going to be a lot of activities, your grandfather is waiting for you in his main hall. By the way, I overheard some servant said that the Supreme Lady is enraged and make a lot of noise in her wing of private quarter"

"What's going on with Number Four now? Is the silk cloth we bring, are not to her liking?"

"Or, maybe, because I move my belonging out of the servant quarter without her permission"

"Don't worry about that, I will see to that matter, and settle it once and for all. Stay in here, lock the door after I leave and don't open for anyone"

"Yes, I will do that" After finishing his morning meal, Virak put some venison strips in his pocket, and walk out toward the main hall, by the time he stepped through the door, wife Number Four and her entourage just filed out of the other door with a lot of noises. At one end of the main hall, his grandfather sat on a mat covered wood platform with Old Vise Man, Vicheyear and a few assistants sat nearby, when he saw Virak, he motioned him to come over with a broad smile on his face.

"Come, come, come son we are waiting for you. Our clan who live at the distant northeast village had bring us some ripe milk fruit, I knew you like them. Did you sleep well last night? It's must be a big change of place and habit right?"

"I slept just fine Grandfather, what was all that noises about with that Number Four?"

"Oh, her, that was nothing, we need to keep the peace and harmony in our domain, when your time come, you need to learn how to do that also"

"Yes, but she doesn't sound like she is in peace, isn't she?"

"It's a small matter; she complained about that you didn't inform her when you move some servant, did you move anybody?"

"Yes, I did, I move Sunthary Devy back to her chamber. She is not and never was a servant. Number Four should not have any business moving anyone in my domain"

"Yes, but since she is a Supreme Lady now you know"

"She is your Supreme Lady not mine, and she should realize that she is not my grandmother. It's time to learn her place from now on tell her to stay clear from my place. And one more thing, you keep Sunthary under your protection, by put her in my domain she is under my protection also, and now she is a governess who is taking care of my area"

"Yes, Ok, and what did you say a governess?"

"Yes a governess, it's just like a teacher, a caretaker"

"What can she teach? Very well so be it" He turned to the assistant to take note. All of his actions and decision were kept in a record book. Virak just grabbed some milk fruits and walked out of the main hall. At the river bank, there were many groups of young men and boys at various ages practiced martial art, weapon and marksmanship with crossbow. Virak went toward a group where all of them were his friends. They greeted each other excitingly.

A warrior-hunter got their attention, he was their master instructor for that day, and he instructed them to start the warm up exercise. Later, they ran around the field, swam in the river until they were so exhausted, and then, they started to practice martial art combat technique. After, they were dismissed by noon; they were so dead tired, sweaty and dirty. On a day like this, they jumped in the river to cool off and clean themselves up. Before they parted, Virak told some of his close friends to come to meet him at his place in the afternoon. Most of Virak's close friends were the son of the warriors and sub clan chiefs from the distant villages, which his grandfather allowed to stay there for training. At his place, Virak was resting in his room, suddenly, there were sound came from the outer edge of the compound, he knew his friends were coming, but he forgot to inform Sunthary about them, she strained her ears, sprung up, pulled her knife out, called his name, and raced toward the edge of the compound; before Virak could react, she already had the first guy by the hair with her knife pointed at his throat. Virak rushed out, and yelled.

"Stop right there! Sunthary let them come in they are my friend" She let him go, stepped aside, and watched everyone of them like a hawk, Virak smile, and brought them to the outer room with Sunthary watched from a distant behind the door. One guy said.

"I thought that a pretty woman like her, she suppose to be soft, demurred and docile, what is wrong with this one? She jump on us like a tigress, what did you do to her?"

"I did not do anything, and there is nothing wrong with her, she just taking care of this place, that is her duty"

"Duty Huh and what else can she do?" They all broke out laughing.

"All right you guy, she is a nice and a respectable lady; now I don't want to hear any of this again ever" At the outer room, Virak had them sat around, relaxed, had some Manat Water, and briefed him of everything were going on in the village and the whole territory. He wanted to know everything happened or going to happen. He never told them to do anything for him, but it seem like they had keen eyes for things that interest Virak, and the things that he should know, for example, the action or reaction that happen inside the private quarter of wife Number Four. Before sunset, most of the villagers went to take their bath in the river, they separated a private cove for women and girls up river, a place for families, and the rest were for everybody else. After the evening meal, the villagers sat around the bond fire under the big roof or at the house cluster. All young women and girls, they learned to cook, do the house choir, and take care of children, read and write and learn some martial art from the older women. For men and boys, we listened to elders or Old Wise Man, who reminisce stories about the thing they heard from around the territory, the world, and the great battles from the long lost "Angkor Empire". Virak's circle of friend, they learned to read, write, hunt, fish, track, and kill among other.

One night his grandfather called him aside, and they went into his private court yard, under the moonlight, Virak still could see the shooting stars, and giant fruit bats were crisscrossing the night sky. His grandfather lit a cigar, blew out some smoke, sight deeply, looked away to the distant mountain, and began to narrate.

"Many centuries ago, we were a part of a great empire. We lived at the center of the Khmer civilization. We received some of our custom, tradition and religion from India long ago before the birth of the "Angkor Empire", under the reign of the long line of the great king "Varman" dynasty. The empire was so waste, the frontier was from China in the north to Malayou (Malaysia) at the south and from Pumea (Burma) in the west to the Sea at the east. The empire started to crumble even before the Angkor Wat was build. First, the Cham invaded from the sea and succeed in the creation of Champa Kingdom (Present day Central Vietnam). Later on, the Siem (Thai), the Yourn (Viet), and the Liev (Lao), they moved down from the Southern China, requested asylum and asked permission from the Varman king to live at the edge of the empire. The three groups were a big help for the empire to wage war against the Champa kingdom. Later the Siam and the Lao adopted the empire custom, religion. The Yourn kept pushing the Champa kingdom with the help from the Khmer empire; they succeed in the elimination of Champa kingdom from the world map.

After the last king of the Varman line, the empire was in declined from infighting. In those days sometime the empire divided into three or four kingdoms. A Khmer (Cambodian) king, the descendant from a guard of the sweet melon patch, let the Yourn used the land along the eastern shore line, today we lost those land to the Yourn forever. The last fragment of the Khmer kingdom shrunk into a small country that almost land lock. Even now a day, I still feel like, we were shrinking smaller and smaller. The foreigners, the wars, the new machines and weaponries appeared closer into our land every day. I think we might see the same fate as Champa in the near future" He trailed off into silent with a puff of smoke; and Virak asked him.

"Grandfather, I know all about the Siam the Yourn through the history class in the lower land school. What about us? They say we are the remnant of the empire. Why do we end up out here in the middle of the jungle and try to live like the jungle people? Why didn't we go back to Join the empire"

"Well it was a long story. Let we go to sleep, tomorrow, I will have Old Wise Man tell you all about it" In that afternoon, Sunthary overheard Virak when he told about the Wise Man story; she expressed her interest and asked to come along. At a corner of the ceremonial hall, they sat patiently waiting for the Old Wise Man. When he came out from the inner sanctum of his temple, he had a bundle wrapped with silk cloth under his arm, he made himself comfortable, leaned back, chew a mouthful of beetle nut, and looked at us one by one, and when he looked at Sunthary on the other side, he was kind of surprise.

"Oh, is that you?" And she replied.

"Yes, just me on this side, Ancient One, if you don't mind"

"No, no, not at all my child, you are welcome to be here, its matter of fact you have the right to be here because the history involve your ancestor as well"

"Thank you Ancient One" His brows came together, it's just like he was in a deep concentration, and he rose his head, looked blankly into the darkness of the jungle, and he began.

"The great Angkor Empire was so waste, its civilization was at its apex dominant in the region, there were only kings of the Varman line could ascended the throne, ever since "Queen Soma" of the Island Mountain kingdom called Chenla. There were many great princes, princesses and generals, who ruled in small vassal kingdoms all over the empire, and they all competed for more power, territory, and favor from the Varman king. It created bad tension among the royal family and top generals, the small incident popped up here and there, eventually, they became full fledge civil war, it weakened the empire. At that time, Buddhism started to gain strength throughout the empire; there were animosities between the old Hindu and the new Buddhist religion. Before the spread of Buddhism, the empire strength was made from the line of fierce warrior and the victorious Varman king.

Every Varman king who ascended the throne, raised great army, crushed the enemy around the empire, and erected magnificent stone temples dedicated to the God who helped them achieved victory. On the wall of most monuments and temples, they depicted the great battle to commemorate their heroes. After Buddhism saturated throughout the empire, the society became pacified and tolerance. Under Buddhist doctrine, they must respect all life forms; they believed the killing of any life even animal is a great sin. So now the empire of the warrior became the empire of the farmer. When Buddhism became the religion of the mass, Hindu religion confined in the royal court as a ceremonial symbol only. The enemies of the empire started to attack everywhere, at one time in our history, the Cham succeed in sacking Angkor Wat before the Khmer realized that the empire was weakened.

One of my direct ancestors, who was a main Brahmin priest his holiness Lord Veravoin, was in Angkor Wat at the time it was invaded, he told the story as how it happened in battle, and how we end up here. The king and his warrior fought bravely to protect Angkor Wat, a retreat from Angkor was not an option, when the king realized that the situation became dire; he appointed a trusted general to get the royal family including the crown prince and the crown jewel to safety. The general was in charge of some five hundred mounted royal guards, they immediately moved a column of horse drawn light chariot toward the northern jungle. The chariot carried the queen, the crown prince, princes, princesses, fifty ladies in waiting, servants, and a unit of over two hundred women royal chamber guards, his holiness Veravoin along with an unspecified number of Hindu priests and their families, and the crown jewel was somewhere in there also.

At the end of the road, the general ordered everyone out of the chariot, and had the guard drove the chariots to many other directions, he knew that the Cham army were not far behind, they went to a hidden garrison nearby, it was a place to train and produce the elephants for the military. The jungle trails that lied further on from here, were the realm of the elephant and the jungle tribal people, so the general ordered everybody and everything, were loaded on the elephant back, and they continued their escape on down the jungle trail, but first, he ordered them to change from their uniforms, silk attires and jewelries to the simple people clothes. He had the guards went to every groups to teach them how to conceal their identities; they must learn to behave like the tribal people. The escapees traveled many days in the zigzag pattern off the normal jungle trail, and avoided the tribal territories. Sometime they decided to stop and set up camp but when the scout informed them about the Cham troop movements near their area, they then broke up camps, and moved out at a moment notice. On they moved to many places until the Cham decided to quit pursuing them and withdraw from the jungle sometime later.

The general decided to set up a semi permanent encampment, concealed themselves as a jungle tribal, and sent scouts to the lower land to gather information from all area of the empire. The jungle camp regularly received mostly bad news every now and then; they were informed how the Varman king and his warriors fought and died bravely to defend Angkor Vat. But one day, there was a good new about the king's brother raised an army to fight the Cham, and now he made head way to Angkor Vat.

A few years later, a big new was finally arrived, the king's brother had liberated Angkor Vat and the empire; the queen immediately ordered everyone to shed the drab color jungle garb, and put back on the uniform, silk attire and jewelry; she went to the river along with her entourage to purify themselves according to her great grandmother the princess Indra Devy's creeds, and she requested the Brahmin priest to set up Bujea on her behalf to the goddess Orma. At sunrise the very next day, she want the young crown prince took the crown jewel and went to Angkor to claim the throne, but the general did not like the idea, so he stopped the crown prince, and sent his scout to the capital to spread the word that the crown prince was still alive safe in some place.

Upon hearing the new, the king's brother made an announcement to invite the crown prince to come to claim his father throne; the announcement was received cheerfully at the jungle camp, the queen was so elated, and she ordered the crown prince and the Brahmin priest to take the crown jewel back to Angkor, but his Holiness Veravoin made a wise decision not to return with the crown prince, and he even advised the queen that was not safe to send the crown prince with the first contingent, despite all the advices, this is what she said.

"My son, go forth, claim your father throne, and after your ascension your first decree must be to build a road from the capital to this camp, and send the royal grand chariot to this place for my return trip because I will not ride on the back of those beasts ever again"

The young crown prince returned to Angkor Vat with the crown jewel, some assistant Brahmin priests, and some guards. The general dispatched some scouts to go along with the crown prince, and posted some along the jungle trail. Sometime later, the scouts informed the camp that the crown prince was dead; they heard that he fell on the sacred sword which was a part of the crown jewel, it stabbed through his heart by accident.

A few days later, the scout team on the jungle trail, informed the general that a sizable army advanced toward their camp. The general felt danger was eminent, and then he immediately ordered to break up the encampment, called everyone to a meeting, and he gave them two choices. The first one was to break up into small band and moved back to blend in with the society, and the second one was to follow him and the queen to retreat deep into the jungle.

Some of the guards, the lady guards and the servants decided to take other routes and return to the civilization. So the rest followed the general and the queen retreated deep into the dark jungle where the old forest and the bamboo forest grew. We had just moved to this place and formed a village just about two hundred years ago, before this they had moved many times to many places, some ancient elder said that at one time, we'd ventured into the realm of the invisible; do not ask me anything about it, I do not know for sure I just recite what I was told, because most of our imported records were destroyed by fire, element or attack. Yes we had been attack many times by the empire soldiers, the wild beasts, the wild spirits, and the wild tribes. That was why they had formed the warrior-hunter clan, who were the production of the royal guard and the lady chamber guard.

I am a descendant of the Brahmin spiritual clan; we are priest, shaman, medicine man, astrologer, scientist, and spy. We can move between the realm and territories, we possessed much knowledge that why your grandfather call me Old Wise One, right now I am not sure anymore with everything going on around the world, and the knowledge I receive everyday may not be enough to understand everything. All of the aristocrat and the chieftain are of the royal clan" And he turned to Sunthary "You too my child you are a descendant of the royal bloodline, your direct ancestor was the great queen Indra Devy, all of her daughter and granddaughter Must inherit the name Devy that was her decree, all Devy mother must bless their daughter by touch to the forehead and run their finger on the… You know the rest.

Throughout the century, there were many things we did that I should not mention here now until you all are more mature. Our clan survives for now but with the new world I don't know how long, it is up to you all younger generation to decide. When the white skin ghost people (The French) occupied the lower land kingdom, I thought that was the end of the Khmer (Cambodian) but later we realized that it was a blessing because it stopped the onslaught of the Yourn (Vietnamese) and the Siem (Thai). Now that the white clan left the kingdom but there are another black and white clan (American) is still wage war in the Yourn country; we do not know what the outcome will be; I heard the Khmer king is at the lost, if he do not play his card right it will be the end of the last remnant of the Khmer. That enough for tonight, you all need to go to sleep; tomorrow will be another busy day"

C2- Making Love Class 101

After a week of living in the village his life became routine, Virak adjusted very well and very quickly to the jungle way. Virak and his friends had permission from the lead hunter to come along on a hunting expedition. The trip was only a few days; it was cut short because his grandfather told them not to take Virak too far from the main village.

At the base camp of the hunting party, they enjoyed eating many kinds of small game fresh cooked meat; for every big game they killed, they will have a feast that evening around the camp fire, and the next day, the rest of the meat will be preserved by smoke dried, salted and sundried. There were no woman allowed to come along on the hunting trip, but on the fishing trip they did allowed lots of women to come; Virak asked the warriors.

"Why don't they allow women to come along on the hunting trip? And why do they allow them on the fishing?"

"Women are forbidden on the hunting expedition, it's a rule; for the fishing, they know how to clean fish better than us, and it is fun to have them around"

"Yes, I can see everybody look happier on the fishing trip, but why many of the women are moaning at night? Are they sick?"

"No, they are not sick, probably, they feel cold at night in the jungle, go to ask your grandfather he has eight wives, he might explain to you better than us" Virak did not quite understand the warrior's explanation, but an older friend said something that painted a different picture.

"A man and a woman, they make love when they sleep together, I saw they rub their genital together to get warm"

When the food supply were plentiful in the storage, everybody turned their attention to work around the village, they fixed houses, built a new one, repaired road throughout the village. The whole community was in the festive mood, they performed pujea ceremonies with dance and song, this is also the time for young men and women paid attention to each other with interest. That mean, it was time to arrange for married and a trip to the Honeymoon Field, yes, a honeymoon field (It's a name I appropriately gave it). It was a place where they went immediately after the married ceremony. The people said the couple will stayed there for a week, a month or more if they got no pressing engagement somewhere else, and most women and girls came back pregnant.

In everyday life or campfire the warriors always mentioned the name and the details of the place, and they may say. "Boy, you all got to work hard and train hard so that you might have a chance to go to the enchanted forest to taste the sweet sex nectar" and at that time, Virak thought what was this sex nectar? Did it ooze out from the tree? Could it be tasted sweeter than honey in this jungle?, then he accepted of what they said at its face value; and they said at the place there was no venomous snake or insect and no tiger, there were many clearing grassy knolls by the river bank, and were surrounded by tall old grove trees and bamboo forest. The small games like deer and rabbit were plentiful, and the river flowed with clear and cold water from the mountain in the high plane, there were flowers bloomed year round everywhere, the place looked mysteriously foggy despite the sunny and clear sky, and it was just like hanging in the cloud where the spirit dwelled" Virak asked them why they didn't build the village there since it sounded so nice. They told him that it was forbidden by the queen decree ever since it was visited by her and the general. Virak tried to understand so he asked.

"And what did the queen and the general doing there?"

"You ask too many questions, I do not know everything, it was happened long time ago"

Tonight they knew it's going to be a big joint married ceremony, because they made a big bonfire near the ceremonial hall. Old Wise Man who was customary at the center of the ceremony, but now he let the other Brahmin priest performed most of the functions around the village, he rather sat in the ceremonial hall with Virak's grandfather and a few elders who smoked cigar and sipping cognac. At another corner of the hall, there were groups of women and children sat around watching the ceremony outside, a few distant away from the group Sunthary sat by herself, wrapped around with dark cape, and watched the function with her heavy sad face. Virak understood how she felt, and he felt sorry for her. Virak's grandfather tried to get his attention, and motioned him to come to sit nearby and tried to explain about the married ceremony.

"Do you see how fun it is to get married? The boys and girls, they sing and dance to show their emotions and how they feel about each other, and that is love" There were hundreds of young men and women sang and danced around the bonfire but only the front line that will get married that night, the young men tried to pass a bouquet of flower to the girls, and when she accepted they were engaged. In the past years, there was more than one girl accepted one guy, but I had never seen a girl accepted more than one guy. Early long ago, parents preferred their sons and daughters married within their own clan, but later something happened, the health and the well being in the village were deteriorated, the chief, the elders and the priest had consulted with the divine spirit, and the answer was the spirit was upset that the equilibrium in the net of our society was not at the balance; they were not supposed to get married only within their own clan or village, they must infused fresh blood into the net of our society, so the solution was to kidnap young men and women from the distant territories and tribes, and got them married with our own people; that was how we adapted to tribal life and survived. As a result today, our people have many shades of complexion and features"

"And after they got engaged, what do they do next?"

"They will go through some Hindu ritual and the ancient Khmer custom, as you see now they are walking around the fire while the priest was chanting, and after the priest announced them husband and wife, they ask the elders for blessing"

The newlywed couple came to kneel and bow in front of the elders who chanted the blessing in unison and threw flowers over them. The second the chanting stopped, the couple sprung up in a flash and dashed out into the night at a break neck speed. It took Virak by surprise, and he asked his grandfather.

"What is happening now? Why they are in a hurry?"

"What? Oh that" all the elders broke out laughing "They are in a hurry to go to the Love Nectar Field to do their deed as husband and wife. Their parents already had set up an elephant stacked with food and supplies waiting for them at home, and the field is just a day ride from here" And then Virak's grandfather turned to him.

"Do you have any girl in mind? If not, I want you to pick some girl from any village to get married. Look son, I am sixty years old now, and I don't know how many more years that I still breathing. I want to see my great-grandson before I leave this world, because I want to assure that my line will continue"

"I don't know Grandfather, I think; I am still too young to get married by the lower land custom"

"No, you are not too young and you are not in the lower land, I was a little younger than you when I married my first two wives. As the chief's grandson, you don't concern about any responsibility, and your only duty for now is to produce some heir"

"I will have to think about it Grandfather" Virak stepped back to a corner, leaned on a pole, and observed the ceremony from a distant. His grandfather and Old Wise Man got into deep discussion in between the blessing to each couple, they whispered in each other ear, looked at Virak's direction and then at Sunthary, and finally they looked at each other and nodded their head. The ceremony finally came to an end with the last couple took off like an arrow, Virak hope they won't get hurt by bumping into the elephant ass in the dark, before they could do their deed as husband and wife in the field of love nectar.

First Goddess Avatar

A week later, Sunthary woke him up very early in the morning, Virak looked out through the window at the eastern sky it was still dark, he turned to Sunthary and asked her.

"Why are we getting up so early?"

"Get up now, please, we have to go to a place away from the village for a while"

"Why?"

"At your grandfather instruction, I will tell you all about it when we get there, and we have to be underway before sunrise; let's go Ancient One and some warrior are waiting for us, you can sleep some more on the elephant" Virak did not want to argue with her despite the tiredness from yesterday practice, he got up, went to freshen up a little bit, got dress and follow her outside. A column of elephants were waiting for them, a few in the front that were already loaded, the last one was empty so some warriors signaled it to kneel, and loaded their supply into the basket, then they climbed on board the platform.

The front elephant started to move forward, and then they signaled theirs to follow, the column of elephant moved forward quietly while the village streets were still empty. The platform and the basket were made from woven rattan cane and liana wine, inside the platform was laid with bamboo strips, it was big enough for two persons lay down side by side, the roof was covered with skin or palm leaves, and there were bamboo blinds hung on the front and rear. They sat at the opposite end of the platform so their bodies swung from side to side followed the elephant walking movement, it's made him feel drowsy, and so Virak slide down the bamboo mat and felt asleep.

When Virak was awake later on he still feel the rocking motion of the elephant, he knew they were still underway on the trail, opened his eyes to the bright sunny day outside, he could see sun rays that shone through the gap of the bamboo blind. After adjusting his eyes to the darkness in the basket, he turned to one side and came to face Sunthary naked knees, her skirt must have been hike up during her sleep, he looked down from underneath and saw her breasts rise and fallen follow her breathing.

Suddenly! She turned on her back, raised one knee up that made her skirt hike up some more that showed her thigh; out of his curiosity, Virak raised his head a little and moved closer to look right into between her legs. Oh! Lord Siva! Behold a magnificent sight that he never saw before in his entire life as long as he can remember, least of all to see up close like this. She was naked underneath like a jay bird, Virak guessed maybe somebody did not order and fulfill her wish list, he remember she had asked for some bra and panty, or maybe Number Four took them all.

He came to think about that, it was all right, if she never receive them that was just fine, Look here! Right in front of him! What a divine glorious sight. Virak bended his neck to observe closer, he could see a small patch of black hair on the top of two thick pink smooth lips, in between those gaps there was something elongated sticking out, it looked like a tamarind seed, so this must be what it look like, the woman tamarind seed (Clitoris) that his older friends in the city always mentioned about.

Virak could smell the wild passion orchid scent from between her thighs so strong, so sublime. The sight and the smell, made his heart beat faster and an instant raging erection. Virak felt dizzy and a tight knot in his abdomen muscle. Virak wondered what was wrong with him, was he felt sick from excitements; it was almost like a bad fever, he never felt exited like this before in his life, is this normal that a sight of the gap in between a woman legs could has this much impact?. Suddenly, his excitement was cut short by her movement when she stirred, dropped her knee, closed her thighs, sat up, and pulled her skirt down. Virak closed his eyes quickly and acted like he just woke up a moment later, he sat up, stretched and said his greeting to her, she replied but with a concerned look on her face.

"Good morning, you were shaking in your sleep and hold your stomach, are you all right?"

"I'm fine it was a good morning nap" She moved closer and put her soft hand to feel his cheek, his forehead, his chest and his abdomen, then she was started like she got an electric shock when her wrist brushed with the tip of the tent pole in between his legs, she retreated quickly to her corner, and pulled her wraparound to cover her red face. She sat folding her legs under and laid out their morning meal with some wild game meat, baked sweet and wild potato, oranges and water in the gourd; they ate quietly and looked at the scenery along the forest. The trail snaked its way up to the higher plateau, Virak can see and feel the changing in the surrounding jungle and in the air; the vegetations were different from the forest in the lower plateau, there were under clear blue sky with the sun shined over head but the surrounding forest was shrouded in the mist.

They came to stop at a crossroad, the Old Vise man came on board, the other elephants moved through a dark corridor on an unmark trail disappeared into the jungle, the Old Vise one turned the elephant onto the other trail toward the mountain. After a few hours later, he made frequent stop, got off the elephant and wondered into the forest.

"What is he doing there Sunthary?"

"I don't know, maybe he gather the ingredients for his medicine, please, don't ask me too many questions now, you will know everything by the time we return back to the village" Virak thought, he was being impatient with all these mysteries unfolding so slowly, but he seemed to realize that whatever will happen it may involve him and it might change his life forever.

At some stop, the Ancient One dug up some roots, and at the next, he pulled out a small hoop net and tried to catch the insects among the flowers. Finally, they returned back to the crossroad, the elephant just went straight into the dark corridor where the other elephants went through. Along the way, Wise Man called Sunthary to come near him and gave her a package wrapped in leaves, and explained some instruction in her ear. Since this was not concern him, Virak stepped out behind the platform, dropped the blind and tried to urinate without getting off the elephant, he was just careful not to wet it back, and he crawled back into the platform, lay down and closed his eyes.

Virak woke up to the rustled sound of the bamboo leaves, he sat up, rolled all the blinds and the side cover dear skin, looking around in this grassy knoll clearing by the river bank, it was surrounded by old trees and bamboo forest, flowers bloomed everywhere, the myriad fragrances of the wild flower accompanied by the sound of the cicada that flowed down from the high canopy, it filled the air and saturated into the mind. The elephant fed itself with those tender bamboo shoots and wild flowers; it went to the river to drink the cold clear water that flowed from the mountain, Virak think this is the place that the warrior were talking so much about.

On this part of the river bank, there was a long sandy beach that lined with rocks and boulder along the water edge, thirty yards from the water edge, the warrior built the shelter from small tree, bamboo, liana wine and varieties of leaves, they must had finished it by the time they get here because everything were still look fresh; the shelter consisted of two roofs, a lower close shelter and a taller open shelter that connected to each other, the open shelter had a fire hast that was already burning at the center of the sitting platform that made from bamboo along the two side of the shelter edge.

Sunthary called the elephant to come near the roof, so they could unload everything from its back. After setting everything under the tall roof, Sunthary started to set up their meal on the sitting platform near the fire; they got roasted rabbit, green papaya salad, baked sweet potato and pumpkin, hot chili and garlic sauce, and the Manat water.

After lunch, they sat around the fire, Virak looked around to observe the surrounding area while Sunthary could not sit still, she adjusted the roasted meat on the fire, checked the boiling clay pot, inside it was the leaves package that the Wise Man gave to her on the elephant. She seemed restless, Virak saw a frown between her eyebrows, and he guessed she had a lot of things in her mind. Virak had a lot of unanswered questions, but he was told not to ask too many questions, he thought he could try to beat around the bush but he did not know where to begin, he started to move around slowly under the roof, looked around and asked her.

"Is this the place where the newlyweds come after the ceremony?"

"Yes, there are a lot of beautiful spots like this one all over this plateau"

"You seem to know this territory very well"

"Of course, since my late husband shoved me lots of places around this plateau, when we came to…… Oh please, do not make me think about the past any more, I try to burry everything behind after my mourning"

"I am sorry Sunthary, I didn't mean to make you upset, I think it's alright and nice to keep remembering beautiful loving memory, but just don't cry over it too much or too long when you lost it, that's what Grandfather said"

"Thank to your grandfather, he is a wise man, I am forever in dept to him that's why I am here. And you, you probably wonder why we are here in this honeymoon field?"

"Oh yes, you'd just read my mind, and why we are here?"

"Because your grandfather asks me to show you uh… no, to teach you uh … Did he say anything to you?"

"Yes, he told me to get married, he want to see his great grandson, his heir"

"Ok, that is what he want me to teach you about. Do you know what man and woman do after they get married?"

"Yes of course, I know my friends told me, they said that the married couple, they sleep together in the same bed, they embraces and they kiss; do you know in the city I saw Europeans couple kiss each other mouth to mouth not nose to cheek like the Asian. And for our people here, when they get back to the village from here most women get pregnant, eventually they deliver a baby, and they live happily as family, right?"

"Yes, but not that quite simple of just sleep together, embraces, or kiss. They make love"

"Is making love more complicate than that?"

"Yes and no, there are more than that but not just that, and it will not be too complicate at all. That's why your grandfather wants me to show you. It will not be like the married couple with the emotional involve. Do you understand? With us here, it's the physical part that will involve. You probably hear people talk about it or you have some idea about what we are going to do here. It will be between you and me alone, do you understand? You will not tell your friends or anyone else from this point on ever, ok, you must remember that.

From now on, it's up to you, if you don't want to do we will stop and forget about everything that's happened or taking place here, and if you want to continue we will keep talking about it, you can ask me any question and about anything, I will do my best to explain to you everything I know one way or the other" She paused for a moment, sat in front of him, looked straight into his eyes and asked.

"So, how do you feel? Is everything all right?"

"Yes, I'm all right"

"What do you want to do?"

"You are the teacher you tell me" Sunthary smiled broadly, her face lit up, she became energetic, and the lesson began.

"Very well, let's do it, the physical part of making love is just like animal instinct, I think the way they do it with no inhibition. You probably had seen dogs, cats or elephants copulated. The elder have said that what the animal do is just an instinct to reproduce, but for human we do it not just aim to reproduce only, most of the time we do it to satisfy our desire of pleasure.

When people make love most of the time we get undress to reveal our body, male and female look at each other body part, that may create the desire, and the desire urge our brain and our body to involve all of our senses like seeing, smelling, touching, tasting and hearing. The last part of love making and the highest point of the excitement is the orgasm. And that is it, if the married couple keep doing it at the right moment and condition the woman will get pregnant. Ok for now, just relaxed, don't think too much about it, your animal instinct will guide you most of the way, and you will know everything soon enough. Let us go to swim in the river, I want to wash off the trail dust, let we get in the room to change our clothes first"

With her last word, she got up, dragged Virak's hand and walked into the shack; inside the hunters had built a bed platform from bamboo and covered it with a thick hay mattress. Virak sat on the bed just like he tried to test the mattress, when he looked up at her she already had the top part of her body barred; he looked at a pair of round perky breast with her nipples pointed straight at him from a few feet away.

She continued to take off the rest of her clothes. Here again, his eyes glued to the triangle area between her legs, he saw again the black patch of hair on the top of a rising mount of thick lips; and of just looking at it, made his heart beat faster. When she finished undress, she looked at him, smiled, and came closer to stand between his legs, patted his cheek to shake him out of his frozen state.

"Come on, get undress, you will have plenty of time to look at me let's go to the river, I feel hot" Virak scrambled to get his clothes off; she gave him a silk krama (A thin silk cloth) to wrap around his waist while she did the same. Virak followed right behind her, observed the movement of her round rear end, her slim legs, her small waist and her barred back that covered with her shiny long black hair. At the river bank, she took off the krama, dropped it on a flat boulder at the water edge, stood fully naked like a river nymph, and motioned him to do the same. Virak followed her; they waded into deeper cold water and started to swim upstream slowly.

After a few minutes, she stopped, turned around, floated vertically and bumped right into him. His now stiff erection pushed right on her abdomen, and her hard nipples stabbed right on his chest, she put her hands on his shoulder, and he instinctively put his on her waist. Under the cold clear water, Virak saw her thighs opened up to wrap around his hip, and the tip of his erection slid madly between her warm thick gaps. They quietly and slowly floated downstream back to the spot where they dropped the krama, Virak's feet touched the shallow bottom rock, he walked up the shallow until her round breasts floated on the surface, he moved his arms down to support her butt up; she looked in his eyes still had her arms wrapped around his neck, her lips were just a few inches from his,

Virak slowly put his lips to hers, tilled his head to one side, their tongue slid in each other mouth, and they kissed tenderly for the first time. They seemed to lost track of time, she moaned softly, put her hand down between their bodies to feel his erection lightly; she suddenly disengaged from him and waded toward the bank.

"What's wrong Sunthary? What's going on?"

"No, nothing wrong, you have made a great progress, I forgot to take the medicine" At the fire hast, the clay pot with the leaves package inside was still boiling, Sunthary poured the hot dark red liquid into two bamboo cups and handed one to him, she sat naked on the bamboo bench sipping the hot liquid with a smile on her face, Virak stood in front of her still dripping wet sporting a raging hard on pointing at her. He asked her.

"What kind of medicine is that?"

"Oh, I am not sure, the Wise man did not say anything much, he just mentioned that's important we must take it the whole time we are here"

After she finished her medicine, she put her cup down, stood up, and dragged his hand into the close shelter. She crawled on the bed with her round butt stuck at his face, Virak watched at aw with her feminine form she laid down on her back, opened her legs to show her wet pink slit with all of its naked glories, and then she motioned him to come on the bed with her. And her lesson continued in earnest.

"Do you remember Love? What I'd said about the animal instinct, the inhibition in human love making, and now we got to be lovers in order to involve with all our mind and body just for now. We got to use our instinct and all our senses. Come here; come on make love to me…"

So, this was the first time in his life, laid naked in bed made love to a beautiful woman. Virak guessed he knew all the things that he need to know. He was instructed to control his urge and to go slowly, since here time moved slowly just like the flow of the river. Virak kneeled between her open thighs with his stiffed erected penis pointing at her wet pink gap. Then, he paused for a moment to savor every second to imprint her naked womanly form into his memory. Her long shiny black hair was spreading and radiating around on the straw mattress. Her brown eyes were half open, looked like she was in a drowsy state, her round breasts topped with the pink erected nipples were risen and fallen follow her breathing, her navel at the center of her small waist, was like a jewel above her smooth flat ab. In between her open legs, what captured his attention the most was her violet tamarind seed on the top and the pink membrane below along the slit...... Virak was so intoxicated with the smell of the Wild Passion Orchid from her warm body...... He looked into her eyes, she looked at him damped with tear, her lips quivered with some hissing sound, and she came with a loud cry that echoed far into the jungle.

"Thank to all Goddess and to you. Oh…It had been so long"

"And thank to you, because you are a very good teacher"

"By the grace of Goddess blessing, we all can become kind of natural born lover with the right partner in the right mood and the right environment"

Virak lay between her legs a while longer, until he decided to roll off to her side. Then they went to swim around in the river to cool off and came to sit on a flat smooth boulder that rises up a few inches above the water level, she came up to stand tall over his chest and then she squad down on...... They both spent at almost the same time with a shaking vibration and a loud cry that stirred a few birds and monkeys in the surrounding forest.

She lay her head down on his chest with her knees folded at his side and her butt stuck up in the air; suddenly, she cried out in pain and put her hand on her lower back, they looked up and saw a few shiny bugs flew back up to the high canopy. On her lower back, there were some red dots, Virak was alarmed and asked.

"What is that? I heard they said that there is no venomous animal around this plain"

"No, it does not feel like a venomous bug bite; let us go back to the shelter"

They finished cleanup, wrapped the silk krama around the waist and returned to the shelter. She immediately, started to prepare their evening meal, Virak told her not to bother with the ritual of the preparation of any elaborate meal, because there were only the two of them, all they needed to do was to cut the food and ate them by the fire, but she still cut up the roasted meat, prepared the fruit and vegetable; and she said that they don't want to live like the savage tribe; they can learn something from them for their survival, but they don't need to live like them one hundred percent. After the evening meal, they sat around the fire, drank the Manat water.

Virak noticed that her body was turning red all over, her breasts got bigger, her nipples pointed out longer, when he pulled her krama open he saw her sex swelled up twice the size that he saw an hour ago, and the clear liquid oozed out and dripping down her thigh, that made him feel concern and he asked her.

"Are you all right? How do you feel?"

"Those bugs are probably a rare kind of bug that the ancient people call them the Golden Love Bug. The stories were told among women in the village, they said it was mostly happen very rarely among women and most likely occurred in this region. Once bitten, the woman body will become thirst for sex all the time for the next seven to ten days, her desire and passion will burn very bright, she become insatiable, it will be contagious to any person who come to contact with her. I don't know everything that might happen to me, because there were many versions of stories and they were told like fairytales. So, I might need your help for the next seven to ten days"

"Anything at all that I can do to help, please tell me ahead of time, so I will be prepare"

"Very well, you may need to eat lots of food especially meat and wild potato in order to boost up your stamina, and you need to make love to me as much as you can for the next ten days. Can you do that?"

"I will do my best"

"One more thing, some story told that the bitten woman may die in agony if she could not be satisfy, in some story told that they need to bring more men from the village to help save the woman; so you will make the call before I become completely insane" She lit up an oil lamp and went toward the close shelter, Virak started to follow her but at the door she turned to him and said.

"I turn in now, and I need to lie down, because I have too much excitement in one day. You may stay out here a while longer if you want to"

"Ok, call me if you need anything"

Virak sat on the long bamboo bench by the fire, cut up some more roasted venison and monkey put on a bamboo woven plate lined with a piece of banana leaf, he used a stick to get some potato from under the ash, and poured himself a bamboo cup of hot liquid from the clay pot. He ate slowly looking around the shelter, he could see everything so clearly under the moonlight, the elephant was standing at the grassy knoll nearby, and the giant fruit bats were flying crisscross the summer night sky. The sound of insect mixed with the sound of water flowed among rocks and boulders in the river, and the bamboo leaves were rustling under the light breeze. All the flowers were still shown their grayish shadow under the moonlight; here, on this high plateau, the weather was comfortably cooler than in the city at the lower land. He added more log into the fire and checked on the roast meat; suddenly, Virak heard a faint moaning from within the closed shelter, he quickly went inside, and on the bed he saw Sunthary lay spreading on her back, her body covered with a thin cotton sheet, and she was moaning just like she was in pain; Virak came to her side.

"Are you all right? Are you in pain Love?"

"Yes, it's so painful but it feels so good. Oh...Goddess have mercy...be gentle please...I know I get what I'd prayed for"

"Are you talking to me or are you praying. Do you need anything? Or is there anything you want to do?"

"Just shut up. Yes, you that what I need...Sorry, make love to me now please" Virak slid on the bed next to her, pulled the sheet off, and he could not believe what he saw, her breasts and her sex were swollen, and turned beet red. An intense strong sweet aroma of her sex permeated the air inside the shelter Virak came to kneel between her wide open thighs…… At the next morning, when Virak woke up he found himself still lay prone between her legs, he sat up looking at her body that it seemed to reduce the swelling a little, but the sticky liquid still secreted from her red gap, he kissed her forehead, she stirred opened her eyes slowly.

"Good morning, thank you for your effort last night; oh…I am so tired, I guess you too"

"Good morning, I am all right, I did not work up so much like you did. Did you enjoy it?"

"Oh, Lord yes, it was heaven and I still feel it, let's go to get something to eat" They held on to each other and walked to the fire hast, she set up some meat and fruit, filled two bamboo cups with the hot liquid from the clay pot, and handed one to him, she motioned him to drink it up before the meal, Virak felt the warm wave coursed through his body and his penis extended to become a full erection, it was bigger and longer than usual that made her eyes glue to it; and then after the meal, she climbed on the bench and squad down over……

At the river, Virak wrapped his arms under her butt to support her and waded into the river while their sexes were still joining; at the shallow area in the water, they separated and while she performed their cleansing ceremony, he started to wash away their sex residues that the river will carry downstream to bless and anoint lovers in the faraway land all over the world beyond all the great oceans.

The morning jungle was still cold, they came up from the river to warm themselves by the fire hast, she sat on the bench and opened her legs wide to inspect her swollen gap, he came to kneel on the ground in front of her and looked closely at the swollen gap and he…... They had some more tea from the clay pot, and she mentioned to him that they should go into the forest to hunt, gather some food, and get themselves familiar with the surrounding area.

They grabbed a couple crossbows, thrown a woven basket across the elephant back, and they rode it toward another clearing that the hunter told them where to find food. In just a few hundred yards from their camp, they had already bagged a few rabbits. In a short distant from their camp, they found another clearing that full of fruit trees herbs and vegetables, the elephant came to stop under the mango tree where he could gorge those ripe fruits, they dismount and continued to roam around the clearing on foot, and they decided that she will gather vegetable and he will find ripe fruit.

Virak went around the edge of the clearing to find the fruit tree; he'd pick a big ripe jackfruit, some mangos, mangosteens, chompou, milk fruits and guavas, there were a lot of pomegranates but they were still too green. When he returned to the vegetable garden with a heavy load of ripe fruit, he saw Sunthary was on her knee trying to dig up some wild potato, and the crotch of her loin cloth was soaking wet from the clear liquid that oozed out from her sex continuously. He kneeled behind her, pushed her head down and pulled the loin cloth aside......

After they'd finished, they got up quickly, adjusted their loin cloth, loaded all the stuffs that they'd gathered into the basket that hung across the elephant back and rode it back to camp. At the camp, they went to the river to swim and make love some more before noon meal. Virak suggested they took an afternoon nap after the meal, he walked behind her with his hands on her waist and help her to get on the bed; she lay on her back, turn to smile at him, and closed her eyes to fall asleep immediately. Virak lay beside her, watched her nipples rise and fall and drifting away himself.

When he opened his eyes Sunthary was already awake, she looked out through the window to the far side bank, it seemed like her mind was million miles away. He lay on his side facing her with one hand on her chest; she spread her legs over his hip to cool off her swollen gap. Virak started to talk to take his mind away from her steaming hot sex for a while.

"Why I never heard anyone mention about this bug in the village before?"

"My mother said, the bug bit mostly women, and it rarely happen, it may occur once every ten or twenty years and that's why it was known only among women just like a fairy tale. I think men feel intimidated when face with strange, strong, sex drives women and that's why they don't want to talk about it. For women, it's a badge of honor, I feel grateful to be a lucky few who get bitten, and the one among us was the Queen mother herself who was the first to experience the affect of the Love Bug's bite"

"Wait a minute the queen! I thought she died from grieves after her husband and her son were killed"

"Yes and no, they said she lost her mind with grief and when the general heard about this beautiful place from the hunters; he thought that she might get well again if she can get her mind off from her misery, so he brought her here, I don't know where exactly. And they said that after the first week, she was still weeping and moping, and she won't come out from the shelter. The general got mad; first he ordered everybody out of the camp and went to wait for them on the road. He begs her to come outside to sit by the fire, but the queen refused and requested for her servants to bring her some water.

The general believe she was mad that she could not realize that she was no longer queen in the palace; she got to wake up and accept the reality. So he dragged her to the river and thrown her in the cold water, she got out of the water yelling and cursing, he ripped all her silk finery off and thrown her back into the river naked. He left her there and returned to the shelter, and when he came back to look for her he saw she laid on a boulder with her body turned red and her legs speeded open wide. Then when they return back to the village a month later, the queen was pregnant. The General let her proclaim her last decree to preserve this jungle for the Golden Love Bug. From then on, they were just chief and supreme lady who rule the extended villages of clans and sub clans"

While listening to her, Virak slid his hand down between her legs, and when she finished her sentence, he slid his body down while she still had one leg over his hip…… They made love on and off until they felt asleep. Every day for the next two weeks, they made love every moment and everywhere, he lost count of how many times they did in one day? Or how many long orgasms she had? Well, they had to made love as much as they could to save her life, they ate much more foods than they normally did, and they kept on drinking tea from the clay pot thank to the Wise Man remedy, and they still drank from it even after the effect of the bug's venom worn out, and also still made love two or three times a day for the next few weeks.

There came the time, they reluctantly agreed that it's time to return to the village, even though they felt that they hadn't had yet enough of paradise. Sunthary felt sad, she had tear in her eyes and said it was a greatest time of her life, and Virak agreed with her it was his best ever. On the way back, they made love for one last time in the platform on the elephant back before they left the high plateau.

Then Virak understood why women were moaning at anytime they were in bed with men. This was her warning of his grandfather's word that they should abide by of not having any physical or emotional attach from this point on. And she said he should pick a girl his age in the village to get married to fulfill his grandfather wish, and she will move out when they arrive to the compound. Virak forbade her to leave the nanny chamber until he said other vice. They hustled to get dress when they saw smoke rise from the tree canopies above the village.

One week after they returned from the high plateau, Virak discussed with his friends looking for a girl in the territory to marry, because they know the territory better than him; and his decision to get married, that will please his grandfather very much. He recruited a few traders who were known to travel far and wide inside and outside the territory to ply their trade. His friends and the traders gave him some names and places of girls that they think he should pay a visit. Virak told the guys to prepare for the trip tomorrow and sent all of them out, he had a list of more than a dozen names of girls and their villages, and he gave it to a servant who brought it to his grandfather.

That night, Virak went to knock on the door of Sunthary room, and when she opened the door he saw she had the dark cloak wrapped around to cover her body, she looked alarm.

"Yes, what'd you want? And what are you doing here? It's late please leave, oh no don't please if your grandfather know I will be in trouble"

Virak did not answer her, he just bolded the door behind him, opened the dark cloak and pulled the hem of her skirt up, he saw she had the ivory laced bra and panty on. He wrapped his arms around her shaking body and kissed between her cleavages, she protested in whisper and tried to push him away, but he refused to leave her. He kissed her lips to silent her, one hand unsnapped her bra and the other caressed her smooth round butt under the silk laced panty. When her resistant ceased, he sucked her pointed nipples and pulled down her panty. He laid her back on the edge of her bed, raised her knees up and opened her thighs wide to look at her sex that he missed so much and hadn't seen ever since they got back...... Despite of her complain about her tiredness and her fear of being discover, he spent the whole night in her chamber.

The next morning, Virak traveled with a group of entourage though the territory escorted by old Wise Man and a band of trusted warriors. Virak decided to marry an exceptionally beautiful girl who was at the same age as him named Soraya Devy, who belongs to a clan which had strong tied to his grandfather, with the old Empire royal bloodline and a full blood Laotian grandmother. His grandfather was so happy to hear the good news he wait to hear upon their return from the Honeymoon Field that Virak's new bride had the morning sickness. That night Virak sneaked in Sunthary's bedroom, he saw her packing all her belonging.

"What are you doing? Didn't I told you not to do anything"

"I had fulfilled my obligation, you are now a married man, your wife may not want to see me hang around your private compound, and beside I have my urgent reason to move out from..."

"What is your urgent reason?"

"I start to have morning sickness a week ago, I afraid I am getting pregnant, thus I got to move out to live with any man who is willing to take me in and give my baby a name. I do not want to stay here that may complicate your marriage"

"You will not going anywhere, I will ask Grandfather for you to be my wife, come with me to my main compound, I will send the servant to move your belonging"

Inside his place, they saw Soraya sat quietly reading the palm leaves manuscript, Sunthary went to kneel by her feet told her about their story and asked her permission to be a part of their family. For Soraya she knew that she had no option but to accept, she came off her chair and gave Sunthary a hug and a smile. His grandfather walked into his area after he sent a servant to request for his present, after he had listened to Virak's wish and request he turned to Soraya.

"Good girl so be it, we will have a ceremony for you tomorrow; I hope I have enough rum and cognac for the reception, and I got to have the builder enlarge your main hall and build wing area for each of you, bless you my children" Virak and his two wives kneeled in front of him put their hands together, he put his hand on each of their head to bless them, chanted some Sanskrit verse and told them to live in peace and harmony, and he left.

The vacation time went on so fast that it was just like at a blink of an eye, and before Virak realized it his time in the jungle was almost over, he got to go back to the city to start classes in the new semester. Before leaving, he had asked his grandfather for the two ladies to come with him to the city but he refused, the reason was he afraid that Virak's parents and the city folk may not understand the custom and the way of life in the jungle village, and they probably will not accept the fact that Virak had two wives at that age; and one more imported thing, was he did not want the two pregnant ladies went through any difficulties of changing place, climate, atmosphere, and the surrounding environment that they had to go through to adjust. His grandfather and Old Wise Man said a lot more things that Virak couldn't understand, argue or reason with them; it seemed like all bet are off, he resigned to the fate and gave in to their arguments.

On an early morning, Virak climbed on the elephant back with a very sad mood, he did not know that it was the last time that he ever see them again; he waved and said his last farewell to his grandfather, everybody else and the two ladies in dark covered cloak held on to each other.

C3-New Found Knowledge

Virak returned to the city of Phnom Penh and started his classes of the first semester. Few weeks later, he started to feel restless and he knew he missed his wives so he sent a message to the jungle village to his grandfather, he requested him to send his wives to the city. He pleaded with him of how desperate and how lonely he was in the city, and he could not live without them. His grandfather replied that he could not send them to him for the same reasons that they had already discussed before he left, and told him to calm down and to be patient. When his grandfather said no that was it, it was hard to make him change his mind. So he just turned his attention to his study and to follow every day events, news and rumors in this ever changing world. There was one thing that everybody paid their attention to was the American war in Vietnam against the communist. The Cambodian people at the border region could hear the rumble sound of the B-52 bomb explosions from the distant and it got closer and louder every day.

Ever since Virak was born, Cambodia had known only one head of states, he was very popular among the majority of people everywhere, but for those who can think and have a common sense will not believe everything he said, and they wondered where he will lead Cambodia to, some people believe that he lost the sense of direction and the touch with reality. At that time in Cambodia, the head of state had all the power as a dictator, a monarchist, he represents everything that the communist fight against but yet he sympathizes with the communist bloc. He declared that Cambodia as a nonaligned country but he let the Vietnamese communist used Cambodian territory as part of the Ho Chi Minh trail, and later on he let the American dropped bomb on them. He openly support and praise the communist bloc, but yet he lock up any Cambodian communist in the country. He used the prime time of the national radio to broadcast propaganda and criticize the West mainly the American, and he praise the communist who struggle for their cause. Most of Cambodian people stay out of his way, anyone dare to criticize his policy openly will be lock up.

Later on in the semester, Virak stopped trying to understand of anything about Sihanouk, the war or politic all together, all he had in mind was to think about his two wives who were out of reach in the jungle, and Sex was occupied his mind the most; he want to make love to a woman any woman, since he knew how more than most of those his age that he knew. Sometime he tried to pick up some girl his age but at that time they were so innocent, too emotionally attach, and they were too squared to let go.

At his last option, he tried looking at some woman who is vulnerable, experienced and discrete. Virak had paid close attention to the ladies in his mother circle; there were a few dozen ladies aged from twenty-five to forty who were the wives of the military officers, the functionaries, the royal families and some diplomats. There were a few ladies among them who attract his attention but in their eyes he was just a tall young boy; from then on, he started to hang around them more and more to make himself known and available to the ladies. He waited to receive them and brought them to his mother's inner chamber or helped them with their errands and needs. Some ladies had started to boast their praise about Virak to his mother that she raised a well manner son who behaved like a full grown gentleman. While she beamed with pride, thank the ladies, and turned to him with an astonished look. The ladies and his mother got together at each other house to do some business, gambling, gossiping or take care of each other problem.

Lady M

One day in particular, some officer's wives confided with each other in a whisper when they were alone together in a small separate secret chamber where ladies can have their one on one session. They did not know that anyone could hear them from a small storage room, Virak could hear the lady's voice very clearly that she complained about how the government sent her husband to study abroad for so long, she missed her husband so much, and she said that she love her husband also and she did not want to rush to do anything foolish, but her frustration of the sexual unfulfilled that made her want to do something to change her boring life. Her last sentence caught his attention, that it made his eyes wide open, his ears strained, and his loin stirred. The other lady said.

"Listen up my dear sister my advice to you is not to rush to do anything in this matter, because it may cause lots of trouble, but if you decide to go ahead and do something you got to think wisely; it has to be guard to the utmost secrecy. Don't pick any man who is too handsome or too well known, because you don't want to attract unwanted attentions, beside you just want to fulfill your need but not to get permanently attached. Be sure to avoid all servant class and uneducated idiot, they cannot keep their mouth shut. You need to count the day in your calendar after your period because you do not want any unscheduled pregnancy, and the one you choose must be clean and healthy. I had heard that the West have varieties of this kind of things, they even have man prostitute. And again, whatever you decide to do, you must be very careful not to mention this to anyone else, I trust you because you are just like a sister to me, take your time to think about it carefully"

Virak stepped away quietly from the storeroom; he believed he had enough information. If he was not mistaken the voice in the room must be that Métis in her mid twenty named Lady M who was a daughter of Prince so and so, and she married last year to an officer. She normally wore dark clothing with classy and stylish touched; she always had sad face and never said anything much at all. Virak thought that she was in mourning but now he knew the cause of her sadness.

He went to wait for her around the corner of the dim lit hallway, when he heard her footstep that sound like she walked alone approaching the corner, he stepped out quickly with his head turned the other way, they collided that she bumped her chest to his and felled backward, he instinctively wrapped one arm around her waist to steady her and the other one was in the fold of her skirt on her crotch, she held his wrist and slowly pulled it out from the fold of her skirt and looked at him sharply; so he quickly apologized to her.

"I am so sorry my Lady for my carelessness; it was my fault, are you all right?"

"I am all right, don't worry" Virak's mother heard the commotion, she came out and asked.

"What's happen sister? Are you hurt?"

"I am ok sister, don't worry, it was my fault"

"Don't worry mother I will see to it that my lady will get home safely"

Lady M refused but he insisted by holding her arm and walked her to her car. She put on her sunglass, wrapped a scarf, and they got in the back seat. The smell of the French perfume from her body, it stirred his lust, and made his shaft got hard like a wooden stick. When they arrived at her place, Virak started to take his leave but she asked him to help bring some packages up to her flat on the top floor.

On the way up, she went up the stair in front of him; he had a few small packages in one hand and followed one step right behind her. Suddenly she tripped and felled back, her butt sat on his chest and his free hand wrapped around her body to steady her, it seemed like she sprained her ankle, so he had her leaned on him with one hand on his shoulder and he wrapped his arm around her hip. Inside her flat, she put away the packages and served him a glass of chilled water that spilled and wet all his clothes. She gave him a silk sarong to change into and took all his clothes to hang dry under the sun light. Lady M came out of her room with a silk sarong wrapped around over her breasts, now he could see the curve of her body outline very clearly that made him had an instant erection, it pushed up like a tent pole from underneath the silk sarong in between his legs; he acted normal and unaware but he could see from the corner of his eyes that Lady M sharp eyes opened wide and she fascinated by the size of the tent in between his legs. She asked him to stay for a while to have lunch with her, because she did not like to eat alone. She turned and went to the bathroom to freshen up, and she knew that his eyes were following her butt movement.

A while later he heard a sound of something hit the floor and her call for his help, inside he saw her laid on the floor near a big bed, she had a large towel wrapped around her body and another wrapped her hair up above her head; Virak helped her up and laid her down on the bed while she tried to hold on to the towel that kept slipping. She said she was all right it was just a little scratch and a minor sprain, he asked her for the ointment so he could apply and massage to ease her pain. Virak rubbed the ointment on her ankle, her knee, and her thighs, at below her butt where he rubbed and massage the longest time; she closed her eyes, turned on her back and let him kept on massage her legs. He moved up higher and higher to push the towel up to just a few inches below her crotch, he could smell her natural clean body scent and the scent that radiated from her sex that smelled like fresh seashell, the scent was so intoxicated that he could not restrained himself any longer so both of his hands crept up slowly under the towel always up to her waist, he could see her clean shaved mount, the slit in between the two thick lips and the tip of a pink tamarind seed for a moment before she held the towel tight between her chest, rolled to lie on her face and squeezed her legs together; he flipped the towel above her waist, laid his hand on her smooth butt, she was alarmed.

"What are you doing? Get out, get off me please…"

"I just try to help to ease your pains; I cannot leave you like this, please, lay still my Lady" He pulled the towel up higher, started to caress and kiss her back down to her butt and her thigh that made her shake and moan but she still protested.

"Oh no, don't do that please, your mother and me we are just like sister and you are just a young boy; I don't want to betray her trust. Get off me please" Virak ignored her plea and kept on kissing and caressing her body, he thought it's time so he yanked all the towels and thrown them to the floor, kissed her neck, and slid both hand under her to grab her juicy breasts. She turned quickly on her back to throw him off, she sat up with both hand covered her breasts and closed her legs together. He kneeled high over her with his erected penis pointing straight at her, he held her shoulder down.

"Oh please, be a good dear boy leaves me alone, if anybody knows about this your mother will know, and when my husband returns I am certain that he will know and he will kill both of us; he own lots of guns"

"My Lady, it is his fault to leave a beautiful young wife alone for so long, we will keep our mouth shut no one will know about this; and your gap cannot talk, your husband will find your gap look just the same when he get back. Don't worry, trust me, just relaxed and enjoy God gift of pleasure. Now just lay back and open your legs wider"

"Oh no please don't... OHH... AHH..." Despite her protest she slowly spread her legs wider, while his finger glued to her tamarind seed.

"Don't worry My Lady; I know you love your husband that's fine, I am not object to that. He can have you when he gets back, now is my turn, I'm not going to hurt you, and you know I admired your sexy round butt, just relaxed"

Virak had not been with any woman for so long ever since he return from the jungle, he missed holding a woman body and feeling the wet warm gap. He got up to kneeled between her open thighs and pushed her knees up......

After her orgasm subsided, tear started to roll down her face with her body still spread open. Virak came to lie by her side, held her to console, apologize, reassure and promise all in one shot. Since then he paid her a visit almost every day until her husband return from abroad. She told him that was the end of their affair after her husband return, Virak reluctantly agreed with her because it was too risky for them to continue.

Two weeks after her husband return, his mother received an invitation to a banquet at Lady M resident. Virak insisted on accompanied his mother since his father was unable to attend at that time. Lady M and her husband received their guess at the door, she hugged his mother and she was shocked when she saw Virak stood right behind but she did very well to conceal her emotion and hold her composure.

The night ambient was very festive; they put out a lavished dinner with good food and good beverage selection. And after the meal guests danced to the modern music and some grouped together to play card, while Virak sat around to observe the activities. He saw Lady M walked toward her bedroom, he acted like going to the bathroom in the hallway, but he passed it and went straight to knock on the door. Lady M opened the door when she saw him she tried to slam the door shut but he was prepared to force his way in. He bolted the door, held her waist and wrapped his arms around her shaking body; for just looking at her face he could read her emotions flashed through, it looked like she was excited and frighten at the same time.

"For Haven sake, what are you doing here?"

"To see you in private My Lady"

"Are you mad? Or are you drunk? Don't you know that over fifty people are outside this room including my husband? Please leave"

"I know, your husband is busy getting drunk with his fellow officers, and I miss to be between your legs My Lady"

"You are crazy to come in here at this time, it's the most dangerous time because whenever he was drunk he always want to make love to me"

"It's OK, I will let him have you after I finish" By the time, Virak finished the sentence he already had her lay at the edge of the bed, her skirt bunched up around her waist along with her panty on the floor; he spread her legs apart and pushed her knees up. With her high heel kicked up in the air, he kneeled down on the floor, bent down...... The idea of getting caught made her frighten, and it's heighten her sexual excitement...... And in just a short time, they both spent in a synchronized orgasm, he lay idle on top of her tried to savor the last moment between her legs but she pushed him off right away and sprung off the bed.

"Get off, let's go, and hurry please"

She put her hand on her gap to stop the leaking, and rush to the bathroom. Virak pulled his pant up, arranged his cloth and ready to stepped out of her bedroom, but something on the floor attracted his attention; he bent down to pick up her panty and stuffed in his pocket, it was for a souvenir because he knew that he may never have a chance to set foot in this bedroom again ever and least of all to get in between her legs.

Virak was at the door ready to pull the latch open. Suddenly, loud knocks came from outside and her husband called out.

"Honey are you in there, open the door, please"

Virak retreated from the door and looked around the room for a place to hide. She came out of the bathroom with a towel rubbed between her legs, and when she saw him she turned pale; and she tried to shout back to him.

"One moment Honey, I'm in the bathroom"

And then, she turned to Virak and whispered.

"Why are you still here? Oh pray to the Lord, we are going to die. Get in there hurry" Virak got in a corner of the room behind tall clothing cabinets near the foot of the bed. She looked at his direction to reassure herself that he was out of sight, and she rubbed the towel between her legs some more and pulled the latch to open the door. Her husband was staggering into the room; so Virak thought she was right he came looking for her after he was already soaked with alcohol. She smoothed her silk skirt and greeted him warmly.

"Oh Honey, you must be so drunk and you need to lie down, I'm sorry that I couldn't open the door right away" He did not reply to her, he just stood in front of her with a wicked drunken smile on his face; he reached down to pull her silk skirt up, and stuck the other hand between her legs. Before she could say anything, he had her lay down at the edge of the bed on the same spot that she just got off five minutes ago. With her skirt bunched up around her waist, he spread her legs apart...... Ten minutes later, he got off her, got dress and stepped out of the door. Virak came out from the hiding place, went to lock the door and turned to look at her; she was still laid on the bed and her skirt bunched up around her waist. He held her, kissed her forehead lightly, and he left.

C4-Vietnam War Spilled Into Cambodia

In March 18th 1970, then the Prime Minister Lon Noll staged a coup d'état to overthrow Prince Norodom Sihanouk. People said the coup was helped by the American CIA. Virak never paid attention to the politic side of this war, all he knew was that a few days after the coup d'état, the Vietcong and the North Vietnamese communist army were all over Cambodia. The American sent the Mike Force unit that was a mercenary force consisted mainly of ethnic Cambodian in South Vietnam (The Kampuchea Krom).The road from the provincial town were cut off and occupied by the communist force. Then Prince Norodom Sihanouk joined with the Khmer rouge.

Virak felt sad and realized the fact that he may never see his grandfather and his two wives, or to set foot in the northern jungle again. He was upset with his grandfather who did not allow his two wives came to join him in the city. He sat on the bank of the Mekong River, thinking for a long time then he realized that his life got to move on, and then he turned all his attention to the war. Despite his mother objection, he joined the new Cambodian army that supported by the American. At that time he believed that if he was men enough to make love to women, therefore he was ready to fight in the war.

The army accepted just about anyone who want to join, they issued them some uniform, showed the new recruit how to use the rifle, loaded them on the long colorful busses and sent them off to the front line within a few days whether they were ready or not. Many of the new soldiers may never see or experience their second battlefield, they either got killed, became disable by their injuries or they will desert the army altogether.

Virak's combat unit was prepared to be sent to South Vietnam for training, they were told that they will be trained by the American special force the Green Beret, and will bring the modern American weaponry back to fight the communist in Cambodia. One morning, they were loaded into the troupes transport boat convoy and went down the Mekong River toward South Vietnam. Down the river, they were received by the barrage of mortar rounds that the Vietcong fired at the convoy from the river bank; some rounds missed the boat by only a few yards. The boat crewmen fired the 50 cal. Machine gun on deck at the river bank. After a day ride on the boat, they were loaded into the C130 transport plane; it was a short flight to the southernmost region of South Vietnam.

The base that will be their home for the next four months was situated next to the seaside town and a mountain range to the east, the defense perimeter were surrounded by rows and rows of sandbags and concertina wire. The first few days, they went through the administrative processing, the issuing of materials and weapons, and adjustment for the acclimatization. They were happy with their first issued M-16 rifle with its light weight and sleek modern look and it's a very accurate target shooting rifle, but they found out later that it was not reliable and suitable for the warfare on all of the terrain and weather in Southeast Asia. They appreciated the usefulness of the M-79 grenade launcher, it's just like to throw grenade at the enemy three to four hundred yards away. At the beginning of the training, the food was somewhat decent; they got rice of course, fried fish, stir fried pork and vegetable, and stew soup. As time goes on, the chow became less and less appetizing, they had made complains to the higher chain of command. A week later, a Major of the U.S. army came to have a meal in their chow hall; they believe they tried to show that if an American army officer can eat this chow, so why can't they? They all kept an eye on him to see how the American enjoys this kind of food. And it was happen as they had predicted, it was about fifteen minutes into the meal, the Major excused himself, calmly stepped out of the door, and he vomited his gut out right in front of the chow hall and rushed to the dispensary to check for food poisoning. Somehow a few days later, the chow became somewhat decent again thanks to the major self-sacrifice beyond the call of duty.

For Virak's group of friend, they had a secret weapon to fight lousy food and hunger; they had Private K a tall, handsome guy who was known to be well endowed. They sent him on a mission, and that he should tried to befriend with the head cook or fuck her brains out if he had to just to get them some food. The head cook was a chubby healthy lady, they wouldn't call her ugly but she was just too plain to be called pretty, and they instructed Private K to take this mission very seriously. Under their clever supervision, instruction and persuasion, Private K accomplished his secret mission meticulously and extraordinary fruitful. Within twenty-four hours, all of them at the command center ate some pork chop, seafood and wash it down with rice vine behind the chow hall, while Private K kept on executing his mission by banging the chubby head cook on the row of sand bag nearby under the moonless night sky that accompanied by the sound of the 122 millimeters mortar rounds fired to the mountain by the allies Taiwanese troupes. The next day they called Private K to their command center for debriefing, and they asked him.

"It was a job well done Private but why we heard the head cook kept spitting continuously last night, was that normal for your style of love making?"

"Thank you Sir, it wasn't my style or anything Sir, she was spitting sand"

"And why was that?"

"I put a sand bag on her face Sir, because I couldn't stand her bad breath Sir"

"Very well private, we think it is OK if she likes it but this is dangerous the sand might get in her eyes, and how about try to fuck her doggy style next time"

"Yes Sir I will, Aiy hai Sir"

"And by the way, ask her to bring some beer this weekend will you"

With the better food, that gave them strength to endure the hardship of the training and the homesickness more bearable. They had the Green Beret unit as their instructors and the Kampuchea krom mercenary as interpreters. The instructors and the interpreters wore the tiger stripe or olive drab uniform and for the Cambodian trainees they were issued the thin shit color pajama that ripped and fell apart very easily after a few times in the field and it bleached the color out that made them stood out like a sore thumb even at night. Before they knew it, they were on the third phase of their training; they had to go to the field training area in the forest where the Vietcong were still lurking so they can put their new knowledge into practice. Most of the Cambodian trainees were used to fight their battle in the open rice field area and farm, and when they saw the deep and thick forest that they had to clear a trail through; it may look very intimidated but they made themselves went through it anyway. To Virak, it was just like a picnic or a hunting expedition; the American had their C ration, and for the trainees they were issued the Asian ration, it was the dehydrate food in the foil bag that they used as cooking pot, and in the foil bag it consisted of a bag of parboiled rice, dehydrate meat fish and vegetable. They tried to overcome these meager meals by adapting the wild vegetable and animal as much as they could. During the maneuver, the training unit was shadowed by some American unit, Virak told the interpreter of how well the unit of American soldier conducted their maneuver in the forest and he was impressed by their fighting skill and spirit. The instructor explained that they were not soldiers but they were MARINES. Then Virak thought to himself that he liked these marines, and it made him felt like want to be one of them.

Benchmark 13

In the forest area that marked in the map as Bench Mark 13 where the training unit conducted their training, they marched during the day and set up a defense perimeter at night. At one area, they came to a sizable clearing a few square miles across with a creek flowed through it. The command decided to set up a defense perimeter and stay put for a while so they could conduct their training exercise.

One evening, Virak's platoon leader gave him a map, and told him to take two squads to an area in the coordinate to set an ambush; Virak looked in the map and found a spot about a few miles from the defense perimeter. It was a good spot where the trail went around on the outer bank of the river bend. He gave the order to move out a few hours before sunset and came to a spot to stage the ambush; he sent a recon team to do the surveillance on the primary position at the river bend where they will set the ambush after sunset. They moved in to the inside bank of the river bend and lined up their position as an arc shape along the inner bank behind trees and bushes; the river bank was sloping about twenty yards down to the shallow water ten yards across, and the trail wrapped around the outer bank at approximately forty yards from the ambush line. It was a perfect position that sat higher than the trail, so it gave them an advantage field of fire that could covered the whole river bend with twenty five soldiers.

They'd set up some Claymore mines and tripped wire illuminator grenades. The ambush went smoothly without a hitch, and when the predawn sky was lifting the darkness by turning slight gray in the east, Virak went to check on every one and told them that he was going to go down to the river to get some water. He squat down on the grassy water edge, filled up his canteens, and dropped a few iodine tablets and put them away in the canteen covers. He laid his M-16 across his lap, and scooped some water to wash his face.

Suddenly, he saw the silhouette of a person walked down from the opposite bank. Virak wondered who that was he thought that he was the first one to come down here, but when he detected the AK-47 assault rifle stock above the silhouette left shoulder of the Vietcong . He instinctively, lay back flat on the grass with his M-16 on his chest, he pointed the muzzle at that on coming silhouette, and slowly opened the safety with his thumb. His heart was pounding so fast and hard, he tried to calm himself by breathing long and deep, and reassured himself that he did not need to worry because there was only one blind Vietcong. The Vietcong came down below the trail level, and Virak kind of lost sight of him for a second in the dark bank. Alas, now Virak could see two Vietcongs one behind the other when they came closer; he was freeze except the muzzle of his rifle that followed their every steps. His experience, knowledge and training were flashing through his head like a rapid fire; now he got two Vietcong soldiers to kill, he must fire automatic and laid the rifle flat on his body with the magazine point to the right and aimed at the Vietcong on the right first; and one more thing, he must spread his legs and flatted his feet so he won t shot off his own toe.

The Vietcong lowered themselves at the water edge but one of them recognized the glowed shadow of Virak's shit color uniform that the outline stood out on the dark grass background. They were hustling to turn their AK-47 from across their back but it was too late for them, Virak blasted a string of about ten or fifteen rounds to drop them both on the spot. And then he rolled to take cover behind the rock and tree, and he shout.

"ACROSS THE RIVER... FIRE!"

Virak took cover hugging close to the rock; within thirty second all weapons on the ambush line must fire at the predetermined kill zone and at any point that they could see sign of the enemy. The sound was deafening by all the gun fires and the explosions of the M-79 round, and when he looked up all he could see was the tracer rounds from their 30 CAL machine gun sprayed across the bank. When the firing ceased, Virak went back behind the line, told the squad members to remove the illumination tripped wire and deactivated the Claymore mines, and he had the radio operator gave the coordinate and direction of the enemy unit position to the command post. The command ordered them to fall back to their secondary position; Virak kept in contact with them and gave them the possible route and coordinate where the enemy might retreat to. In less than a minute, when they were safe at the secondary position, the artillery supports fired a few dozen rounds over their head. The company came out from the defense perimeter to catch up with them; they joined the formation and advanced to the river outer bank. A marine unit combed the forest area beyond the trail to assess the result of the artillery fire. The company got to do the body count directly across from the ambush primary position where the Vietcong bodies were still in their hammock. At the water edge where the two Vietcong bodies laid, Master sergeant of the Green Beret debriefed Virak; he asked what had happen, how he killed the two Vietcong and so on. His last question was how the hell they did not see or hear over fifty Vietcong came to sleep right in front of their line? His face turned red like a monkey; and Virak replied.

"We all know that Vietcong are expert on the subject of cover and concealment but last night they did not see or hear us. There were always half of us who stay awake at all time. You might forgot that we were soldiers before we became your trainee here, then we had killed our share of Vietcong. If there is anything wrong I'll take full responsibility but leave my squad alone"

"Hey hold your horse, I did not blame your squad of anything, by the way congratulation. It was a job well done and you had killed a high rank North Vietnamese officer. Now I have something to write home about and something to brag to the higher command" Master Sergeant and the whole detail of the Green Beret instructors shook Virak's hand. And then the Master Sergeant asked Virak.

"So now, do you want anything for you and your squad?"

"My squad wants some cigarette and I want to get out of this shit color uniform"

"Consider done plus a few days off when we get back, I will treat you with a day of R and R in town. Don't say a word to anyone is that clear?"

"Yes, Sergeant"

The unit completed their field training in two more weeks, and then they break up camp, and marched to the main road where they loaded on a convoy of five ton truck and returned back to the base at Long Hay.

The battalion received a few days off including a day of R and R at the sea shore; Virak's squad members received a carton of cigarette and a set of brand new uniform each. One evening a Kampuchea Krom mercenary approached Virak and said that Master Sergeant want to see him. They went through the back gate into the American compound behind the tall fence area at the center of the base. The mercenary handed Virak a set of a tiger striped uniform with a pair of jungle boot and told him to get change. When the Master Sergeant came out flanked by a few Green Beret members and the Kampuchea Krom mercenary, he looked at Virak and said.

"You look smart in the tiger striped uniform and the jungle boot, how do you like it?"

"This uniform is much better than the shit color one I was issued"

"How come you say like that? Many brave men die in that uniform"

"That why they die in that uniform, I guess they all died by gun shots wounds"

"Of course, they all die in battle but what make you say that?"

"That uniform bleach out color after a few wash, had you ever notice that all the Cambodian trainees were kind of glow in the dark? They stick out like a sore thumb; it will make an easy target for Vietcong" The Green Beret looked at each other and nodded.

"Come to think about it that was true, you all were kind of glow in the dark. Thank for bring this to me, I'll talk to the Colonel about it but in the mean time let's we go to town and have some fund". And all of the Green Beret cheered.

"Yes let's go to town and raise hell"

"Let's go to kick some ass and take name" They filed in an old two and a half ton truck with a mercenary driver and a machine gunner at the ready. On the road to town, Virak talked with a mercenary and he told him that his unit was called Mike Force it was funded by the CIA and trained by the Green Beret; the CIA form the mercenary force among the ethnic minority groups.

The town was named something that Virak couldn't remember; the street was lined with bars, restaurant and brothels. Most of people who walked on the street were American GI who had some liberty to get away from the monotonous life on base or in the boondocks somewhere. This red light district catered for American GI, and all of the Vietnamese on the street were working even the small children; they sold cigarette, gum, and condom or shine shoe. Most Vietnamese men who stood on the street were trying to coerce the GI to come in to their bar and brothel. For women, if they looked older most likely they were working women who sell or serve food, but if they were young and to be on this street they were considered prostitute. Master Sergeant brought them to this establishment with a unicorn sing that had their restaurant-bar over the river and brothel operated in full swing on the upper floor. At the rear of the bar they had separate banquet rooms that connected to the open decks overlook the river where Virak could see the reflection of the moonlight and the busy boat traffics. They had set up a private banquet waiting for them; there were trays of hot Chinese and Vietnamese food lined up at one side of the room next to a bar. They sat at a long table with a platoon of Vietnamese hostesses mingled among them. As the banquet went on, they were served and satisfied at every whim by the girl hostesses. When they were just started at the beginning, some GI and the mercenary already took some hostesses upstairs. A mercenary officer offered Virak some whisky but he refused and he said he never had any whisky before, and preferred beer instead, and so the hostess quickly served Virak a bottle of St. Miguel beer Number33 label.

"It doesn't matter what you drink, if you can lead a squad of soldier and kill Vietcong you can seat at my table any time and drink whatever the fuck you like" He raised his glass up to propose a toast "Cheer, fuck the Vietcong" Glasses raised and the alcohol flowed to dull their sense, Virak thought to himself that they might literally fuck some Vietcong tonight; they never knew may be there were some of them among the hostesses. They partied late into the night, they ate, drank, smoked and groping the hostesses; they frequently, pulled the hostesses from the table to the room upstairs and sometime a guy took two of them at the same time. It was late and Virak never drank so much beer before he was kind of feel more tipsy than usual, so he turned to thank the Sergeant and bid everyone goodnight he guess they will continue until daybreak. The Sergeant told Virak to pick a hostess who will be his bed companion for the night; the sergeant asked him.

"By the way you are not still a virgin are you?" Virak did not answer he just laugh and looked to pick among the available hostess; and the sergeant said.

"If you are it's time to get rid of it, I'll have a few hostesses to make sure that you will bust your nut tonight many time over to get rid of that disease" Virak picked a young hostess in blue miniskirt, she quickly dragged his hand toward the stairwell and before they went up she whispered and giggles among other hostesses, Virak heard some French word like ORIGINE he realized she thought that she got herself a virgin to toy with tonight. When they were inside, she called a servant came to change the bed sheets and the pillow cases; they took a shower together and slipped into silk robe. She laid on her back, spread her legs, and with opened arms she motioned him to come between her legs, and lamented that she did not get pick to come up stair tonight so she needed an urgent pounding, but Virak shook his head lay on his back and pointed to his erected penis, she nodded her head, and came up tried to impaled herself over him but Virak push her face down to his knob. She got down to perform her job quite well despite she still groaning her displeasure; Virak had never been with a prostitute before, and he had heard about all kinds of the venereal disease, so he was kind of afraid to do anything with her until she expertly rolled a condom on his shaft then he reluctantly gave it a try. That night, Virak had lots of alcohol drink, cigarette smoke and stayed all night frolicking with prostitute, and he went to sleep with an unsettle dream; at one point he dream of dark shadow chasing him and tried to bite his nuts off.

C5- In the Cambodian Army

Finally, Virak's unit was at the end of their training after almost four months. Now, they prepared for their departure back to Cambodia. The American had issued them some new equipment, material, ammunitions and the same shit color uniforms. Virak asked the American that why they still gave them these uniforms after they told them about its condition, reason and consequence. Their answer was that they already ordered them, they were available in stock. There is nothing else they can do about it. So, Virak asked some more about the M-16 rifle.

"We'd use this rifle for a short period of time we know right away that this M-16 rifle is not fit for all terrain and battle. In these parts of the world are covered by wet land and most likely we will fight our battle in the muddy rice field; every time we had to crawl dragging our M-16 through mud it will most likely become unserviceable and proof unreliable. I know they cannot do anything for the Cambodian trainee, but how about the American troupe here in Vietnam. Why don't they do anything about it?" A colonel of the US army answered to his question.

"This rifle was ordered to be use as main rifle for all arm force by the secretary of defense. They'd test it and experiment it in many ways and places. The study show that the soldiers like it. This M-16 is light weight so they can carry more ammo and chow; it is a very accurate shooting weapon. Is that answer to your question?"

"Sir, I agree that this rifle is a very accurate shooting weapon. With due respect Sir you and your secretary of defense may never crawl in the mud and drag this weapon through to fight Vietcong. If you had done it you probably experience the difficulties with this weapon Sir" The Colonel turned red; he was just smiled and changed the subject.

"And you don't need to worry about all the materials like spare parts and ammunitions etc…because within four or five months American troupe will be all over Cambodia, and we will fight the communist side by side" (They find out later after they went back to Cambodia that what the colonel said was not true, it was a big lie. There were no American troupe ever sent to Cambodia, and it was sad and disappointed to realize that the American did not intend to stay fighting to win this war).

They were loaded into the C-130 cargo transport plane, and made a short flight to Pochintong airport near Phnom Penh. Virak's unit was immediately put under the command of the reactionary unit to help reinforce any place that came under attack. They were based in an installation near the capitol, and every few weeks they were out somewhere in the countryside engaged with the Vietcong and the North Vietnamese regular army. Virak request permission to keep their old weapon like the AK-47 and the Gerent M-1 etc… For just in case they may need them when their M-16 should act up during the wet season.

They kept all of the enemy weapons every time they killed or captured them. In their first few battles after they got back from the training, they had lost some of the original troupe who went to South Vietnam with them. The high command replaced them with some raw recruits that they had to train them to try to get them up the par with the unit. Despite of their effort, those haft trained recruits were getting killed like flies, because the high command did not give them enough time and equipments to prepare them properly.

At a battle South of Phnom Penh, they were just about to send to engage with a North Vietnamese regular unit, and the rumor said it was led by a famous one breast woman commander. Upon hearing this famous name at the briefing many of the officers and NCOs looked concern and sweating. Virak was afraid that they might transfer this mood to their troupe. So he stepped up to offer a motivate cheer.

"Hey, cheers up sir don't be alarmed, we'd beat the NVR before and there is no reason why we cannot beat this one just because they have a one breast woman as their commander, this does not mean that they cannot be beaten. The rumor said she had a magic spell that her and her comrades could not be killed by bullet. Sir, tell your soldiers to get this superstitious out of their mind. I guarantee that if we believe in ourselves we will aim straighter and the round will hit the target more accurate.

And one more thing as we know that our M16 is a good target shooting weapon, the NCO must check them to make sure that its clean and they must know how to clean it with CLP and to know how to aim with sight picture and sight alignment. Do not assume that they all know you must ask them and have them demonstrate. When we know our enemy and know ourselves, this will give us confident, and with the preparation of our weapon, logistic and intelligent we know we can defeat any enemy whether Vietcong, Vietminh, one breast or two it does not matter"

Everybody was quiet and looking at Virak, he felt like he had done something wrong, and he turned to look at the battalion commander who stood up and shouts.

"All right you heard him. You got two hours to prep your troupes. That's an order. DISMISS!" He looked and pointed straight at Virak.

"You, come here, front and center. Who are you?"

Virak came to stand at attention in front of him, and before Virak can answer he nodded his head and said.

"Oh you, you are the squad leader who kill the Vietcong in NAM"

"Yes Sir, I am sorry Sir that I get carried away and open my mouth without thinking"

"All right, it was a good motivated speech, I wouldn't have said it better, but you must request permission to speak. Is that understood?"

"Yes Sir"

"Your name is T, is Colonel T your father?"

"Yes Sir"

"Do you know? Your father and I we are good friend"

"No Sir, I did not know"

"I thought you were his son I was right. Be careful and take care of your soldiers. DISMISS" Virak gave a salute, do the about face and when back to the company command post because he got a feeling that the company commander might want to see him. Virak stood at attention in front of the company command in his tiger striped uniform, jungle boot, his full load of the 782 gear, his M16 at sling arm with one round chambered locked and loaded. The company commander came to stand in front of Virak with his hands on his hip, and he shouted.

"What do you have to say for yourself, Mr. Know All?"

"I am sorry Sir that I speak without asking for permission. I got carried away when everybody hear the name of the one breast bitch they look resign and sweating, and I was just try to motivate sir"

"Just try to motivate you said. The best you can do was keep your mouth shut, and everybody was sweating because the GODDAMN tent was hot. I better not see your face at any other briefing ever. Now DISMISS!"

Virak did the about face and step out from the company command post (Virak did not see the commander's face again until he was killed a few hours later). This battle, it was just like they receive an invitation to a fight or the one breast bitch tried to lure them to their grave. The NVR occupied a district town and kept thousand of civilian in it, they had set up the defense perimeter and stayed put for the last few months waiting for the government next move. He thought the high command had weigh in all options, they couldn't call American plane to drop bomb on the position because there were too many civilian there, and now they decided to send in the reactionary force.

The brigade had set up an installation on the main national route. The supreme command sent in a few batteries of the artillery and set up the communication and logistic, a heliport and a field hospital; it seemed like they expected a big show down with heavy casualty. The latest intelligent information they received from their recon unit that they had set up in layers of belt and the belt were split up in pieces and spread out all over the countryside. The NVR knew that they did not have enough troupes to make a long line, so they break the line and spread them out that way we could not move around to attack them from their blind side without running into the small line.

Fifteen minutes after Virak's unit stepped out from the installation the artillery started to sound off, fired dozens and dozens rounds over their head to the enemy positions. A few battalions marched directly to the district town but Virak's company went through the forest and hilly terrain on the wing of the brigade formation. They moved quickly through the low shrub and sparse bamboo forest, along the way they met some resistant from small band of NVR. They knew that they'd met this NVR unit a few times before, now they could recognize their behavior and their profile easily from hundred yards away.

The NVA wore green or black pajama, green smoky hat and sandal made from the old tire and tube; sometime they could predict the numbers, movements and directions by just reading the sandal track. Virak knew they regrouped whatever left of the small band, because when the wing formation came closer to the first small mountain the tire sandal track got heavier and more numerous, and there were traces of blood mixed in. At the edge of the mountain there were a few hundred yard of clearing where Virak's unit came to stop at the edge to observe the terrain, this was a perfect spot to ambush any unsuspected knuckle head; they tried to get the fire support from the artillery but they said the coordinates were out of range, and for the air support was out of the question, it will take too long and it will be too late; so they had no choice but to move up and engage with the NVR head on.

The company opened up in the buffalo horn formation and fire M-79 and 60 MM mortar rounds at the top and the side of the mountain. In less than an hour despite some resistant, they swept through and put the mountain behind them with some casualties, and they followed the trail of blood toward the district town. At approximately a mile away, they saw the broken lines of NVR formation carry their wounded comrades. They quickly fired the 60 MM mortar round on their line or in front of them. They saw a few bodies dropped from the NVR line formation every time the round exploded. One round was exploded in the middle and took down the whole line because they bunch up too close, Virak quickly pointed out this mistake to his squad. And for those enemy soldiers, who did not get hit with the shrapnel, ran real fast toward the bamboo forest ahead because that was the only way to survive.

In the previous battle, they had bad experience when they came upon the death or wound enemies, the wound NVR had grabbed the machine gun and sprayed on us, or sometime they planted the grenade trap under their dead comrades. Now a standing order was when they saw the dead or wound enemy they must pumped some rounds to their head to make sure that they were dead and some round into their body hopefully if there was any trap under the body it will set off. At fifty yards away, some wound NVR surrounded by five or six of their dead comrades, Virak stood behind some new soldiers and when they hesitated he gave them a firm order.

"Do you all see those? Don't ever hesitate for a moment to put some rounds on their heads and bodies. Now to the head, AIM! Fire! To the body, AIM! FIRE! "

Virak felt uneasy right before they went into the wooded area from the open field. They fired some round of the M-79 and the 60 MM into the bamboo forest. Suddenly, two M-113 armored troop carriers came from behind to reinforce them, which they were glad to let them have the honor of blasting at the bamboo forest with their 50 CAL machine gun, and the 75 .MM non recoil canon ahead of the formation advance. The NVR realized that the element of surprise was lost and these soldiers were not some foul to be foul with or falling in to their trap, so they felled back to their secondary position deeper into the bamboo forest and resumed to fight back; many time that the government soldier had push them out from a position they just fall back to the next secondary one, dug their heel and fought back with all their might.

This seasoned unit of NVR had shown the tenacity and the experience of a battle test unit that was why they had a reputation as a force to be reckoned with. At one point, the company formation came upon a barrage of RPG round explosion that the NVR fire at them nonstop for a minute that made their new troupes disoriented and unable to respond to order or fired their weapon off without aiming at anything, but for the seasoned soldiers they knew that this was an act of all out defense of their last strong hold, it came to a point of do or die for them a self-sacrifice so the main body could retreat.

The best action for this was to take them out first and fast before they rain down the RPG rounds to wipe out the unit formation, so the seasoned soldiers knew what they supposed to do by taking charge of the green troupes to calm them down and have them used the M-16 for target shooting by aiming at the enemy neck; and they advanced closer to get a better sight picture for a sure kill. The RPG launcher was a shoulder fire weapon so they must aim just right below the RPG round to put the M-16 round on target; they could not use the AK-47 for this job, now they know why the NVR did not even fire a shot from their AK-47, it was an all out RPG for them.

A few minutes later, the RPG explosion was quiet, Virak could only hear an occasional M-16 rifle fire; he knew that his soldiers had executed their predetermined order from training very well. He nodded his head at them to show his approval and admiration for the job well done. The unit got up and advanced to take over the real estate that they were entitled to; some of their new troupes were puzzling at this situation, and they asked.

"Why did they retreat so fast? We only fire single shot compare to their hundreds rounds of RPG"

"No, they didn't retreat, you will see why in a moment. Have your weapon ready at all time" Virak told them to wait and see for themselves, and when they came to their line of defense in the bamboo forest, they saw the dead and dying NVR soldiers in every foxhole with head and neck wound on all of them, fresh warm blood was still oozed out from their wounds. They were ordered to finish them off on the spot and gathered all of their weapon and ammo especially the RPG; they piled them up on oxcarts that were found behind the enemy line with a side of beef carcass, rice and cooking utensils that were going to be theirs.

The platoon commander ordered the company to move out and, Virak knew immediately that something happened back there. He turned to look back at the old spot of company command where body parts and a part of a motionless face of the company commander still lay stewed around the bush. The platoon commander came to pull Virak out from his squad and appointed a corporal to take over, and he pulled him aside to tell him.

"Our company command was wiped out by the RPG rounds back there and the armor track vehicles are taking our dead and wounded soldiers to the rear; I want you to help me in the command post that I have to create and fill in the command structure before we regroup with the battalion" Virak gave him a few names of NCO that he knew well and capable of filling in the slots.

One of them was Sergeant BT who was a few years older than him and he'd known him since before the war started, BT like to drink alcohol, smoke cigarette a lot and visit the brothels every chance he get when they are in town; he may be a little lazy but he was courageous, faithful, reliable and the ability to get the job done.

At the district town, the brigade was order to dig in surround three sides of their defense belt. Virak's company was the last one to join the battalion formation with the most casualties, so they were assigned at the rear defense line and spread out behind the battalion command.

Before they reached the battalion position, Virak had suggested to the acting company commander that they should distribute all the beef and rice to the troupe before the battalion lay eyes on it. The acting commander agreed with Virak and he told him to go ahead to act out and give order with anything that deem necessary and kept him informed. Virak immediately commenced the distribution and asked BT to take a scavenging detail of fifteen soldiers and an empty oxcart to the nearby abandon village to look for anything edible especially fruit and vegetable, and also take anything useful like utensils, tools etc...

They stopped the formation in the shade near the abandon village to cook and eat their meal immediately, and Virak had BT crew cooked the beef bone making it into vegetable soup. Virak was right about the food, they had finished their meal before they arrived; the battalion sent an officer to receive and inspect them, and when he saw some beef bones left hanging on the side of the carts he asked.

"Where are all the beef?"

"I guess probably the Vietcong ate them, that's what left when we found them"

Virak replied to the officer immediately before the acting commander say anything unsounded; the officer went to inspect the bones and saw the fresh cut mark with little flesh left on them, he turned to Virak with a disgusting look on his face. Virak knew that the officer knew he lied to him but he didn't give a damn because he knew what he did was reasonably all right to feed his soldiers first before he let the high command got their hand on the beef. The acting commander tried to console the officer by offering the bones to him, but the officer did not want any of it, he turned red and barked.

"Cut those disgusting bone down, throw them away, and move all these carts to the command center immediately!" Right after the officer left with the weapon carts, a battalion clerk came to get the acting commander to report; Virak gave him the soup pot to take it to the battalion commander, but the clerk pointed to Virak that they wanted him to report also. Virak told the clerk to go ahead and they followed at a distant that he could not hear them. Virak turned to look at the acting commander concerned face and reassured him.

"Staff Sergeant Sir, you are our commander acting as an officer, you don't bother yourself with the detail of food and logistic because you are busy taking over the command. Let me take full responsibility if they ask anything about all the detail and the beef, and we deny everything and just say what beef? What are they going to do, shoot me? Don't worry about it Sir after the battalion commander fill his belly with this soup every things is going to be all right"

At the command post, the acting company commander went in to report, Virak look around the post and it seemed like it became a brigade command center because he saw the high radio antenna blended in the bamboo bush and a Jeep-A2 with a one star plaque on it. Virak asked somebody and they said it's true that the brigade took over; he was surprised and concerned about the officer might report them always to the general command.

While Virak sat sweating under the shade holding the soup pot, a clerk called him into the command bunker. All kinds of ideas and cases scenario were flashing through his mind, he was thinking about ditching the soup pot but it was too late, he was standing at attention in front of the brigadier general and the colonel his battalion commander who sat at the table, and they were looking up at him and at the soup pot.

"What do you got in your hand Sergeant?"

"Soup Sir"

"You are not bringing a pot of soup to bribe us do you?"

"No Sir not like that at all Sir, I just bring it here for you to taste our field vegetable soup made from beef bone left by the NVR Sir, and it cooked by the troop of company B Sir"

"All right, let have it, let see how the food of company B taste like" Virak stole a glance at the acting company commander who stood at attention just a few feet away, he was sweating profusely and Virak was alarm when he saw his staff sergeant chevron was on the table in front of the general. Virak's eyeballs shifted slowly to the general who seem to try hard to swallow the vegetable soup but our battalion commander seem to enjoy it, he look down to his bowl and kept on eating with a slight smile on his face.

The general motioned to the officer who came to receive the company, ripped the chevron from Virak chest with a sinister smile on his face he did it with a vengeance. Virak's heart dropped down to the bottom of his belly, he thought that was it, that was the end, and he wished he should have pee in the soup pot if he had known that it's going to be like this.

He thought that the worst they could do to them was to demote them down to second class private and send them out in the field. Virak drifting imagination was cut short when the general finish his soup and wiping his mouth with the colonel follow suit. They got up came to stand in front of them and he started.

"You two had done it… Staff sergeant, sergeant, you had shown your courage, dedication and leadership traits in acting as company commander and assistant commander you had brought victory to company B despite all odd. A victory over the reputed battle test NVR, the elite force of the One Breast Bitch. From this day forward in this battle field of this district town, I Brigadier general… promote you two to the rank of lieutenant and second lieutenant in charge of company B"

To everybody amazements including Virak, it was a relief for both of them. They pinned a lieutenant rank insignia on the acting company commander chest and a second lieutenant on Virak's, and that made them felt relief and glad that they appreciated their effort and hard work. All of the officers in the bunker came to congratulate them including the officer with a sinister smile and the two commanders came to shake their hand again for the job well done and to give their compliment to the cook of the company B field vegetable soup and told them to submit the name of those soldiers in the company B who should be promoted to the battalion commander.

They were dismissed moment later, felt relief and glad to get away from that bunker undaunted; when they went in there felt like crawling into a snake pit but now they came out felt like floating on the cloud with gold stripe on their chest. On the way back, they congratulated each other for their meritorious field promotion, and the newly promoted lieutenant said to Virak.

"Congratulation to you young Second lieutenant, I knew I pick the right man and thank you for the job well done"

A week later while the battle was still in full swing a battalion clerk told Virak that the battalion commander wants to see him in private at the bamboo bush a hundred yards from the bunker. And when he got there the commander said.

"My wife had sent me a message, she said that your mother is gravely ill, pack your bag right now and go home to take care of your mother. Now go" Virak packed his bag and reluctantly left his unit in the middle of an operation.

C6- A Break from the War

In Phnom Penh, Virak thought about going to knock on Lady M door but the consequence of getting caught made him changed his mind, so he gave up for the time being and went straight to his house to see his mother. When Virak arrived home, he started to ask everybody about his mother condition but it seemed like nobody could give him a straight answer and they were unwilling to say anything else, so he went to peek at the inside of her inner camber. There she was sitting holding court with half a dozen ladies, and they were chatting like a flock of bird, and it didn't seem to have any sign of ill condition like the commander's wife said in the message at all. And now Virak could understand it is a mother instinct that she will go to great length to get her son home safe and sound, but he felt disappointed because his unit was still engage with the one breast bitch unit in the battle field right then, and here he was safe and sound and horny at home.

Virak walked in the dark hall in front of the chamber, and there stood the person he wished to see the most it's Lady M, she was just about to open the chamber door. Virak rushed to hold her hand, wrapped his arm behind her, and walked her from the door of the chamber toward a storage room at the opposite side. She protested quietly and kept greeting him in low tone of voice.

"Oh hi, when did you get back, your mother miss you terribly... oh no please let me go?"

"Hi, and I miss you too come in here for a moment please" Virak dragged her pass the chamber door through the dark hall; he pushed her into the storage room and close the door behind them, she looked alarm and begged him to let her go.

"Oh please be good be a dear let me go, I must see your mother, we got to stop this; they will hear us"

"Just be quiet so nobody could hear us, there are a dozen noisy ladies in there and they are not going to miss you; it had been so long My Lady"

Virak held her shaking body in his arms and they kissed passionately, a moment later, she started to relax, Virak sensed warmness coursed through her body and her round full breasts crushed on his chest, his hand moved lower to caress her round butt and pulled her restless crutch rubbing against his erected shaft.

He released her for a moment to unbutton her shirt and unsnap her bra; he put his face between her cleavages to absorb the womanly scent. He reached down to pull the hem of her silk skirt up to her waist and let her held on to it, and he pulled her panty down and let her stepped out of it. While kneeling, he admired her naked slender woman form from the waist down and absorbed the fragrance of Chanel No 5 that she had anointed between her legs......

While lying down, she pulled her knees up with her legs wide apart she pulled him over and urged him to get on top of her...... Virak reared back to admire her naked form with her silk skirt bunched up around her waist, and her breasts rise and fall follow her excited short breathing...... his shaft sheathed tranquil in her soft and warm depth and everything seem to fade away from his mind the battle, the troupe, the One Breast Bitch Vietcong commander and at that moment even the sound of chained explosion from the B-52 bombing could not get his attention away from this ultimate pleasurable moment between her legs. She had her legs wrapped around and her heel dug on his butt.

Virak left his rod drill deep and he relaxed on top of her in a state of sublime ecstasy. When they heard the noise of the ladies leaving the chamber, then she quickly pushed him off, arranged her clothes, smoothed her hair, and hesitated to listen for a moment and she stepped out quickly.

Lady S

Virak waited for a minute before letting himself out but before he could close the storage room door, the chamber door opened and there stood Lady S looking at him pulled up his zipper with her eyes wide open. Virak recovered himself and quickly apologized to her, close the storage door and walked away. Lady S closed the chamber door quickly, came to push open the storage door, called to him in whisper, pointed and motioned him to get in, and he had no choice but to comply. Lady S closed the door behind her, she looked around the room and turned to look at Virak with a smile on her face she licked her red lips and she asked.

"What were you and Lady M doing in this room?"

"Lady M is she in the house? I do not know My Lady"

"Ok and how about you, what are you doing in here? Don't tell me that you come to pee in this storage room"

"No Mme, I come in here to adjust my pant"

"Adjust my foot, this room smell reek with sex, and when she walk pass me she smell just like this; and even before her husband came back from oversea she look glowing and gleaming just like a cat had just swallowed a canary. I knew that she was up to something or some man had his thing up hers. Now tell me the truth, how long had you been screwing her?"

"I don't know what you are talking about My Lady, you must be mistaken me with somebody. I never have anything to do with Lady M or anyone else"

"Ok you sounded unbelievably convincing but come to meet me at this address tomorrow afternoon, we will discuss about this matter quietly. Don't tell anyone or I will bring this mater to your parent or Lady M's husband"

"OK Mme I will see you tomorrow" Now Virak had another lady to deal with, Lady S was in her early thirty, she was a tall woman with large breast, slender waist and big round butt. She had no children and she inherits a lot of wealth and properties from her rich diplomat husband who pass away a few years ago. There was a rumor among the ladies that there were a lot of the upper class aristocrat men try to court her but they said she contemplated married a foreign diplomat and move to live abroad. She was an influence and a well connected person in the upper crust society. Virak thought he must be very careful because she was a force to be reckoned with. He got no idea of what will be in store for him, and he wonder why she want to see him at this address, it must be one of her property.

At an appointed time, Virak came to ring the bell at a private entrance to a five stories building near the central market. This building was just like any other in this area, all of their ground floors were shops, offices, restaurants and hotel lobby. In between those stores shop, there were private entrances to the upper floor apartment flats and offices. He punched in the code she gave him to open a steel gate to a stair that went always up to the penthouse.

When the last door open up, Virak was surprised to see a different version and style of Lady S, and she stood at the entrance hall with one hand on her hip and a drink in the other; she greet him with a smile on her face and she seemed to be more friendlier than before. She wore a stylish black bell bottom pant that showed the profile of her curvy big round butt and a white long sleeve shirt that tied a knot above her bellybutton. She looked more attractive in this attire than the silk skirt that she normally wear when she come to his house.

She looked relaxed and friendly but he didn't know what to expect, and there was one thing for sure the reason he came here was the discussion about him and Lady M in the storage room, and he thought he knew what to do was to deny everything and to maintain his innocent. Virak put his hand up together to greet her and acted sheepishly looking down to avoid her sharp searching eyes. She came to stand in front of him pushing those two large breasts under his nose; the sight of her cleavages and the fragrance of French perfume from her body had made his loin stirred. She put one hand on his shoulder and the other to lift his chin up, she spoke softly.

"Hey, don't worry, relax, I am not going to tell anyone about it, it's a secret between us, consider me your friend but some little favor I need from you" She paused for a moment; he look at her just like a prisoner who waits for the verdict.

And then she opened her red lips slowly to give him the whole deal.

"First, you must keep everything under secret, and second you must do what I told you to do. Don't worry there will be all pleasures; serve my every whim, if you please me I will set you free and you will be reward handsomely. Do you understand? And do you agree?"

"Yes Mme, I understand and it's OK, I would love to be your friend"

"Excellent answer let me remind you again that we must guard our secret friendship under utmost secrecy, when we are in front of other people I am you mother's friend OK"

"Yes Mme and I'm just an innocent young man"

"That is an intelligent thinking superb; you seem to be more mature beyond your age. You are a rare gift for me and I start to love you already my friend"

They already had their arms around each other the whole time they exchanged their deal, her big round breasts rubbed lightly on his chest, and he took a liberty of sliding his hand down to caress her smooth round butt, and she kept rubbing her crutch on his now stiff member under his pant. She suggested that Virak should make a phone call to his home to inform them that he will spend his weekend at a friend's place.

After he'd made the call, she motioned him to follow behind her, she walked slowly with a glass of Hennessey Cognac mixed with Perrier water on ice in hand, and she swayed her slender hip and her round but toward the bedroom. Inside, she started to unbutton her blouse and told him to get undressed; his eyes followed her every movement and when she pulled her bra off to reveal a pair of huge breast with the pink hard nipples sticking out that made him had an instant stiff erection.

"How many girls or women you had sleep with"

"None, I never sleep with anyone Mme"

"Do you have any notion of man and woman makes love?"

"Yes, I guess so Mme, I listen to my friends talking "

"What do you think between me and Lady M?"

"I think you are very sexy, Lady M always has sad face it's just like she was in mourning all the time"

"Good answer, now come here" Virak walked into her embraced, put his hand on her big round butt and they kissed. She opened her legs to accommodate his stiff erection and with her hip squirming, she made the tip of his staff slid and slide madly along the wet lips of her warm gap. She stepped back, put her hand down to hold his erection and pump back and forth that made it became stiffer.

"You are a boy who possesses a man tool, lucky me, I will guide you through all these pleasure things, first let me taste this…HMMM"

She got up pulled him onto her four poster bed; she leaned against the headboard on the plush pillow, she spread her legs and pulled her knees up to present to him her big lips clean shave puff up gap, and it was coincidently smelled like she also anointed the Chanel No 5…… After resting for a moment in her arm, they went to the bathroom to continue their pleasure in the shower.

They came out in silk robe and went to the dining room to eat the hot food that she had order from the specialized restaurant. They fed each other roast duck, bird nest soup and washed them down with rice vine from the jug full of root bark and animal parts; she said it was Chinese traditional medicine and it's good for their stamina and prolong pleasure. Virak said he was all for it any things for the pleasure with a sexy woman like her that made her beamed with pride. They made love on and off for a few days before he reluctantly went back home by her persuasion and the promise for more. When he got home everybody including his mother thought he was sick because he looked so pale, she had an herbal doctor came to examine him and ordered some herb medicine to boost his strength; the doctor just smiled and suggested a few days bed rest. So Virak had to stay in bed for a few days to make her stop worry.

How to connect the baby arms and legs

One morning, while Virak was still on bed rest, his older sister and a bunch of girls came in his room, even though he wasn't happy to see anyone but it was her habit to ask him what he want from the market before she went to do her shopping, and among the group a fully lactate large breasts woman with a baby in her arms caught his attention, so while his eyes captivated by the large lactate breasts he replied to his elder sister.

"Milk, fresh warm milk that's what I want"

"OK, I will look for it; I don't know if they have what you want... OH shut up; you are so mean" When she saw his eyes glued to the mother with full lactate breasts, she frowned and they all scrambled out of his room. The sight left him with a raging hard on under the bed sheet. Virak tried hard to think and dig deep in his memory, he guessed he had seen her face from somewhere but he could not place her until he inquired with his elder sister later.

"That was RV don't you remember? She is my friend be nice to her, remember she had been through a lot in her short married life"

OH yes, now Virak remember her, she was more slender then and now she is more curvier that's why he couldn't remember her, RV and his elder sister knew each other since elementary school; they were five years older than him. About a year ago, RV's mother arranged for her to marry a wealthy gentleman in his fifty who live at the next building. A few weeks after their wedding, one night there was a woman cried for help from the old man flat. When their relatives busted the door in they saw the old man lay naked motionless between her legs and RV tried in vain to get herself from under his dead weight.

At the interrogation, she said that the old man made love to her every night before they felled asleep but that day he made love to her more times than usual and that night his ejaculation was so intense that it may caused his heart to skip a beat; so he might have passed out and died on the top of his new young bride who thought he was resting on top of her after their orgasm, not until he became cold, stiff and heavy when she tried to wake him up but he won't regain consciousness, and then she realized that she was in trouble because she felt suffocated under his weight and his penis still lodged deep between her gap. They tried diligently to pry his corps and dislodged his penis from her gap. The old man relatives thank haven that he died at the apex of his pleasure, and what else can a man ask for?

A few weeks later, his relative announced the miracle; they were so happy that RV got pregnant and the old man had left his legacy behind in RV womb as proof for the fruit of his labor. And this is where the story comes to play since her baby was born without a father stay around keep making love to the mother through the pregnancy to connect the baby arms and legs. So this is a joke about the people in the old era who were so superstitious and ignorant, even now a day, there still are uneducated people believe in that fashion as the story went.

Once upon a time, there were two friends who live in the remote countryside; the older man who was a traveling merchant, his profession took him away from home for months at a time and left his pregnant wife at home with relative to take care of her. And for the bachelor younger man who was a farmer, and being a hard working farmer he stay close to home all his entire life so he had little knowledge about the fact of life. Customary, a newlywed couple supposed to make love at the first night they share their bed. So at that crucial first night he asked his friend for some advice; and the older one said.

"Don't you worry about a thing brother; I will check it out first to make sure everything will go smooth for you"

"Gee thank you very much; you are just like a big brother"

"EH don't mention it to anyone and what's a friend for; all you have to do is just put out the light, come out so I can get in to check to make sure that it's safe for you" In that fateful night, the younger man put out the light and slipped out, and the older one slipped in to take care of the young bride. He caressed and warmed her up, and stood at the foot of the bed, spread her legs, raised her knees up and performed his deed. Haft and hour later, he came out of the room with sweat on his forehead. The younger one looked concerned and asked.

"How was it? What should I do?"

"Perfect, you got nothing to worry about, it's all clear for you all you got to do is just go in there, stand at the foot of the bed, spread her legs and shove it in, and if she say anything you just keep your mouth shut and keep on pushing" The younger one rushed in, spread her legs and tried to follow the older friend advice in between her legs. The bride was surprised and glad to guide him in.

"You are very quick to recover for another round, you must be special my darling" The younger one kept his mouth shut, pounded into her until he spent. And then he put two and two together, he realized that his friend had his way with his wife first. He was so furious that he pounded between her legs all night until she complained.

A few weeks later, the older man left home to ply his trade. The younger one who waits for this occasion went to visit his friend's pregnant wife, and he acted surprised.

"OH no. why did he leave home while his wife pregnant like this?"

"What's wrong with that brother?"

"At an early stage of pregnancy like this he supposed to stay home to connect the baby arms and legs or the baby might born without any limb, he probably look like a squash"

"Oh no, what should I do?

"Well, a relative or a close friend may help"

"OH, would you please, since you are his best friend"

"OK, I will try my best, what's a friend for but don't tell anyone even him"

"Why? Don't you want everybody know your good deed?"

"No, because it's taboo and bad luck may befall upon us all; we must keep everything under secret"

"OK, can you help me now?"

"All right, let's we get in your bedroom" He had her laid on her back, spread her legs and he shoved his shaft in her gap to help connect the baby limbs. And so the younger man do his good deed ever since and they all live in harmony happily ever after.

And now, we returned to conclude Virak's good deed with the young widow RV and her baby. One day when he caught both of them alone in the hallway, he acted concerned and asked her to come in his room and locked the door behind him. And then he inspected the sleeping baby arms and legs very closely. She looked concerned and she asked him.

"What's wrong?"

"No, there is nothing wrong, this baby is lucky. Who help you during your pregnancy?"

"Help me to do what?"

"To connect the baby arms and legs" And then she realized that Virak was joking about the old story.

"OH, get out of here, there is nobody OK" She just laughs, turned red and look demurred down at the baby; and he continued to push.

"Nobody help you! You take a lot of risk, you should have asked me, I will help you to connect anything, and I even give him some extra limb"

"It is too late now, and he seemed to be OK. You were always away from home and even if you are home, you are my best friend young brother"

"It's not too late, I assured you that I may look young but I am very capable, and beside I still need some fresh warm milk" Virak's hand followed his word; he reached out to hold and feel her ample breasts. She was nervous and turned toward the door. He followed her and pinned her from behind at the corner, he reached around from behind to rub her hard nipples, kissed her neck and pushed his erected penis on her butt outside her sarong. Despite her protest, he turned her around, unbuttoned her blouse and her bra and bent over the baby to suck her nipples. She protested quietly until the baby started to cry, then he had to let her go and he whispered in her ear.

"Come here alone in the afternoon" She just casted her eyes down and walked away slowly; Virak was not certain that she will ever come back but he believe that she got to feel horny sometime, and she could not get relief by just played with herself alone; a woman who had a hard penis went through her gap once there will be no substitute. In this hot tropical climate, almost everybody will be inactive and taking a nap in the afternoon. At some afternoon, she came in the house but she avoided Virak because there were still a lot of people in the house.

He almost gave up on her but one afternoon when almost everybody in the house went to attend the ceremony at the temple, she came in his room with the baby was still sleeping in her arm, and she said she needed a cool and quiet place to put her baby to sleep. Virak pointed at the rattan cane couch; she put the baby down on the cushion and still sat there looking at the baby.

He went to sit next to her, and started to caress her shaky body to feel her reaction, she still protest out of fear but he still believe she came in his room to get her itch between her leg scratch but one way or another he got to bang her right then and there. He unbuttoned her blouse and unsnapped her bra, and pushed it open to take a moment to admire her large full breasts.

Virak weight both of her globes and bent down to suck on her hard nipples, and then reached down to pulled the hem of her sarong up and slid his hand between her smooth thighs to feel her soaking wet panty. He got up, dragged her to his bed; on the way he pulled her sarong and her panty off, and laid her on her back at the edge of the bed, he fumbled to drop his pant, hooked the under sides of her knees over his forearms……. And that was considered his good deed to fill in the gap for the husband duty in connecting the baby arms and legs according to the old story. Was it just a joke? Really? OH well, at least he could help the mother……

The Princesses

Virak's parent tried to send him back to school but he did not think that he still have any interest in studying anymore. Despite the lack of interest, he went to school anyway to make them happy and to catch up with the social activity that he had missed. The school had a long tin roof behind the classroom building that used to park the bicycle and motorcycle sheltered from the sun and the monsoon rain. That morning it was raining very hard, so Virak just sat under the tin roof waiting for the rain to clear up a bit because he didn't want to get wet. Everybody left for class because it was almost the time for starting bell sounded.

Suddenly the window in front of him swung open and there in the middle of the window frame was a beautiful sight he ever saw, it was a pretty face long hair girl with a slender body and the fragrance of frangipani permeated the air around the window. She was gloving like a ray of sunlight in the middle of the dark stormy night. Did he say night? Yes he did and it was just like that.

He was so captivated by her beauty that he could not move or looked away from her. He could not hear when the starting bell rang and somebody reminded him that it was time, he guessed then time had no meaning to him at all, and all his attentions were following her every move, when she returned to her seat next to that window that gave him the side view of her perky breast, her long shiny black hair decorated with frangipani flower of course and her gold emerald earring hypnotized him by swinging back and forth. The teacher and everybody in the classroom except her, they were watching him and amused at his sense of lost.

Virak knew she sensed his present still at the window with all the commotion in the class, she bent her demurred red face down and casted a glance at him from the corner of her eye that flashed like a lightning bold through his heart; the teacher waved his hand across his face.

"Don't you have any class to go to?" Virak did not hear his question at all; until everybody were laughing very loud then he came to his sense.

"AH OH yes, it must be the storm"

"Yes, I know it's the storm and the rain, and why don't you just go to your classroom"

Virak moved away from the window slowly with his head was still floating somewhere in the cloud. He walked into his classroom, took his seat and did not pay any attention to his surrounding or to the teacher who was barking at him about his tardiness, all Virak could see was his finger pointing to the door. He walked from his seat and was still lost in his thought; then he was thinking out loud.

"Who was that girl?"

All his classmates erupted in laughter but the teacher was turning pale it's probably from his extreme anger and with his lips was quivering and he seem to have steam coming out of his ears, and then he shouted "Get the hell out of here!" That night, it was an unsettled night for Virak; he had so many excited dreams, and it's a matter of fact he was dreaming all night.

In the next morning, he woke up tired but he was not too tired to stand outside the classroom window with almost all of his classmates who want to know which girl he was talking about. After waiting for a while, the window was opened but by a chubby plain looking girl, everybody around inside or outside the classroom busted out laughing. Virak was speechless with his jaw dropped open; then his classmates asked.

"Is that it? Is that the dream girl you 're talking about?"

"Hell no, that one is definitely not the one"

Virak looked pass the chubby girl into the classroom, there stood his dream princess smiling; he tried to get his classmates attention and pointed to her, and by the time their eye met her smile varnished.

After what happen, he stopped going by the window because he felt kind of embarrassed, then he only observed and admired her from a distant. The girls in his class started to tease him.

"What's happen now Romeo, we heard that your beautiful dream girl was turning into a toad?"

"You all are my toad dream girls now"

Virak got up and playfully chased after them; they all shrieked and fled away. One of them in particular who had the most developed hip and breast named SR ran slowly behind the other because her fully developed butt slowed her down.

Virak caught her at under the bottom of the stair, he wrapped his arms around her from behind, pulled her butt rubbing against his loin with one hand rubbed her breast inside her shirt, and the other one reached under the hem of her mini skirt to rub the front of her panty.

She was squirming and trying to push his hand off but it kept on worming down the waistband of her panty to scratch the short fuzzy hair, and when his finger touched her tamarind seed all of her movement ceased, she relaxed her legs, opened them up a little to let his middle finger had access to her moist slit. Virak moved her chin and kissed the corner of her mouth, she closed her eyes and low moan escaped from her lips.

He heard a lot of commotion from the upper floor, and then he started to release his grip and held her waist to steady her now wobbly legs and buckle knees. The girls yanked his arms off from her and they pulled her away. They all pointed their finger at him like a bunch of angry mop.

"Why did you do to her? We were just joking; now we will report you to the administrator"

"What did I do? I did not do anything, ask her" They all looked at SR; she was still looked flushing red and had her arms over the girls shoulder. He noticed her hard nipples poked through her white shirt, she looked at him, lower her eyes and she let out a few words.

"He didn't do anything"

"UHH why do you let him off the hook?"

She just turned and walked away with all the girls followed behind. At that moment, Virak realized that she is his only friend among those hostile girls; then he started to look at school in a different perspective.

He kept low profile, involved in school activity, and improved his grade but he could not get rid of the bad boy image to the girl in his class; so he asked for their forgiveness. The girls was still could not accept it until he apologize to SR in person and in front of everybody but SR want it to be in private because it's between her and Virak. So when everyone was out of the classroom for the physical education class. They had SR and Virak inside the classroom and they stood outside to guard the door. SR looked nervous; he came to stand in front of her and asked.

"SR I am sorry for what I did to you would you please forgive me?"

"It's OK, you don't need to do that, I did not tell them anything, they'd set up all this, this is not necessary, by the way I should thank you"

"You are welcome, what's for?"

"For made me feel like a woman"

Hmmm if he was not mistaken with all these set up look like she wants another dose of therapy. He held her hip and pulled her to his embrace and they kissed like the movie star in the European movie. Virak pulled the blue baggy gym short for girl at that time and her panty down, he rubbed her tamarind seed and slid a finger through her moist gap that made her winced with a surprise look on her face.

"Don't go too deep it's hurt" Then he realized that she had not been penetrated yet, so he want to put her on the table to do it properly but she refused.

"No not here, not now, it's risky" She was right; the girls were starting to call them.

"SR, are you all right in there? Teacher is looking for us" She did not respond but adjust her cloth and walked out of the classroom. Virak peeked through the window slate, he saw the astonishing look on those naïve young faces and they asked SR.

"What did he say?"

"He said, he was sorry for everything"

"Why did it take so long?"

"Because he went on and on apologizing before I let him go"

"Why you are flushing?"

"It was hot in there with all the door and window close"

Virak suggested to SR that they should get together some time to finish what they had left off, but she said she was afraid that her fiancé will find out at their wedding night that she was no longer a virgin. She told Virak that her fiancé is the son of the high ranking official in the government, they were arranged to be married when he returned from Europe after he graduated. They love each other and she doesn't want to cheat behind his back because she kind of feels sorry for him. When he was still here they used to find quiet time together petting and feeling each other body that made her want more but he did not want to go all the way because he want to wait until their wedding night. Virak understood her need and want, and also just being there at the right time, so he tried to reason with her.

"What do you think what we did in the classroom, we had already cheat on him. I just want you to feel the ultimate pleasure. You cannot help it; you cannot wait for him for so long. Don't worry about your virginity because now a day girl play sport, you just write to him and tell him that you had feel sharp pain and bleed a little while playing soccer. I am certain that he will understand if he doesn't see any blood at your wedding night. I guess you already know how to mark your period on the calendar to avoid any unwanted pregnancy. I will make an arrangement for our class to have a picnic at the jicama plantation (Chamka pekourk) on the east river bank. You can bring all you friend to have fun at the plantation, and I let you know how to come to meet me in the bamboo trail to the river bank"

Virak picked one of her safe day and a day that a lot of their classmate could come because he want many people to be there, so if she slips out from the picnic nobody will pay any attention. He told her just keep low profile and let the other organized it, and she just went along with it.

And now Virak asked his friend BT to help him make all these happen. Do you remember? Sergeant BT, the older friend, he is just a little lazy but smart and capable. BT and Virak went to see the farmer to make all the arrangement necessary for the picnic on the day that Virak had chosen plus he paid a deposit for the seclude shack at the bamboo trail by the river bank. BT knew exactly what Virak was up to but he did not ask him anything. Virak also had BT rent a mini bus to transport those classmates who does not have a motorbike.

On the appointed date, Virak went to the plantation early in the morning to make sure that the farmer had the food ready and he went to get himself familiar with the seclude shack at the river bank, and then he paid the farmer to finalize their deal. Virak put a few coolers full of food and drink in the shack, locked the door with the padlock and chain.

And then, he went to the city to check on BT progress; he saw BT started to load the mini bus and everybody were happy to have a picnic at the jicama plantation, when they saw Virak they ask if he want to come along but Virak declined for reason he was busy, and he also saw SR who was ready on her Honda scooter, he knew she stole a glance at him from behind her dark sunglass and she probably already wet her panty with anticipation, he thought she dressed down with kaki pant and wide brim hat to avoid drawing attention and that was a proper attire for a picnic and a romping in the wood.

Virak was satisfied the way his plan went so he left them and went to the market to get some beer, whisky, cigarette and a box of condom for BT, he did not know why BT want all these thing for but he did not ask, he just get them and bring to the seclude shack at the river bank.

The seclude shack was not small the way it sound like at all, it was a big long roof with almost haft of the floor was made into a semi open porch where they hung a few hammocks and they built bamboo bench around for sitting and laying, and there were tables and chairs all were made from bamboo, and the terracotta stoves for wood and charcoal burning, was placed at one corner to serve as a small kitchen. Inside, there were a large sitting room and a few small rooms with bamboo platform build in them covered by colorful reed woven mat only and that why he brought along a few cotton blankets. And in the rear there was an enclosure bathroom with a few water storage urns and it connect to an outhouse. So everything was set to have a decent comfortable home away from home that made entirely from bamboo, wine and toddy palm leaves.

Under the porch, Virak started the fire in the terracotta stove to announce human present in this dwelling place, and boiled some water just in case they might need some tea later on. He walked around to check everything to make sure the place is clean and safe; he thought the farmer had done a good job of taking care of it. He move his bike inside to keep it out of sight because he didn't want any of his classmates know that he was here, just in case any of them might wonder around the farm and come upon this place by accident even though there are "No Trespassing" signs all around.

After, Virak was satisfied everything was in order, and then he came to lay in the hammock waiting for her. He looked at his watch its ten o'clock in the morning, and according to their plan she should leave the plantation to return to the city for some reason and she should be here by now.

And suddenly, he heard a Honda scooter engine humming along the bamboo trail and it came closer by the second. He stepped outside to wait for her with anticipation, and finally, there she was with a bright smile under that wide brim hat. Virak took the scooter from her and rolled inside to park near his bike. She took off her hat and came in his arms, they held each other without saying a word but he could feel her fear in her quicken heartbeat; a moment later she cooed.

"OH Sweet heart, I was so afraid came down that dark trail

Still holding each other arm in arm, she looked in his eye searching for reassurance, and slowly they kissed tenderly. They knew what they were here for, but first he must make her feel like they came here to have a casual picnic, after all they knew that they had all the time in the world in this jicama plantation of this Little Heaven.

They walked outside hand in hand; and sat at the bamboo table and set up their light noon meal, they had cold cut sandwich in baguette, chilled bottle of 7UP and some jasmine scented Thai pastry for her(Once she told him she love this pastry), and he certainly will indulge a woman with anything she love. By the way, it works just like a box of chocolate to woman in the West, and it may be a key to open her heart and her legs as well.

They ate and talked listening to the bamboo leaves rustling under the light breeze and looking over the river to the distant city beyond the west bank. After finishing their meal, they walked to the river bank, he pointed to her some part of the city over the far bank, and they talked about school and how she managed to get away from her friend, they joked, they laughed, and relaxed under the shade of the milk fruit tree where they came to stand face to face looking into each other eye. Virak wrapped his arms around her slender body, held her tenderly and they kissed.

Inside, it took him a few seconds to get naked; he spread some cotton blankets and sheet over the reed mat on the bamboo bed, and then he sat at the edge to watch her slowly getting undress. He hooked his finger inside the waistband of her panty and pulled it down to her ankle, with her hand on his shoulder she stepped out of it. He still kneeled down on his knees and his face was just a few inches from her sex; the fresh seashell scent of a woman body was intoxicated all his senses...... After their climax subsided, they held each other a while longer savoring their sublime moment.

And after she left, Virak grabbed some snack and a tall glass of Tiger beer on ice and he went to the river bank, sat on the bamboo bench under the milk fruit tree looking away over the river. The boat traffics were crisscrossing the river to every directions but an occasional bush of the water hyacinth that always floated down stream followed the river current. He wondered where these plants originated from, and where will they end up at? Or what might happen to those bushes along the river.

He looked far away upstream, and he was certain that some molecule of water in the river must had came from the highland jungle where he received his first lesson in making love from Sunthary, and during their cleansing ceremony where they blessed its flowing water with their love residue to anoint lovers everywhere. Now he was at the river bank in the lower land far away from the jungle, and made love to somebody else. Oh Sunthary, where is she? Is she safe? When will he see her again?

Tear rolling down his face unknowingly; he cursed at the war that brought pain and misery, and he cursed at the Vietcong that came in Cambodia and at the American who helped Lon Nol to overthrow Sihanouk. He cursed at Sihanouk who chose the wrong path, made the wrong move and the wrong decision. Damned the war, he felt so miserable at the moment.

The Mamasan

Virak heard footsteps from behind, he knew that BT is coming; he wiped his tear quickly, slipped on his sunglass and trying to act normal.

"What's the hell man? Why do you sit your sorry ass here alone? And where is the bitch? Oh excuse me, I think I know who she is, the one on the Honda scooter right. The guys said she is the daughter of Prince so and so; be careful man with that one, they may be no longer royalty but they still have a lot of powerful connection. Well quit crying over her man if you didn't get to bust your nuts, come on I got a bunch of women in the shack, and I bring more beer and food lets us party"

At the shack, Virak saw five women four of them were in their late teen or early twenty and the one sat by the stove looked like she was in her thirty. He turned to TB and asked.

"Why do you bring that odd old woman here for man?

"She is the mamasan, my old teacher she can cook man, she just want to step away from her business for a while. And these women they are not the sex slave from the whorehouse, they are free spirit women who banded together to work for themselves. I invite them here as my guess, remember to treat them nicely OK"

"If you say so"

BT introduced Virak to all the younger women and the mamasan; they were already got the party started, many kinds of food and drink were laid out on the table, BT grabbed a glass of whisky, pulled a woman from the table and went inside the room.

Virak get another beer and join them at the table; the women did a lot of talking it seemed like all of them tried to engage him in their conversation at the same time, at the time Virak was not in the mood so he just smiled to be polite and sipping his beer. These women were so aggressive that they turned him off; one of them asked him to go in the room with her or with her friend or with both of them but he declined, one asked if he was still a virgin and the other one wanted to give him a blowjob right on the spot, he just apologized for his tiredness and told them he might join them later. BT came to his rescue by drop one off and took the other two back inside.

Virak excused himself from the table by just telling them that he was full, and came to join mamasan who was still busy beside the stove; she had a completely different manner from those young women. After she had finished her cooking, they still sat by the stove at the corner talking; he took a good look at the thirty years old woman, and he was surprise to find her attractive, she may not dressed provocatively or put on a lot of make up like those younger women but she is unmistakably a pretty woman with a refined manner.

Virak was still wondering whether she was a school teacher like BT said or she was just a retired whore who teach him how to make love; so he asked her that BT had told him she was his teacher and he wonder why she worked in the brothel with those women, she just smiled and narrated to him her life story.

"I know people always misunderstood that I work with them they think that I am also a prostitute, that is all right you are not the first, some of the customer had come to request for my service numerous times I get use to it by now but I always decline and explain to them that I am not a prostitute. Some years ago, yes I was a teacher near the northern provincial town; and after my husband of two years passed away those rich and powerful men want to force me to be a concubine or a kept woman, that was why I had to escape to this city ever since.

Five years ago, I rescued some women who was about to be force into sex slave prostitution, and since their status and honor were already ruin and we were motivated by financial need they asked me to open up my place as a brothel but we share the profit instead of I own them like the sex slave whorehouse. They all feel free to come and go we do it so well that right now we own our own place; and BT was my student when I still teach in school until I decide to open the brothel and then I quit teaching"

"You have done a very noble thing for a good cause for those disadvantage women Madame"

"Thank you for your understanding of our plight, despite at such a young age your thinking is much more mature. You are so different from BT but yet you two hang around together"

"BT and me, we know each other all our life, he is my friend we need each other that why we still hang around"

"But it seem that you two don't hang around together when BT come to the brothel that why I never see you before"

"No Mme, I don't like to hang around in a brothel, it is a matter of fact I never go to any brothel with him or not, because I love to be friend with older woman like you"

It took her by surprise of what Virak had just said to her, she turned to take a good look at him, and with a smile on her face she said.

"Oh boy I am flatter, you are so very bolt for a shy young man who didn't say anything much, don't you think that I am too old for you?"

"No, you are just the way I like in older woman"

Later, she got up and mentioned that she wanted to take a shower at the rear of the shack; Virak volunteer to show her where everything were, on the way she reminded the young women to clean themselves even though they were not on the job every time they get lay.

When they were inside, Virak held her from behind and feel up her body despite her feebly protest, and then he showed her to one of the room at the rear that were divided by thin wooden board and where she will spend the night. He went around the shack to light all the kerosene lamps, and then he picked a room next to hers, got himself change into a cotton krama and went to the rear to take a shower naked next to her.

She was surprised to see him but kept on pour water over her head while she had a big krama wrapped around her body over her breast. Virak pulled his krama off to let her see his erection at its full glory and continue to take a shower just like nothing happen, it may be a little bit dark but he knew she could see his naked body with the light from the hall. After finishing the shower she changed the wet krama with a silk sarong and dried herself up watching him lathing soap on his body for a moment and then she left.

He went outside to tell BT and the young women not to disturb mamasan in the room across the hall and they could have the other three rooms. He went to his room made her feel his present so she could floating her thought about how excited when she saw his stiff erection or how will it affect her body if it stab between her legs through her gap.

He knew she could not help but to mesmerize about the suppressed exciting memory of the long ago past, the memory of how excited when she had a man in between her thighs, and all these memories could triggered the awakening the dull senses of her sexual excitement that she had suppressed for so long came to life.

Virak played a cassette of Sinsisamut love songs in the player and went to knocked on her door asking if she want him to bring her anything; this was a crucial point that he will guest by the reaction of her answer, if she said no that mean she is a dull boring old woman after all, but if she reply yes she want something then he will knew immediately that her body become alive her slit is wet with anticipation, and she might want him in between her legs.

"UHH……… yes please I want some cognac on ice"

Voila! That was an open Sesame type of magic word; Virak went to get some drinks and a plate of roasted meat and he went back to knock on her door. Inside he closed the door behind him, pushed the latch in, put the food and drinks on the bamboo table and stood there for a few seconds to look in her eyes and gauging her mood that will decide his next move should be. He could detect a spark in her eyes when she looked up and thanked him for the things he brought to her, and she asked him why he played the cassette left in his room? He sat on the bed next to her and he replied.

"So they won't hear us talking and not knowing that I'm in your room, isn't that what you want?"

Virak made her known that he intent to be discreet for what might go on between them; she did not answer him, she just smiled looking at him from the corner of her eye and reaching for her cognac glass. He also grabbed his beer and they toasted; she asked him what are they toasting for? He told her it's for them and their exciting moment to come. He dimed the light and kept on talking until he noticed her restlessness and her hip squirming, then he could feel her anticipation of the inevitable…..

He humped in between Mamasan legs on and off until the early morning wee hour before he decided to resign and slipped back into his room. Nobody knew that their celibate mamasan had her fun with him that night and he didn't tell BT that he screwed his teacher until they were on their way escape to Thailand, and he still didn't believe him then.

C7-On the Bank of the Mekong River

It had been a few weeks since SR sacrificed her virginity in the shack at the jicama plantation on the Mekong river bank. At school, she looked serene, content, and most of the time she was quiet and also talked with a soft spoken manner.

Every day, she dressed classy even in her school uniform and looked more prettier, curvier, and most of her friend took notice and talked among themselves that SR had acted like a grownup lady ever since they returned from the jicama plantation. Whenever no one noticed, she looked at Virak's direction with a forlorn and longing look in her eye. He responded with a little nod and a smile to let her know that he understood her want and longing.

Virak immediately, initiated a plan so they can be alone together somewhere in private. He remembered Lady S had mentioned to him last week that she needed somebody to take care of a furnished building at the riverside that she want to keep it vacate for renting to the foreign diplomat.

He immediately volunteered to take care of it so he could have a quiet place to study and wait for her at their appointed time every Saturday; she was very happy to hand him the keys, told him the place was his to taking care of and she will see him on Saturday.

Virak gave the address to SR and told her where he will wait for her; he brought some servants to clean up the place, rearranged the furniture and stocked some food and drinks in the refrigerator.

The property had a three stories row houses front building with a wide driveway on the side that lead to an huge backyard that was overgrown with shrub and vine covered by tall fruit trees, palm and coconut, and the driveway continued always to the two stories building at the river bank that he made sure they cleared the driveway out always to the river.

A day before their rendezvous, Virak spent the night alone at the front building to make himself feel at home; he climbed up the stair in the back and came down by the front one, each floor had its own complete one bedroom apartment unit.

In the living room, he found an old phonograph and a stack of record that left there from the previous tenants, there were French, English, Italian, and German music titles, he'd played some of them that he liked and became absorb in them like the music of Johan Straus The Blue Danube, The Four Seasons of Antonio Vivaldi, Sumer time of George Gershwin, and various titles of Wolfgang Amadeus Mozart.

Virak woke up the next day to a cool breezy morning, and he went to a restaurant around the corner to have his morning meal, he had a bowl of seafood noodle soup with a piece of long fried dough and a tall café au lait on ice, and he also bought some dishes to take out. At the apartment, he changed into a more comfortable silk sarong and sat by the window waiting for SR. After waiting for a while, he heard the humming sound of the Honda engine scooter came along the side driveway.

At last, there she was her cute face under the wide brim hat and a thin kaki jacket over her school uniform. Virak opened the back door to let her inside the apartment with the scooter and all, inside she dropped everything and rushed into his arms, she lay her head on his shoulder with tear welled up in her eyes she cooed softly.

"OH my darling, I miss you so much" He held her body tenderly, raised her chin up and looked into her eyes.

"But baby, we see each other every day at school"

"I know but it isn't the same, we're so close but yet so far because I cannot hold you or being hold by you in your arms. My darling, please hold me" They kissed and held each other for a while until he felt her hard nipples pushed at his chest, and then he showed her the bed room where she could change.

He came to sit down on the couch looking out through the window over the backyard to the Mekong River beyond that was full of life activities; he followed a lone patch of water hyacinth that was brought from somewhere by the water current, now it floated slowly followed the river to some where unknown; it was the same as their life and all lives on earth, it seemed like a high degree of uncertainty awaiting for them all. He turned on the old phonograph with the record of Straus beautiful music on the turntable, it was the Blue Danube. At the time, Virak did not know what kind of music it was, all he knew was that it sounded beautiful despite an old phonograph disc it still sounded beautiful and flowed like a river.

Suddenly something equally beautiful was blocking his line of sight, SR came to stand in front of him, and she had on a saffron and green silk sarong with one of his long sleeve shirt that tied a knot above her navel; the silk sarong showed the profile of her round butt and her sexy hip. He held her hip and pulled her close to inhale the fragrance of jasmine scent from her body that permeated the air around them. She slid herself to sit on his lap and to make him hold her slender body.

Virak offered her some drink she shook her head, he offered her some food she shook her head, and then asked if she want to make love she just smiled and hid her face in his chest. Virak started to unsnap her bra and pull her panty down, and when he made her stand up all the shirt and sarong fell to the floor, she stood there naked look like Venus just came out of the sea, and then he told her to turn around to admire her beauty in all of her naked glory. Despite her fear of being seen from the window, she turned around and rushed into arms, he picked her up and walked naked into the bed room.

While the Blue Danube was still playing in the living room, he laid her down in the middle of the big bed; and sat up to admire her nakedness and then after a lengthy and thorough foreplay he kneeled between her legs, raised her knees up and...... Later after the shower, while she dried herself up Virak walked naked to the living room to retrieve their clothes.

In the living room there Lady S sat on the couch looking out of the window with SR's panty was hanging on her finger, and she looked up at him and his member with a gleaming smile on her face.

"So, what have you been up to? I thought you need to be alone to study, and what is this? Is this yours?" Virak smiled wryly gathered all the clothes and sat next to her, and then she tossed the panty to him, he replied to her.

"Yes my Lady, I do need to be alone, but I can't say no when a classmate need my assistant on a project"

"Of course, and I presume that's a she who need your assistant. That 's OK, I understand but I can't wait until Saturday, because waiting is not my strong virtue, and I'm sorry for barging in like this, so tell her to wait for a few minutes because your aunt need you assistant on the top floor immediately" Virak caught SR by the bedroom door, walked her to the kitchen, and show to her the food and drink. SR was alarmed when she heard footstep on the stair.

"Who is there? Is there somebody else in the house?"

"That's OK, It's just my aunt, she needs my help upstairs for a few minutes, there are foods and drinks on the table, just help yourself, OK Baby" He gave her a kiss and went upstairs to the top floor. Virak went to open the bedroom door but Lady S called him from the rear living room with a big window that looked out to the river. She had already changed into a pink silk robe and looking out of the window with her back toward him.

"I'm sorry to bother you like this but just like I said I can't wait, give me some now, hurry, I don't have much time, beside you may not want her to wait too long either" Virak sat on the couch behind her for a moment to admire the profile of her big round butt and her small waist under the silk robe…… She leaned forward to put her hand on the window sill, pushed her butt back, and spread her legs apart to present to him her gigantic puff up gap that was already wet…… Virak make her spend with loud shouting without spending himself. And he went downstairs to see SR in the kitchen, who had a worry look on her face.

"I heard your aunt shouting, I am sorry if I get you into trouble of anything; should I leave?"

"No don't worry about it, everything were already taking care off as we speak, and she will get over it soon"

They heard the front door open and close; Virak went to push the latch locked from inside to assure SR that no one will come in by surprise. They enjoyed their meal and each other company; they talked about school, their life and their future. She said that her fiancée had applied for her visa so she can go to live with him in Europe. Virak told her that it will be great for her, and he hope for her to have a happy life with her fiancée in Europe. She said that she will miss him, he told her she will not miss him but their love making and she can call him any time she come back to visit Cambodia, or he can go to visit her in Europe when the war is over. They became quiet and wondered when will this damn war be over? He looked at her face she had tear rolling down her cheek; Virak wrapped his arms around to hold her tender body and kept on chewing the broiled stuffed frog sausage. One day, SR came to see him with tear in her eyes. She said that she received the visa that will allow her to go to Europe to reunite with her fiancée, and she left for Europe.

Virak went to the second floor of the wooden building at the river bank; he sat by the window, looked over the Mekong River flowed, listened to Straus music the Blue Danube, and shed his tear quietly alone. He did not foresee that he could feel this way so bad, if he had known that he will be in so much pain of missing her, he probably shouldn't let her go."

OH Lord Visnu, I miss her so much, I miss her jasmine scented body, her tamarind seed"...... Virak sat alone many days at the window listening to the same record of the Blue Danube; one day he could not hear anymore music but some kind of scratchy noise, he pulled the record from the phonograph and thrown it out of the window watching it splashed and disappeared in the river. Everything became quiet; he leaned back on the couch looking up in the sky. Suddenly Lady S came to block his view and drop her clothes to the floor.

"Where have you been? I was looking all over for you; I need you for one last time"

Virak did not pay attention to a word that she had just said he just looked blank through her. She kissed him and climbed on the couch to rub her breasts, her navel and finally her thick lips gap on his lips. Virak held her shapely butt and lost himself in between her legs. After a while, she got off, lies back on the couch, spread her legs wide, and pulled him over her body. She impatiently, guided his hard shaft through her wet…… They made love vigorously and had their thundering orgasm together, he shot his load deep in her liked the river flowed, and then he put his face at her neck and blurted out loud.

"OHH…SR, I love you so much….." Lady S pulled his face up, looked in his eyes, waved a finger in front of his glazed face and warned him while he was still squirting deep in her.

"EH…Watch out, not so fast Honey, we may have a lot of excellent times together but keep love out of this do you understand? Fall in love with girl your own age OK. What's happen to your fellow student? The owner of the panty who was at the house the other day; And I am sorry, it is too late for you Honey. I had found my prince charming, we just got engage last week, here look at my ring. And we will get married at the cathedral next week. I will be Mme… and we will move to Europe at the end of this month. Don't feel bad, don't cry OK Honey. We still can see each other and get together anytime I come back to visit Cambodia"

Virak reared his chest up, shook and kissed her hand to congratulate her and her husband to be while his hard shaft was still lodged deep between her legs. Virak had a blasted at Lady S wedding reception; he just had a few drinks despite his mother warning about alcohol consuming at that age, then Lady S came to his rescue.

"Don't you worry sister I will put him in the hotel room upstairs" She walked Virak to the elevator; while they were on the way up he told her he didn't want to be in the hotel room, instead he asked her to spend the night with him at the river bank place.

"Are you out of your mind? This is my wedding night and my husband is waiting to screw me after this reception over. I hold him off until tonight" Inside the room, she pulled all his clothes off, and she walked toward the door; Virak grabbed her hand and pulled her onto the bed.

"Don't leave yet My Lady gives me a ride for old time sake"

"I don't think you are in a condition to ride me I will ride you" She stood over his chest, pulled the hem of her gown up, and she squatted down on his waiting......

Lady S moved to Europe a month later; she sold most of her properties except her residential home and the riverside place that she let Virak taking care of it. Lady M and her family were also immigrated to Europe after she delivered a healthy baby boy.

Princesses Devy

At the school yard one day, a group of girl approached Virak and asked.

"Hi, can we ask you a question?"

"UH…OK, yes"

"Why you don't come by our class window anymore? She is kind of upset; we think she is looking for you"

"I don't know what you all are talking about or whom do you all refer to"

"The princess, we call her Devy"

"I'm sorry; I still can't remember the name"

"You saw her at the window of our classroom, do you remember? The pretty one"

"OH yes right, the angel with frangipani in her hair"

"Right, now you remember, she is Princess… Devy, she is training to become an Apsara dancer"

"I thought that after the coup d'état the republic had abolished everything royal"

"Yes, that's true but we don't care about that, she is still our princess but we don't come here to debate about that. We just want to let you know that after the day that you were at the window, every day she look kind of upset because when she open the window you weren't there"

"Did she ever say anything?"

"No, she never said anything but…"

"That's what I thought, I don't have time for another joke, have a nice day, I got to go, bye" Virak started to walk away, all the girls had disappointed look on their face except one of them she was so persistent that she came after him, grabbed a hold of his arm and said.

"No, no joke, would you just listen for one minute please, I am serious this is not a joke"

"How about you let go of my arm"

"I am sorry"

"I see that you are very dedicated to your friend well being, and who are you Miss?"

"Hi I am Princess RD, and you?"

"Hi, I am Virak Emperor of the universe"

"OOPS! I am very sorry, I forgot, I don't have any title anymore"

"And I am sorry, I lie I never have any title at all"

"Seriously, let we get back to talk about my friend, I'm afraid she may be dying if she never see you again"

"You got to be kidding right, she never said anything to you, and how do you know she want to see me? Or she is dying, is that what you just said?

"Yes, at least she is dying inside, and we know her because we are her best friend ever since first grade. She'd never been like this before you were at the window; we think that her unhappiness is cause by you"

"Cause by me? Now wait a minute Your Highness, I did not do or say anything to her, and I just looked at her at the window that's all"

"We know that's not entirely your fault but would you please come by the window just once, so she won't look like a wilted flower anymore"

"Doesn't it occur to you that she is upset because she lost her royal title?"

"No, it's not that, we'd lost our royal title too, we never get upset about that at all, and we prefer to live like this equal with everybody else"

"All right, I'm just kidding, I'm sorry"

"We are serious because we are concerned about our friend happiness and well being"

"What's about your happiness princess, and that I want to know"

"Never mind about us, we are here to tell you about our friend, we just want you to know about this, what you are going to do is up to you, and if she is dying from her unhappiness it will be your fault"

They left Virak there speechless; he thought that these girls were naïve that they got the gut to come to talk to him about their friend unhappiness. Was that he the cause? Virak didn't think so; he remembered that he didn't do a damn thing, not even a word exchange between them. She must be upset about something else, well, he can stop by to say hello and will see what will happen.

A week later after the girls came to talk to him; Virak went to sit on the step outside her window that was a foot higher than his head. After he sat there for ten minutes, finally a pair of slender arms pushed the window panes out. She leaned out looked to the left look to the right, and before she saw him Virak jumped off the step, put his hand on the window seal, looked into her eyes and greeted her.

"Good morning Princess, how are you this morning?"

She was startled, jumped back with her eyes wide open.

"Good morning I'm fine thank you; and you"

"I'm fine thank you; Princess"

"Please, don't call me like that; I don't have any more title"

"OK, you still look very much like a princess"

Her face turned red and she replied.

"Thank you, but I am no longer…."

"By the way I am Serey"

"I am Devy"

They just stood there looked in each other eyes and they were kind of lost of word. The atmosphere around them was so thick, tense and quiet that they could hear a pin drop. Virak heard whisper inside the classroom. "He is here at the window, be quiet, don't look"

A week later, a couple of girls who claimed to be Devy's best friends stopped Virak after school and asked him to join them at the café nearby. Virak went along to a café a few blocks from school and he wondered what were these girls had in mind. They kept telling him how happy Devy was ever since he went by the window; and Princess RD seemed to be the leader of the pack who kept on pushing all these nonsense out of her concern about her friend well being.

"Hi girls, Princess RD I'm so glad to see you, and you look so fine today even in this school uniform, I would love to see you in the royal silk and gold outfit..."

Virak grabbed and kissed Princess RD hand, the other girls turned pale because he had breached their royal protocol and violated haft dozens of other rules, but RD seemed to be unfazed by his attention to her, she went on pushing thing about her friend.

"Thank you very much, how nice of you to say; you should come to see Devy practice in Apsara costume she is really like an angel, at school she looked so happy and so radian. Why didn't you come by again? It had been a week that you did not show up and now she start to look restless again. She might turn into depression and become sad like a wilted flower and might die just like the character in the Wilted Flower story of Nou Hach"

"Wait a minute your highness, not so fast I know that she is not going to die from depression anytime soon, because when I saw her she didn't look upset or anything that show she have a depression. I don't want to make a fool of myself, one time is enough. Besides, she is royalty and I am a common person, we have nothing in common and we have nothing to talk about"

"You are wrong about that one, you don't know her, and you never sit down to talk to get to know her. How do you know that you two have nothing in common?"

"Is that so? And how the princess is going to have time to talk to me?"

"That can be arranged; we will have a garden picnic and play some game at my house. Be there Saturday after school"

The house was a huge colonial style villa surrounded by flower garden, manicured lawn, and fruit tree orchard. When

Virak got there the game were already in full swing, there were the badminton on the lawn and tennis table near some kiosk. There were a few servants who set up tables to serve some snack and drink nearby. He greeted Princess RD, grabbed some drink and joined the ping pong table.

A girl from the pack, came to get him from the table and told him that the princess want to see him. Virak grabbed his drink, followed the girl to see RD who want to show him the garden. They walked along the rows of fruit tree like milk fruit, jack fruit, chompou, and mango; there was a small pond near the orchard that was full of lotus flower and at a corner of the pond, hidden a kiosk under the shade of the bamboo bush near the brick wall at the back.

"Would you wait here for a minute, I almost forgot there is something I need to do"

"Of course, by all mean your highness"

"You don't need to say those royal term if my friend come by don't kill anyone with royal joke just be nice OK"

"OK RD, don't worry, I'm not that uncivilized"

"I know you are not, that's why you are here" After RD left, Virak sat under the kiosk looking at the lotus flower in the pond with an old foot long gecko crawling on the beam kept him company. Ten minutes later, he heard a footstep came from the orchard rows and a voice called out.

"RD...Are you in there?" This voice sounded familiar, and then he was surprised to see Princess Devy stepped inside, and she was also equally surprised.

"OH, good afternoon, the girl told me that RD was waiting for me here"

"Good afternoon your highness; and RD also told me to wait for her here" They looked at each other, and then realized that it was a set up, Virak just smiled and nodded his head while she turned red and turned away to hide her face.

"Your highness, you have a lot of very good and loyal friend around you who are so concerned about your well being. They said that you might die from depression just like the character in the Wilted Flower story if you can't see me at the window"

"Please don't use those royal term anymore, and don't believe everything they said"

"No, I didn't believe everything they said but I want to hear from you; your highness" She did not say a word but she just smiled and looking down to the floor while he stood in front of her.

Suddenly, the old foot long gecko that hung on the beam started to croak "Ghec… Ghec… Ghec… Koooooo, Ghec… Ghec… Ghec… Koooooo" She jumped to grab his arm, and she looked so much squared.

"OH please, get me out of here, I am so afraid of that creature" Virak wrapped his arm around her to let her seek refuge in his chest, and he grabbed a stick nearby and thrown at the old gecko who crawled outside the roof and jumped to a nearby tree. She still had her hands covered her eyes and hid her face.

"Devy, the creature is gone" She opened her eyes and looked up around the roof; his hand lifted her chin up and he planted a quick kiss on her lips, she just closed her eyes and stayed motionless in his arms. Virak kissed her again slowly and smoothly, this time everything around them came to a standstill, she wrapped her arms around his back and they were kissing until they heard chatting sound from the orchard rows. She broke their kiss, pushed his chest, and stepped away from his embrace, and she went to sit at the other end of the kiosk and used her handkerchief to dap her face and her neck that made his eye followed every move of this beautiful Apsara while she stole a glance at him from the corner of her eye. Virak sat at the other end of the kiosk, looked at the lotus flowers and acted like nothing happened. The girls leaded by Princess RD, barged in the kiosk with astonished look on their face, and they looked at Devy and Virak back and forth. RD sat near Devy talked to her and sniffed at the same time, and she looked at the girls giving them a smile and a wink, and then came to whisk Virak to the outside of the kiosk, she thank him for the job well done and sent him back to the ping pong table; he overheard the girls giggled and whispered.

"RD smell guy scent on her"

C8-Return to the Battlefield

This was a darkest chapter in Virak's life it was full of sorrows and miseries; he was not prepared for the calamity event that unfolded all these tragedies had given him a big surprise or it's just like a big jolt of the electric shock. It made him felt more matured beyond his age, and he was more humble and aware of living in easy life ever since he was born. And he felt an urgent sense of the uncertainty of the future and more responsible to others than just thinking or concerning of himself alone.

The first tragedy was unfolded when Virak woke up one morning; while he was looking up at the sunrise in the east he heard the commotion at the front gate of his family compound, and when he came outside he saw a soldier walking barefoot, and he recognized him as one of his father driver-bodyguard. The soldier informed them that their mother was dead and their father was presumed dead from drowning but they had not found his body yet; suddenly the sound of wailing and crying were echoed throughout the compound. Later in the evening, the news of his father demised was confirmed, they'd found his body at the bottom of a pit twenty feet under water. They drove into the enemy ambush while on their way back to the capital.

A few days later they had a double funeral procession at a Buddhist temple where his father used to live as a monk. They were cremated and their bone fragments were kept in two marble urns. For Virak and his sibling who were less than eighteen years old, were put under the guardianship of some elder relatives. Virak was exam from the military service but he chose to stay with his old unit.

Few months after his parents funeral, Virak was on the east bank of the Mekong River about thirty miles from the capital, and the mission was to protect a bridge for a few days so a brigade in front of them could retreat along the Mekong river bank road. A week had passed they were still holding the bridge despite they were under the constant attack by the North Vietnamese regular army. They were ordered by the high command to hold the bridge a little longer so the retreated unit could pull out all of their wounded soldiers and equipments. They were informed that they will be resupplied by air.

The American plane the C-130 had made a perfect drop tons of ammunition in the middle of their defense perimeter. The Cambodian air force used a Dakota twin engine to drop them some food; they dropped from a very high altitude that the wind push the parachute off target, some were landed in the river and majority of them were swept away with the wind.

Virak didn't like the situation that they were in one bit; he want to ask the battalion commander but he hesitated because he thought they were just like soldiers anywhere who received order and executed with no question asked. Yes, they were the soldiers in the field did the execution while the high command made the decision; so all they could do was to execute order and report the situation in the field so the high command could make their decision and issue to them the next order, but at the situation they were in right then they may never receive the next order because they did not have the mean to report their situation, since their radio communication were destroyed by the enemy mortar round explosion. It seemed like they were in a bad situation just like a sitting duck.

The high command could not take any action by guessing about the situation the unit was in; they might think that the battalion was probably wiped out because the NVRA force could root out a brigade so the battalion will not stand a chance. Even though, they may knew that they were still alive they will not have the capability to reinforce because they sent the battalion here to help save a brigade on retreat and they should have fall back right behind them, but the high command want them to hold the bridge longer so the brigade last fragment unit could be saved.

Last night, the last fragment unit was annihilated or pushed into the river by the enemy attack just a few miles from the defense perimeter. Now, they knew the battalion couldn't fall back along the river bank even if it want too according to the recon intelligent reported that the enemy massive buildup right behind their position.

Virak knew that they could not just sit and wait for the high command or the NVRA to decide their fate; he looked in the map and studied it down to the small detail, in any particular area that he was not sure about he brought it to clear with the recon scout.

This abandon town was build around on both ends of the bridge along the river and over the creek that flow under from the lake and swampy area a mile inland, and in the flood season when the Mekong River water level rise the creek will flow in the opposite direction to replenish the lake and swamp. Next to the town, there were big field of potato and vegetable and some large fish ponds along the creek always to the swamp land.

The town and its vicinity were situated on a strip of dry land about less than a mile wide paralleled to the river, and also the only one main road that went through it. Virak asked the company commander if they had received any word from the battalion command, but he said that they were just on the standby mode for now.

Virak knew he got to do something and he was compelled to take action, but first he got to talk to the highest authority here the battalion commander. Virak took a moment that the enemy mortar and the artillery attack were slowdown a little bit to go to the battalion command post to ask the commander for a private talk; he was surprised and displeased when he saw Virak.

"Why are you here mister? I thought you were exam from the service; anyway if you change your mind and want to go home it is a little bit too late, it might have to be delay"

"I had made up my mind to stay in the service Sir, and after all I still need a job to support myself. I come to see you concerning our present situation that we are stuck with little food supply and the uncertain future"

"What do you mean our uncertain future? I had sent a few agents downstream to the capitol to bring my report to the high command. In the next few days, we will receive the air support, food supplied and reinforcement. We are not in any danger of any heavy attack, so don't worry about it we will be back at our base by next week"

"Sir with all due respect Sir, this could be a big mistake and a false hope. I believe the reason that they won't attack us here because they knew we are an experienced well prepared unit, and it will cost more to attack our defense position, so they'd rather attack the less experience frontline unit closer to the capital. They know that we are short of food supply, so this will leave us little choice, we can take our chance to sit here and wait for reinforcement or move back to face the enemy unit buildup a few mile right behind us.

Sir either way, this is our uncertain future. The high command may already think that any unit beyond the frontline, were already wiped out, and that's why they concentrate their resource to hold the enemy there; they may or may not receive your message, and even if they do receive your message and know that we are still holding up right here, they do not have any more capable unit to come out to rescue us.

As you can see Sir, they send us to help a brigade in retreat from a formidable NVRA because they believe that we are a capable and experienced unit that can get out of a tight spot, they did not expect that it can turn out to be like this because we take our order down to the letter, and that was not our fault it just the way we operated. And one thing for sure Sir, we cannot sit and wait for the high command or anyone to decide what we should do next"

"All right, I kind of understand your explanation so let me hear what you think?"

"Sir, we know that the enemy artillery and mortar are very accurate because of their recon surveillance in the forest surround our position. We can send our recon team to eliminate them with our silent weapon"

"What are you talking about silent weapon? The American did not give us any of this silencer stuff"

"No Sir, it is not the American's stuff, it's our homemade crossbow and poison arrow. I had order the crossbow for all of our recon members, and I hold on to this Two Steps and Cobra snake venom that I can issue to them at a minute notice.

After we have clean up the surrounding forest, we need to readjust our defense perimeter to outside of town and along the outside of the fish pond earthen berm always to the swamp land beyond this forest, that will give us higher field of fire and a better kill zone in time of all out assault as this enemy unit are known for.

We need to take the lumber from these civilian abandoned houses to build strong cover for our bunker and foxhole; yes Sir I know we have a standing order to keep our hand off all civilian properties but we are in a situation of dire need for the survival of our unit, if we don't take this course of action we may not get out of here alive to fight another day.

And for the food supply Sir, we cannot wait until we run out of food we must harvest the fish from the ponds and river to preserve by smoke dry them, and move the defense line beyond the field during the day so we can move and replant all of potato, cassava and any vegetable that we can get our hand on to the plot inside our defense perimeter.

We need to send a few soldiers who know and use to live along this river to the capital to give the high command the enemy precise coordinates and our request for precise actions to be taken if they want us to live.

They need to have the American bomb the enemy units build up a few mile right behind us, and the carpet fire by the American gunship in the forest beyond the swampy area that we know the thick forest where they rest their main force who probably lay around in their hammock without any cover because they know we could not reach them.

And for your command post Sir, I suggest that you move away from those concrete building, because they seem to be easy target for the enemy artillery fire at any time since they already know and plot them in their map that was why we lost our radio communication"

They just sat quietly under the bamboo bush shade, the commander was in deep thought looking down on the map for a long time, Virak had said everything that he needed to tell him and he took a sip of water from his canteen waiting for his reaction. Fifteen minutes later, the commander got up and motioned Virak to follow him into the command post. He called all officers and enlisted men in his staff to gather around put his hand on Virak's shoulder and he gave them the order.

"In our present dire situation as you all know, I temporary appointed this young capable officer to take temporary command of the recon unit and logistic. I want you to inform all companies to fully cooperate thus he carries my authority to pull and utilize anyone in the unit and he will report direct to me. That's all gentlemen get to work"

First Virak pulled out BT and a squad of soldier that he knew to protect his back. Next he went to assume command of the recon unit with the assistant battalion commander; the unit commander was so shocked and upset, despite the battalion XO reassured him that the change of command was temporary and necessary for the present situation. Virak asked him to help on carry out the order or get out of the way; the lieutenant gathered his thing and went toward the battalion command post.

Virak immediately assemble force recon unit of over a hundred strong most of them knew him from the training in South Vietnam, he explained to them about their task before hand and he had them dipped the tip of their arrows in the poison bottle under his close supervision.

Virak assigned the area of responsibility to the platoon leaders, and had them tell him their course of action to make sure that they understood the mission and the way he wanted them to follow from A to Z to get it done within twenty four hours.

His last course of action was to form the logistic unit; first he appointed a senior staff NCO to carry out the task of pulling out about a platoon of NCO and enlisted men who had background as cook, fisherman, hunter and gatherer. And for their first mission, he ordered them to break into all houses and buildings to gather all useful items from food like rice, condiments, dried fish, and stinky preserved fish like Phaork and Prahok to tools, cooking utensils, and clean cloth for bandage, rice vine and any alcohol for antiseptic, and cigarette.

Virak place all confiscated items under the senior SNCO control despite BT's complained that he should be in charge of the cigarette and rice vine, Virak had to convinced him to accept by slipping him a few packs of cigarette with his promise that no one will see or smell any cigarette smoke from him. The carpentry unit started to disassemble the houses to get lumber for the bunkers and foxholes cover.

Thirty hours later, the recon teams reported to declare the initial step of the mission was accomplished, they had secured the area from the river bank to the swarm land over a mile from each end of the bridge and continued pushing outward. The companies started to take up position to build the covered bunker along the fish pond berm, the outside of town always to the river bank.

And for the big task, Virak requested the battalion commander to order the companies to secure the forest line beyond the planting fields and for all available hands to help harvest and replant the potato, cassava, taro, yams and any kind of edible plant that they could get their hand on. The logistic NCOs marked the spots and count the amount of the kind of items so they could estimate the amount of food they got on hand.

The senior SNCO of the logistic unit had already set up the kitchen-storage-headquarter under the bridge; they used parts of the house roof to connect to the bridge so it could block the light of the fire so they can burned all day and night in the big smoke house according to the smoke cook specialist, and Virak had them built the wooden platform across the shallow creek to the other side as a staging area right under the bridge, at the other side, they flat the area under the bridge to make a storage and resting area.

By the time they had finished the logistic kitchen fish came by the ton every few hours from the pond and a few hundred pounds a day from the row of large dipped baskets in the river; so the logistic machine started to process, preserve, smoke, cook and distribute to the whole battalion. A week later they had preserved most of the fish from the pond, and they still received the fresh fish from the river every day. The specialist cook used a huge casted iron vessel to cook batches of sour fish soup or kind of steamed fish stew like called "Amok" to the appreciated soldiers and even the battalion commander came to the logistic kitchen to give high praise of appreciation comment to the cooks personally.

The hunters had found large population of wild rat some as large as small piglet and snake like cobra and boa constrictor to add to their smoke rack and their menu. They had kept some poisonous snake alive to extract poison for the recon team to use in set up the poison bamboo stick booby trap to ensure the silent kill.

Since the enemy lost their eyes and ears they rained the artillery and mortar rounds in the town area at random; the battalion command was watching the houses burning from the safety of their bunker under the bamboo bushes. The commander asked Virak to returned the command of the recon unit back to the lieutenant but Virak asked for a few days before he returned them and a promise that the commander continued to send the team out to patrol and to lay booby trap throughout the forest to ensure that the enemy will not sneak up on them; the battalion commander gave him his word.

Virak brought half of the recon unit at a time to under the bridge and gave them their choice of meat from the smoke rack, a few ounce of rice vine from the stone urn, some cigarettes and twelve hours rest on the spot. He had given the rice vine and cigarette to the whole logistic crew every few days and BT who was always at the front of the line and later blended himself in line to get a second serve, the senior SNCO always looked at Virak and he nodded his head in approval to give him Virak's ration.

A few days later, the American planes had drop bombs and attacked with their gunships at the enemy positions a few miles behind them and the position beyond the swampy area. Everybody were so happy they believed that their lives and their unit were out of danger; Virak forgot the dateline that he had to return the recon command, so he sent the recon to go throughout the defense perimeter to tell them not to let their guard down, and he had them help laid the last few hundred of the Claymore mines that we'd receive from the American air drop.

They must laid them the way to stop the enemy assault en masse by tying each of them to the tip of a bamboo pole and by using the lever to push the other end down when needed to trigger the mine a few feet in the air or at any high they desire. They had used this technique to stop Vietcong and NVRA's assault before, and it proof to be very effective.

On the evening of the second day that the American plane attacked the enemy positions, the battalion commander called Virak in to return the recon command back to the lieutenant. With BT at his side, all the officers in the command post came to shake Virak's hand for the job well done, and when they were on their way back from the command post BT kept on complaining about something that Virak could not make out what he was talking about; and he turned to him.

"And what the hell are you mumbling about BT?"

"I just say that don't let all those attentions get to your head. All those "Mthfkers" in the command post are still thinking that you are just a foul young guy, who does all the work to save their ass. They appreciated what you are doing right now but you mark my word when we get back to the rear, they will be the one who get decorate and promotions. It is unthinkable for them to report to the supreme command that they let the boy to do the man work to save every one of their ass it will be an embarrassment for them"

"I don't want anything, and I don't give a damn what they think of me, I just do what I need to do to save my ass and yours. Let's go get some sleep, because we haven't had any good night sleep ever since we come to this place"

Song Krear Mear

Virak lay down thinking about the Vietcong across the swamp, and he kept asking question in his mind like what will they do? And what should we do? What will happen if…? And he drifted to sleep but he felt like his eyes were still wide open looking at the Bo tree leaves in the canopy.

His eyes followed a colorful butterfly flew to the far side of the creek. Suddenly the whole surrounding area became foggy and chilly, he could not make out the fire at the smoke rack or the bridge but a big man on a horseback appeared through the fog, he rode across the creek and came to stop near Virak's bedding, then he asked him.

"Uncle where do you think you are going? This is a war zone; it is very dangerous around here"

The man wore an ancient style shiny silk cloth with a red silk krama wrapped around his waist and an ancient sword hung across his back, and then he replied.

"Never mind about where I am going I don't believe that you can sleep at a time like this, there are thousands of Yourn (Vietnamese) are lurking in the forest"

"Ehh, and how do you know about the Yourn here? Who are you? This is still a dangerous place and you shouldn't be here Uncle"

"Fear not son, there is nothing can harm me now, I'd already spilled all my blood on this land, I am SONG KREAR MEAR, this is my land, this is my duty to know when the enemy set foot on it, now get up"

Virak heard thunder of the footstep of men and animals in the fog just like an army was on the march, he turned to look at the man on horseback but he could not see the face clearly, the man appear to have thick moustache and a saffron color silk krama wrapped over his head, then Virak asked him about the footstep.

"Who are those men Uncle?"

The horseman pulled out his sword that was still dripping with blood and he reached down to tapped the flat side on Virak's shoulder, he instinctively ducked and tried to move away from the sword but it'd already touched his shoulder, Virak was irritated and wondered of what was this horseman up to? He sheathed his sword and said.

"Never mind them they are my men, now get up"

And just rode passed up the creek bank, Virak crawled out from his bedding and looking around up the creek bank but the horseman was disappeared including the sound of the footstep and the fog was clear from the air of the evening sky. It was clear and warm, and the Bo tree leaves were moving under the breeze from the Mekong River that made a distinct sound from any other leaves.

There was only BT who came out of his bedding and looked kind of lost. They ran up the creek bank, and looked at both directions of the road there was nothing out of the norm; he thought that somebody had played a prang joke with them, and then Virak absentmindedly touched his shoulder on the spot where it was tapped by the bloody sword he could feel wetness, and when he rubbed his thumb and forefinger together and looked at them to his horror and astonishment there was fresh blood on his fingers.

Suddenly, something hit him like an epiphany, he felt like the Vietcong will attack their unit at any moment. They went down to wake up everyone under the bridge, and then Virak ordered them to cook triple amount of the daily ration of dried meat fish and potato, and they must immediately distribute them around the perimeter.

He asked the recon commander to pull all of the teams to come in behind the defense perimeter and laid mines and trip wire at all of the avenues of approach in the forest. He shown the heavy mortar crew the predetermine coordinate along the forest line closest area to the perimeter and asked them to fire at anytime that they come under attack.

At the battalion command post, they were laughing at Virak; they believed that he must be drunk with rice vine; the commander looked at Virak, shook his head and said.

"Go back to your area and try to get some sleep son, you had work too hard, go ahead get some rest OK"

Virak went back to the bridge; the place was quiet because the senior SNCO had the crews took the position at the creek mouth in the covered bunker along the bank overlook the river. There was only a group of wounded soldier stay behind to tend to the smoke rack. Even though, they didn't expect much that the Vietcong will attack them from the river, but they had learn always expect the unpredictable innovative enemy.

Virak went to check on the logistic crew position in the bunker overlook the river bank; the bunkers had the advantage field of fire but in the dark moonless night like this one they could not see the Vietcong at the water edge until they come up over the steep bank and the tall grass. Everybody think that Virak was worry too much and the Vietcong never attack from the river, and it will be too much trouble to cover these areas.

Despite their displeasure, Virak sent everybody down to the river edge to set up the trip wire of illumination and the fragmentation grenade, and he had the wounded soldiers laid the Claymore mines to cover the creek mouth, and he placed an M-60 machine gun on each side of the creek bank. Virak was still on edge even after all of the preparations; the senior SNCO came to reassure him.

"Get some sleep Sir, I will wake you up if anything happen"

"I couldn't sleep chief; I feel that the attack is eminent"

"Pardon me Sir may I ask how do you know?"

"I will tell you when we get back to our base"

Suddenly, illumination trip flair was popped and it lighted up the whole river bank; the wound soldiers manned the machine guns and plugged the trigger to the Claymore mine wire. Virak ran up the bank to the bunker where the flair was popped, they saw the fresh water otter dove back into the river.

Virak heard the crews were laughing, he was irritated and had the senior SNCO went through the position to tell them to keep their mouth shut and their eyes open. He sent BT and his men to check on the bunker that the otter came up to replace the burnout flair by setting some trip wire in the deep crevasses on the bank.

Virak just felt a little relaxed and confident that everything had taking care of to the best of their knowledge; when he started to lie down on the bedding he heard grenade exploded in the direction where BT and his men went. Virak ran up on the road to lay prone behind a big jackfruit tree above the bunker, and he saw BT and his squad fire their M-16 and M-79 into the crevasses.

Virak yelled at BT and his squad to take cover in the bunker but they replied back that they could not see the Vietcong came up from the water edge, one of his men who stood on the top of the bunker got hit with the AK-47 round and his lifeless body just rolled off the bunker cover down the river bank.

And then Virak saw BT and his men scrambled to get into the nearest bunker or any hole on the ground. Virak was certain that they could take care of themselves because they were instructed to get familiar with the terrain at their position so at night they will recognize anything that was out of the ordinary, and all of the bunkers had the grenade sump dug below their sloped floor to absorb the explosion of the enemy grenade.

When Virak came to the bunker over the creek mouth above the wound soldiers position; the Vietcong had used the bamboo poles to trigger most of their trip wire and then they rushed up the bank after all the illumination flair were burned out.

The battle had begun, the wounded soldiers triggered the Claymore mines, fired the illumination flair up in the air from the M-79 launcher, and the M-60 machine gun sprayed at the Vietcong who rushed up the bank and those who were still in the water, they shot their heads and watch them carefully to make sure that they sank into their watery graves, and they still dropped grenades and fired the M-79 rounds into the crevasses.

Within fifteen minutes they had eliminated the fierce Vietcong trigger force of over a hundred men. Virak knew he had lost one brave and cocky soldier for sure for this initial round of battle that sent a signal to the rest of the Vietcong assault force to attack the rest of the defense perimeter.

Now after they had done their part, they still kept their eye at the water edge and listening to the symphony sound of artillery and mortar rounds explosion mixed with the explosions of the M-79, the fragmentation grenade, the Claymore mine, along with the rattled of the M-60 and the 30 cal machine guns, and they also could distinguished the exchange between the M-16 and the AK-47 including the Vietcong battle cry (YO DIH).

Yes the Vietcong shout their battle cry when their assault line charged at the position, and they were cut short by the Claymore mine explosion that it happened just like Virak had envisioned. All soldiers were trained to keep their mouth shut because they were busy aiming their weapon and doing their job to defend their position, and after the battle was over they can shout their battle cry and basking in victory if they were still alive.

The Vietcong assault on land was different from the one wave of the initial assault from the river; they attack the defense line with the intensity of waves after waves of assault as long as they have those little Vietcong soldiers in black pajama to fill in their rank and file. At some point, they had succeeded breaching the defense line but they were fallen into the fish pond that was full of bamboo thorn and barbwire just below the water surface where they were eliminated by the machine gun at the secondary defense line on the creek bank.

Before sunrise, a few American gunships came on scene to pay a visit and assessing the situation; they knew that these Vietcong main force from beyond the swam had move to find safety in the forest near the unit defense line, and with the signal from the ground to let them recognized the outline of the defense position, the gunships laid carpet of machine gun rounds on the forest and fields a few hundred yards from the defense line.

After the sunlight had cleared the morning fog; they were still covered in smoke from the fires that still burning in the forest and the last remnant of the abandon town. They were ordered to keep a close surveillance on those piles of the dead and wound Vietcong that were lying around just a few yards away.

They had experienced that some wounded Vietcong who lost hope of recovering and with many parts of his body missing nodded his head or waves at the soldier in the foxhole to finish him off on the spot. The soldier turned to look at the officer who gave a nod of approval, and then the soldier sent a merciful single M-16 round to honor and grant the enemy last wish.

Since they had realized the unit existence; the American sent them some more ammunitions, food and medical supply. For the next few days many soldiers and Virak, they enjoyed chow down the Asian rations that the American had dropped, but to Virak's astonishment the majority of the soldiers were still request for the food from the logistic kitchen.

So the logistic crews had to go down to the river to pull up the dipped baskets; they got more fish than usual because they hadn't pulled them up in the last few days and there were a few dead Vietcong bodies added to the bait in the baskets. They cooked the sour fish soup with green tamarind and the Spicy Amok dishes; and then they sent them around the defense perimeter where they started to bury the enemy dead.

A week later, the battalion was tapped out by a replacement unit; they hurriedly grabbed some ammo, food ration and the rice wine stone urn that now became the unit victory drink jug that was full of root, bark, spices, a few dozen of mean cobras, some of other animals and unknown body parts. And they quickly put some distant between them and the bridge battle field.

The battalion returned to their base near the capital and was immediately granted the triple R. Yes, they deserved the triple R of readjustment, rest, and recreation after returning from a battle like this one. The first phase of the Readjustment was the treatments of body and mind in that order; the doctor checkup to treat any wound and the body cleansing of bugs and parasites, and general hygiene that they haven't had in the last few weeks.

And the second phase of the Readjustment was the treatment of the mind by rewarding and praising for the job well done, counseling for those who bear deep scar in their mind from the battle field, and sending those who need spiritual blessing and meditation at the sanctuary of their religious belief.

For Rest and Recreation, they left to soldiers own device; for example BT planned to go straight to his teacher-

Mamasan establishment to invite some girls to join him for a picnic at the jicama plantation shack by the river.

Before, they all partway to their rest and recreation; the battalion command thrown a big victory feast for everybody. It was kind of mess night at separated tables for officer and enlisted men.

And before anything else started to begin; everyone must pay their respect to the unit victory drink jug by taking a sip from it, standing silent for a moment as a remembrance to their brothers in arm who did not came out alive from all battle fields, rendered a salute, took one step back and execute the about face.

After a whole night of feasting and drinking, Virak woke up late the next day as usual after a night like that, he started to pack his thing ready to go to the capital to see his family and let them know that he was still alive after a return from long absent in battle.

A battalion clerk came to stop Virak at his door and told him that the commander want to see him at the private quarter behind headquarter; so Virak just followed the clerk and wondered what and why.

Inside the living room, the commander and his wife sat on the couch, and at the other corner Virak saw a young woman in her early twenty, a girl of fourteen and ten years old boy; they all sat on the floor crying quietly.

He greeted the commander who looked like in a deep thought while his wife was busy chewing the beetle nut and "Mlou" leaves, and then Virak took a seat on the chair in front of them. The commander's wife looked up smiled and received him warmly; she turned to spit the red beetle nut juice in a silver spittoon and said.

"OH, Hello, come here my son, I am also still feel sad from the lost of your parents, your mother she was like a sister to me, and how's your family cope with the tragedy? You should not go to the field anymore since you are exam from the service.

I hear only high praise from my husband and the officers; they told me how you help our unit at the difficult time and how you behave mature beyond your age. And now that we have your good character in mind, that's why we need to talk to you with some matter concerning the lost of our soldiers and the family members whom they left behind"

"Yes my lady, of those soldiers that we'd lost in battle were tragedies to all of us and their families which we treat just like a part of our own"

"Good, I am glad to hear your noble sentiment point of view. Just call me aunt, consider me like your mother's sister"

"OK aunt, so what can I do for you?"

"OH yes son, let me introduce to you these three young people here who lost their love one at the bridge battle. The young lady Sovana had lost her husband, the girl and the boy here lost their father.

Their known relative were cut off and are still stuck behind in the enemy zone, and they have no any mean to support themselves. We don't want to ask the others to take them into their family, because my husband and I don't trust that they will decently treat these young people well the way we intent to. I don't want to see and hear later that they end up as concubine, servant or worth in the brothel.

For you and your brothers and sisters who are orphans just like them so you all will understand how it feels when you lost family member. I hope that you and your family are kind enough to give the boy and girl a decent place to live but they want to come together despite I try to tell them that it is hard to find a place for them in one family"

The young woman who is in mourning with a black shawl over her head came to kneel by Virak's feet.

"OH please Sir my lady, I can be a servant in the family, and I don't want to be a concubine or end up in a brothel, I am willing to do anything to live a decent life"

"Don't worry dear, I will not let you end up in a bad place; that is why I try to ask this kind heart young gentleman, and don't you interrupt me"

"I am very sorry my lady"

"Aunt, if this is up to me I can take all of them but I am not the head of the family, and so as of now we are under the guardianship of the elder relatives"

"OK, I understand son, how about you bring them to see your family and also ask the elders for their permission, and if they reject for some reason, I will find them someplace else"

"OK Aunt I will do that, and let sees what happen"

"OH thank you dear, may the Lord Buda bless you"

With tear in their eyes all three people came to kneel at Virak's feet to thank him profusely. He motioned them to get up and pointed them to the commander's wife of whom they should thank for her concern and effort.

C9-Divine Celestial Dancers

Virak brought the three people to his house to meet his family; they were received warmly by his brothers and sisters, they had made room and found space for all of them to stay in the house. The hope was short live because the elders opposed the idea of adding more people from the different class to live among their family and they also pointed out about their cousin.

"We don't want to see you bring just about anybody into your family. It is too much trouble just like your cousin Kheng; he is married to a Vietnamese woman whose family had connection with Vietcong. The authority wants to deport her, and now they seek refuge inside our compound that will bring more trouble upon us. As of now, we are no longer having your father good name as shield to insure the military police, so their vehicles are now parking at our gate as we speak"

Virak went to meet the military police outside their compound before they charged through the gate to apprehend cousin Kheng's wife. He asked them to standby for a moment so he could do some fact finding before he let them come in. Fifteen minutes later after he listened to the story, Virak went outside with his M-16 lock and load at the ready position to show to the military police that no matter what they decide next he determined not to allow anyone force through the gate alive.

"Yes it's true that they are Vietnamese but she had shown to me some pictures and document to prove that she was born here. Her family moved here over twenty years ago; she had no any knowledge of her father's connection with Vietcong, and he had been deported along with everyone in her family. Right now, she is married to my brother she is my family member. I will take full responsibility. It doesn't matter if anybody thinks that she is a Vietnamese or a

Cambodian but I am certain that she is not responsible for her father action, and I believe she tell the truth. Sir, I just came from a battle over the east bank; my unit had killed numerous members of the Vietcong and the NVA, I can tell a Vietcong when I see one, and she is not she belong to my family and she is pregnant. I will not let you take her. She stays here"

The military police agreed with Virak's statement; so they let him singed a few pieces of document and they left. So now he had responsibility of five people lives and they were not allowed to stay in the house. Virak did not want to argue with the elders, so he had no choice but to place them temporary at his secret hang out in the riverside place. He sat on the couch looking out of the window on the top floor and thinking about what to do next. He'd given some money to cousin Kheng to buy some food and things that they need to live there for the time being. Virak had already assigned their space, cousin Kheng and his wife stayed at the ground floor with big kitchen big open living room, and the young widow, the brother and sister stayed at the second floor with a lot of room to spare, and he kept to the third floor by himself. At the table, they ate their meal quietly, Virak looked around the table at everybody sad face and with their eyes casted down on their plate, it seemed like they were resigned to the fate of the circumstance and the uncertainty of their future that rest on his shoulder. He was thinking it was up to him to cheer them up but for now he let them eat at their own leisure.

After the evening meal, Virak asked everybody came to sit at the back porch that overlook the backyard; then he asked everyone to tell about their life for the reason that if they were going to live as family they need to know one another, and he also emphasized that nobody owe him any obligation whatsoever, and they were free to do whatever they want and go wherever they wish; and while they stay here he will do his best to make this place a family home. Cousin Kheng was an office clerk for a foreign company but was fire after they had learned from the authority about his wife background. And his wife name was Nguyen T. H, and she was working as a cook at a restaurant in a big hotel but she lost her job when the government agent told her employer about her father involvement with the communist that she had no any part or knowledge of. They met each other before the war started in Cambodia, and they decided to get married just six months before she lost her job, and right now she was four months into the term of her pregnancy.

The young widow named Sovana, she was married to her husband less than a year ago and they were from the northeast province, and came to the capital after most of their relatives were killed by the B-52 bombing at the area near the Ho Chi Minh trail. The brother and sister lost their mother three years ago, and their father left them with Sovana to look after while he went on the mission with the unit. Now Virak understand why they want to stay together. Virak asked cousin Kheng to act as the legal guardian for the brother and sister so he could enroll them in the public school; and he also promised the young widow, cousin Kheng and his wife BT that he will actively looking for job for them.

Virak went back to the top floor and sat on the couch at the back window looking out over the back yard, then he was thinking what in the world did he get himself into, involved with these people lives, and most of them are older than him how he was going to take care of them? And where he was going to find jobs for them? What he was doing here concern about them? After returning from a battle he should get drunk and banging between a woman legs any woman maybe Mamasan, Yes why not? He had screwed his teacher behind BT's back, and he didn't see any harm in trying to do it again. Suddenly the vision of Lady S leaned on the window, pushed her butt back at his face to present her big fat moist cunt lips that made his loin stirred...... No, No, No, wait a second, he didn't want to go there yet, he was in the middle of trying to help these people, and they are his family now, and he got to do something to help them first, everything else can wait but it was so hard since he had no woman for a while. Well that can wait; right now he needed to think of anything for them to do. What? Where? How? He was thinking about Phnom Penh and the situation that they were in then. All of the national routes were practically cut off or destroyed by the enemy, and all of the commerce ground transportation had to be escorted by the military convoy. Most of the countryside and distant rural area were control by the communist it became an impassable enemy zone. Before the war, people in the city used to move freely to the countryside to escape the hectic city life, but now the only open space they could hang out was the river bank in front of the palace royal. Most of the employment were in the military, restaurant, bar and brothel.

Virak was looking down on the big backyard at about two to three acres full of trees and shrubs from the back porch always to the river bank, and Lady S told him to take care of it but he couldn't do anything except looking at it. What if he asked her to make something out of it? Make what? How about a garden? A place that people could come to hang out by the river and have a drink or two to escape from the reality of the war. Yes, a small eating and drinking place by the river bank, and they could sell comfort food to go with beer and so on……Yes how about a beer garden or a place to party with friends and love one to honor peaceful moment and to celebrate life. How about that? He thought he will talk with them tomorrow.

Virak told them about Lady S who is the owner of this place, and asked everybody what they think about the idea of having a business in their backyard. Cousin Kheng said that was a very good idea; and TH was so happy that the restaurant business was her specialty, she guaranty to put out good tasting comfort foods that customer will come back to ask for more. Sovana said she had experience with bookkeeping for her parent grocery store, and she could help at any capacity to make the business run since she express her gratitude to all of them that accept her as a family member. The brother and sister were willing to help with anything but Virak made it clear that they must stay in school to concentrate on study was their first priority; he would rather hire other people to do the job. Cousin Kheng said he could revive his old contact with the food supply line and the material need to create a restaurant. Virak shown to them the vision and the plan for the backyard, the river bank and the kitchen in the ground floor and the back porch will need to be expanded to become their main floor, but first they started to open small plan of eating and drinking place with good food in a relaxed garden ambient that people like to hang out and party, that way they won't need to have a big capital to start with.

They started from the very next day to clear the shrubs, saved all the palm and fruit trees, planted flowers and decorative yellow bamboo bushes, built the roof with bamboo and peralta grass over the river bank and the walkway, poured some cement under the roof to make the ground look clean, and they began to serve foods and drinks as plan.

They invited people from all walks of life to come to enjoy their place; people gave them rave review about their food, their service and most of all the ambient setting that created an atmosphere of exciting mood. Only a few months later, they were forced to expand from public demands, they had to build more big roofs and kiosks to accommodate bigger and more numerous parties. They had to hire few dozen more wait staff put under Sovana supervision, and over a dozen cook staff to work for TH, and cousin Kheng took charge of all day to day operation as the general manager, and Virak preferred to stay unanimous watching every aspect from the background.

They had done so well that Virak tried to send some amount of money to Lady S in Europe but she replied "You do not need to send me anything; I have heard high praise of your place. As far as I am concern the Riverside Garden is yours. Good luck sweetheart" So instead, Virak used the money to help the temple, the battalion and his family. The Riverside Garden became very busy that customer had to arrange and book their parties in advance with Sovana who became indispensable to the operation.

The mamasan and her girls came to have their meal at the garden very often, there was not a day passed by that they haven't show up at anytime with big or small group, Virak told Sovana to reserved a kiosk for them anytime they show up with or without reservation, but he told BT not to reveal about his involvement in the garden to mamasan and the girls. One day at noon meal time, the garden at the river bank was full of office workers, students and military personnel; were enjoying their meal and the view over the river. Virak was walking on the side trail along the fence to the building on the river bank; he used to go up to the second floor to have a quiet moment and sometime he observed the whole garden through the side window.

Before he reached the building, Mamasan called him from a seclude kiosk surrounded by flower and bamboo bushes. Virak went in the kiosk and saw the Mamasan had her noon meal alone, and she smiled at him from behind the dark sunglass. They exchanged pleasantry but in his mind all the memories of her naked body at that night they made love in the shack at the jicama plantation, had flushed through his mind just like watching a fast forward film. His loin started to stir and he could feel the warm sensation coursed through his body, Virak felt like want to grab her right there in the seclude kiosk but then he remember they agreed to have the secret affair for one night only. She said that she couldn't get a straight answer from BT of who was the owner of the Riverside Garden and river bank building because she had an idea and a proposal for a business venture. BT brought the Mamasan proposal to Virak and cousin Kheng, Mamasan said some young women who lost their respectable decent family do not wish to become prostitutes and when she saw the vacant river bank building next to a popular restaurant she believe it could become a respectable night club that could create a lot of jobs for those decent young women as hostesses and server, and if sometime any client who need a sex partner the club can make the necessary arrangement with her establishment discretely of course.

So the private club was created, Virak had BT running the show behind the scene. They hire respectable men who had close contact with government, the supreme command, and the diplomat corps, to help them established the high echelon clientele. The club had their own bar but all of their food will came from the Garden kitchen with high quality dishes that demand high price by cousin Kheng. For the security matter, BT hired some disable veterans who were no longer be able to perform their duty in the field to guard the club. The Garden and the Club were running smoothly with very high yield profit. Jobs were created for hundreds of people, and everything that Virak had planned to do or had not plan, were accomplished in a short period of time. One day, while he was sitting at a table with some of his classmate from school in the quick service area, Princess RD approached him.

"Excuse me; I need to talk to you"

"OH hi RD, of course excuse us guys" They walked to a seclude kiosk at the back by the wall behind the jasmine and bamboo bushes. RD turned around facing him and Virak could see anger in her eyes.

"So, what the guys at school said is true, you hang around here all the time, we thought that you were still in the bush somewhere fighting Vietcong, but you are here, why don't you come to see her?"

"It is not like what you see RD, I had been so busy and I just have my hand free recently. I will go to see her, please, tell her that I'm sorry"

"I don't know, she is in Apsara costume waiting for me in the car, I didn't expect to see you here, and how about you go to tell her yourself?" There were a lot of car in the parking lot and Virak did not know which one belong to them. So he grabbed some drink at the quick service and went back to the kiosk to ask RD. while on the walkway he sensed that everybody in the Garden stopped whatever they were doing and turned to look at something behind him.

Virak turned around, and suddenly he felt like he was hit by the shockwave of a bomb blast, the glass dropped off from his hand, his ear turned deaf and ringing with the sound of silent, all of his surrounding became foggy and the only light he saw, was the radiant light from an Apsara a celestial dancer who just came off from the wall of Angkor Wat, without her golden crown her flowing long hair that adorned with frangipani, and with tear welled up in her eyes she floated swiftly into his arms, hid her face on his chest and started to cry softly. Virak was awestruck by her sudden appearance. He just stood there holding her tenderly in his arms and absorbed the fragrance scent from her slender body. He lifted her chin up, looked into her eyes with tear was still rolling down her face, and her lips that open up like rose petal.

"Oh sweetheart, I miss you so much"

"So do I you Baby, so do I" Virak leaned down to kiss her lips, and then they were dragged down from the cloud by RD who patted their back and whispered to them.

"Cut it out children, not in public OK" She looked at Devy.

"Calm down girl, not so fast" And she turned to Virak

"What do you think you are doing Mr.? Let's get out off the walkway, come on" They hardly paid any attention to RD at all; their eyes could only see each other. They went in the kiosk behind the jasmine shrubs where RD had order some food and drink, and after a few minutes for Virak to say pleasantry to her friends they were unknowingly started to melt in each other arms, they seemed not to care for anything were going on around them. This phenomenon was very unusual for Virak to fall head over heel this way, because he always had a high degree of control over his heart and his head most of the time before. He guessed in his condition the jungle people can say that he was intoxicated or poisoned by her love. RD interrupted their sweet moment with a worry look on her face.

"Hey children, it's time, and you young lady not so fast, one step at a time OK, let's go" They walked out to the car in the parking lot; Virak started to feel like a piece of his heart just about to leave his body. At the car, all the girls were waiting inside and the driver had the engine running, Virak held her and gave her a kiss for the last moment that they were together, and he whisper in her ear.

"I love you" All the girls in the car were giggling except RD who look kind of worry; Devy got in the car and turned to smile at Virak with tear welled up in her eyes. Everybody around the parking lot saw his helplessness when the car door closed and it started to move slowly away; he was just a little shy from crying. Inside the living room behind the restaurant kitchen, cousin Kheng tried to comfort Virak by saying.

"Oh don't worry; she will be back, after a kiss like that any girl will come back for more right?" He turned to look at his wife for support but TH shook her head with disapproval and signaled him to go away. Virak just came to sit at the table next to Sovana who patted his back with motherly concern look on her face.

At the very next day, RD sent a message to Virak that he must be very careful since Devy and him, had shown their love affection in public especially the driver, and if Devy's parent heard about it they all will be in trouble especially Virak. Sure enough a few days later, Devy's mother came to the main floor of the Garden with a dozen of uniform armed guards to forbid Virak to see Devy ever again or he will face consequence. Once again, his heart had fall to pieces; he sat at the living room table near the kitchen sulking and moping over his desperation of not being able to see his Princess again. Virak had glass after glass of Hennessy cognac on ice mix with Perrier water, and listened to cousin Kheng who tried to persuade him not to do anything foolish that might bring harm to all of them, and he said that Virak should forget about her since he was still young and there were a lot of girls out there who were far more prettier than Princess Devy. Virak just shook his head and drank some more cognac in hope that it will help to ease his pain and cousin Kheng joint him with the cognac since he had nothing else to say. TH came to clear the table and set up for the evening meal; Virak was irritated and wondering why the kids did not come down to help TH set up the table since she was too far into her pregnancy now and she could not do everything by herself. Cousin Kheng told Virak that the brother and sister had found their uncle, and he came to claim them in that afternoon. Virak was upset and asked him.

"Why I was not informed? And they left without saying goodbye after all I had done for them"

"We thought that it was not necessary to bother you since you are in the middle of all these troubles and pains; we told them to come to see you later, and Sovana did not want to go with them"

"I decide not to go with them even if they begged me, because they had found their relative not mine and I don't have any responsibility for them anymore. Look at you, you drink too much, you should finish your meal first please"

Sovana knew of Virak's bad habit that he tent to drink beer in his normal happy mood and he drown himself in the stronger alcohol drink to ease and forget his pains and sorrows. Over their evening meal, they talked about many different subjects more than usual, but Virak knew they tried to get his attention away from his pain, and cousin Kheng mentioned that many important clients and business associates who want to offer Sovana for the arrangement of a married proposal, but she won't reply back to anyone of them. They all turned to look at Sovana who was shy and embarrassed, and she demurred casting her eye down on her plate.

"I did not know how to reply back to them and by keeping quiet I guess they know that I don't want them. Yes I do want to remarry again but I don't know what to decide, I want to ask you since you are my guardian but we all are very busy and now you are in a lot of problems..."

"It doesn't matter how busy we are you can always talk to one of us since we are family, and I already told you since we got here that I cannot be your guardian. Can't you see that I am still too young to be a guardian?"

"Yes, I remember what you'd said, but the commander's wife had also said that you are mature beyond your age; you had brought me out here from headquarter; and you support me with food and shelter therefore you are my guardian. I don't have anyone else" Then her tear started to flow down her face and she cried softly; Virak wrapped his arm around her shoulder to console her.

"Oh come now, stop crying, you have a whole family here; cousin Kheng and TH can be your guardians and I also will be here for you always. You have to make your own decision and ask us if you have any doubt. Whenever you decide that he is the one tell him to send a go- between to come to see cousin Kheng and when everything are finalized, we will see to it that everything will be arrange for your married to whomever you choose. And don't you ever let me see tear on your pretty face again from now on"

"Thank you so much" She cried harder, hid her face on virak's chest, and her hand laid idol on his laps.

"It's all right, everything is going to be all right, I have enough excitement for one day, and I am the one supposed to cry. How about let we all forget about everything and let have a good time OK"

While she was still crying and hiding in his chest, then suddenly Virak felt that he had a massif erection between his legs and her hand was on it; she was kind of caressing it with her soft fingers, she stopped crying, sat back on her chair, took a sip from her glass, and she looked at Virak with a funny expression on her face. He just kept on drinking to enjoy the night away, but alas, his erection was still there and it's getting harder than ever. It was a relief when Sovana turned her attention away to talk to other people, but a few minutes later her hand once again laid innocently on his laps and when he moved to try to adjust himself the tips of her finger nail poked sharply on his erection. Virak had to excuse himself to go to the restroom to try to adjust his pant so it won't be too uncomfortable.

A second Virak sat down on his chair, her hand was slowly right back on stroking his still hard penis under the table. Now Virak knew this is not her innocent act, it's a kind of an invitation, a proposition or an easy explanation that she is horny. That's it, she haven't had a man to take care of her need, her itches ever since she lost her husband, but Virak thought wait a minute, didn't he suppose to be a mature beyond his age guardian. He had rejected the idea of being her guardian, that's right he is not her guardian and he did tell her to forget about everything and enjoy life at the moment while they could. Yes, he thought he did said all that; Oh well, now this is the moment, her moment, so be it, wait and see what is going to be unfold. TH had a dishwasher came to clear the table; and cousin Kheng said he had enough to drink so he need to turn in early. Virak started to slow down on alcohol intake ever since he started to have an erection to keep his head clear. He said good night to them and walked up to the top floor and that he didn't want to stay up here alone; Virak was thinking about sneaking out to beg Mamasan for an encore. Suddenly, there was a light knock on his door, and he was wondering who could that be, he hope it's her, and when he opened the door, there stood Sovana in her pink silk robe. She just stepped in and closed the door while looking at him.

Unexpected Goddess Avatar

"Are you ready to go out?"

Sovana just smiled, let her long hair loose, untied the robe belt, pulled her robe and dropped it to the floor. She had only the silk sarong that she wrapped below her belly button, her bare slender upper body that radiated the scent of jasmine fragrance; Virak could not take his eyes off her round perky breasts with the hard pink nipples pointed straight at him.

"So you think I am pretty, I did not realize that you ever pay any attention to me before"

"Yes, you are undeniably very pretty, I knew it won't be long someone will ask your hand in married"

"How do you know?"

"I knew because you are very attractive to be ignore"

"Well yes, some day someone might come along, but I need someone now. You had said that to let you know if I need anything, you had provided me with almost everything, but I still have my need of physical love"

"I had promised the commander's wife that I will take care of you but not to sleep with you or to take advantage of you at your vulnerable time since I suppose to be a mature beyond my age guardian, it seem like it doesn't look right don't you think?" She interrupted him by stepping closer in his arms and put her finger on his mouth.

"You are not my guardian, you'd said it remember, you are my savior, and I am always in dept to you that I can never repay, but I think I can taking care of this if you don't mind" She put her soft hand on his erected penis before she finished her last sentence.

"You are not a virgin aren't you?" Virak did not replied "you are too calm and confident to be a virgin"

"Sovana are you sure about this?" She nodded her head and stepped closer to stab her pointed nipples on his chest.

"Yes, I am sure without any reservation. I want your tender kiss and love affection just like you and that Apsara dancer, when I watched you two it made me feel longing. She can have your heart but I need you now tonight, I don't mind if you call her name while we make love"

"What's about the suitors? That you were talking about"

"They can wait; I will make my decision some other time" She dropped the silk sarong that was her last piece of cloth to the floor, wrapped her arms around his body and looking at him with a longing passion in her eyes. Virak quickly shed his clothes, and came up to kiss her luscious lips. A while later, they broke their kiss and still held on to each other…… She lay her head on his chest with tear welled up in her eyes.

"All you women, why do you have to cry every time and at everything" She smiled and said.

"I shed tear of happiness. Oh, it had been so long that I hold a man in my arms"

"So do I, it had been a while that I make love to a woman"

"I don't believe you; your look, your life, I had known almost everything about you, but you still are mysterious"

"What is it so mysterious about me?

"I don't know, it's just like today that I will never believe in a million years that I will end up in your room and in your arms, and hopefully will be in your bed"

Virak pick her naked body up and walked toward the bedroom; while he was intoxicated by the jasmine fragrance mix in her womanly natural body scent; he lay her down on the edge of the bed with her legs were still hanging down to the floor and reached to turn on the lamp on the night table. She raised her heads up and was surprised to see her naked body reflected from the mirrors on the wall. While kneeling on the floor between her thighs, Virak bent down to kiss……

One afternoon, Virak had just finished the first session, Sovana turned to her side to present her round butt to him that was still wet with their love juice at her gap. He held her waist, pulled her but toward him, and they felt asleep in spoon position with a sweet relaxing dream. Suddenly, they heard commotion from down stair and came up toward his flat; he could hear Princess Devy and cousin Kheng on the stair outside his door, and then loud knock.

"Sweetheart I know you are in there opens the door for me please"

"He is not in there your highness, would you please come downstairs and have some meal we have nice fresh roasted duck. He is still in the field your highness. I will call Sovana for you"

"Mr. Kheng pleases stops talking to me in that royal term, I am no longer a princess, I don't want your roasted duck, and I don't want to see Sovana. I want to see him I know he is in there. (Loud knock) Sweetheart would you please open up"

Virak let Sovana out through the front door stairwell that was rarely used, and when he was sure that she got in her flat, he came to open the door to the inside stair; and there stood Devy with tear in her eyes. She rushed into his arms and was crying uncontrollably. He held her tightly and nodded his head to cousin Kheng. Virak walked her to the couch at the back window and he told her to wait for a few minutes that he need to freshen up. He went in the bedroom to replace the bed sheet and went to the bathroom to wash off Sovana body scent. When he came back to the couch and found Devy was already changed to a green and saffron silk sarong and a thin white shirt; then she said.

"My family will move to Europe in the next few months, and I don't want to go with them I want to stay here with you please don't send me away, because I love you so much"

"Yes Baby, I just learn to love you more than anything else, and all I want to do is to hold you in my arm forever, but our love is up against so many odds, as you know your parent don't want us to see each other, you mother came here with armed men and she threat to hurt me and people around here that made them fear for their life. I think you should go to Europe with your family, I hope you will be happy there"

"My life couldn't be happy without you; it doesn't matter where I go"

"I understand but we are still too young, and later on in life we will see thing differently, we got to learn to cope with it, we have responsibility and obligation that we need to take into consideration, it may not all be pleasant the way we want but we will cherish the memory that our life have cross path"

"I don't understand a thing you said, but come here, give me some memory" Devy got up and dragged his hand to the bedroom; in the bedroom, she stood by the bed, dropped the silk sarong to the floor and pulled the rest of her cloth off while looking at him.

"Make love to me; make me feel like a woman" She came to undress him while he was trying to reason with her but deep down he felt that he was fighting a losing battle.

"But Baby if we do that, it will complicate everything further, I think……" She put her finger on his lips, and she walked backward dragging him toward the bed; Virak thought to himself who is he to refuse this beautiful angel wishes. She got up on the bed, laid her body with all of it naked glory at the center of the bed. He stood by the bed looked at her like he was in a trance. She reached to pull him up on the bed…… They lay for a while holding each other.

Later she went down to sit alone at the table in the main floor having her meal, and then she left that brought a relief to cousin Kheng. A few days later, she had cut class and come to visit his bedroom more and more often; cousin Kheng had warned Virak about the plain cloth undercover agents of unknown source had set up a surveillance network around the area. One day, Devy just stepped in his room and told him that she will go to Europe next week and she missed her period. Suddenly, cousin Kheng came to knock at the door, and he whispered to Virak that a plain cloth agent left the main floor quickly upon seeing Devy came up stair through the side door, and he suggested that Devy should come down to the main floor and sit at the table having her meal just in case something might happen.

Virak reacted quickly sent Devy down to the main floor, and he went down to a storage room under the stair where they had a small secret room to keep a safe box right behind Sovana office desk that he could hear the noise from the busy main floor. Virak crawled through a low door behind Sovana desk that startled her; after he explained to her what was going on they went behind the blind on her office door that opened to the cashier booth. On the main floor, it was busy and noisy as usual, and at a corner Devy sat by herself eating earnestly acting like any other customer. Suddenly, Devy's mother stood in front of her with her hands on her hip and asked her.

"What are you doing here young lady? And where is he?" Virak did not wait to find out what her answer will be because the sound of a military five tons truck pull up and the combat boot of a few squads of soldiers rushed in and went up to all the floor. Sovana pushed Virak back through the low door and put something in front of it. He leaned on the safe listening to the thunder heavy foot step of the combat boot and touching the Smith and Weston revolver under his arm. She told him to move quietly into her flat where she hid his uniform and combat gear.

When Virak went in Sovana's flat for a few minutes cousin Kheng came in and told him to escape with the delivery truck in the early morning, but Virak refused his idea because if something happen not according to plan; he don't want to kill fellow soldiers in order to protect himself. Virak assured cousin Kheng not to worry that he will be out of here by morning; and he told him that he will stay with his battalion for a while and he will be back.

Sovana gave Virak a krama and a silk robe; so he could change and to get freshen up. When he get out from the shower, Sovana had already set up his evening meal, and it's probably his last meal at the garden for a while; Virak ate quietly while Sovana looked on and cried silently at his side. After the meal they laid in her bed talking in whisper; he told her about his plan and his suggestion for her to prepare herself. They knew that they will not see each other for a while and tonight is their last night in bed together, so while they were talking their hand and mouth were busy exploring one another body......

C10-Chained to the Pig Pen

"Welcome back lieutenant, I knew that you couldn't stay away for long, and you come at the right time that we are just about to mobilize on another mission. You have an option to stay back if you want too, but if you miss the smell of gun powder and want to come along I will be honor to have you stand and fight Vietcong at my side" After he gave Virak a long welcome speech, he spread out the map and pointed to him the imported coordinates.

"The high command wants us to establish our present here, and the intelligence report that there are some NVRA in this area along with some Khmer Rouge unit. If you are interest in coming with us I want you to tag along on the company patrol, make an assessment, and report back to me" On the day of their departure point, BT shown up at Virak's quarter, so he had to take some time to listen to his reports, messages, and complains.

"There is nothing new happen except that the pretty widow she looks kind of upset after you left, did you screw her?"

"Hey, shut the hell up BT, the commander's wife entrusted her for me to take care of her, Sovana is a hard working respectable woman, and she will get remarried soon. Don't you ever let me hear you talk like that about her again; you just stay there taking care of the club and come here to see me every week, and ask Sovana to send some food for me"

"All right, I just concern about her miserable loneliness that's all; and you, why do you have to go on the operation with them? Why don't you just stay here? And what's the matter with the American? When we were in Nam they'd said that they will be all over Cambodia in six months, and that was over a year ago; and now there is still no American here, what's the hell with them?"

"It's probably they change their mind"
"Is that right? And what's about us?"
"We will keep on fighting I guess"
"Fight with what? Our bare hand"
"All right, calm down BT, why don't you have your hostesses at the club find out from your high echelon clients in the diplomat corps; those people from outside, they probably know these kind of information better than us"

Virak went along on patrol with the third company; and only a few miles in the bamboo forest, they were engaged in skirmish with a Vietcong unit. The order was to retreat and call for artillery and air support, it sound so simple but the company command was too slow to react, and it was pinned down at a rice field dike. Virak asked the platoon commanders to hold the Vietcong at their present position then he moved a platoon to get the command post out. They got them out all right, but the platoon was panic they became disorganized and retreated too fast. Virak grabbed an M-60 machine gun from a freshly killed soldier, took cover behind a tree and started to fire at the advanced Vietcong line.

Suddenly, Virak felt a sharp object poked on his neck, he rolled around on his back then he was looking at the tip of the bayonet on an AK-47, was pointing at his face by a Vietcong soldier, then he got no other choice but to raise his hands. They quickly tied his wrists and elbows together behind his back, cut off his combat gear from boot to helmet, and they brought him to a holding place behind their front line with the other captured government soldiers from other battles. In less than five minutes, that Virak separated from his weapon he became a tied up prisoner, he tried to look around to get his bearing but a communist soldier pointed at him and shook his head, and then he realized that his chance to escape at the present was slimmed.

All captured soldiers were turned to the Khmer rouge for questioning; they interrogated everybody, beat up most of them and killed some on the spot. Then the Khmer rouge tied each one of them to an end of a bamboo pole that had a hammock hung in the middle, and they loaded the hammocks with their wounded comrade.

They made them walked in column with the bamboo pole on their shoulder, and marched west to northwest toward the Kirirom region; it was probably their base somewhere in the mountain. The Khmer rouge soldiers only stop at meal time twice a day and six hours rest at night; it take like ten days to get to their base. After dropping off their wound at the hospital, they loaded foods and ammunitions in the hammocks, and march them back to the different frontline.

For a while, that was all the captured soldiers did was to carry their wounds, foods and ammunitions back and forth between some bases in the mountain and their frontline somewhere. On the road, they gave them some food and water sometime at irregular interval it depended on the time and place and the supply on hand. The prisoners all knew that they were still alive because of their usefulness as beast of burden; some prisoners who were too sick or had leg wound that they could not walk or carry load will be shot and thrown in the bush.

Anyone could get sick or kill very easily here if luck was not on his side, because in this region was one of the cradle of malaria and a whole host of other strange diseases. Many prisoner lost their life to snake bite or poisonous plants, but there was the menace creature of all was the jumping blood sucking leach, it was always the ever present on the jungle trail. The Khmer rouge soldiers used their knife or machete to scrape it off their body, but for the prisoners their hands were tied to the bamboo pole. Sometime they were lucky the creature hung on the easy spot that they might just get it off by rubbing against the tree trunk, but most of the time they hung on the spot that they could not do anything about them, just let them had their fill and they will drop off on the trail like a pouch of blood, and those were the prisoner blood. Many times, each prisoner had ten or more of them blood sucking leaches hung on their body at the same time.

There were a few times, the Khmer rouge column was attacked by the American or the Cambodian government planes near the front line, and the captured soldiers were smacked in the middle of it with their hand tied up to the bamboo pole. Virak lost count of how many trips he'd made back and forth between the mountain and the frontline. They were very tired, it's a matter of fact they were beyond tired it was a living hell; each of them walked like a zombie, there was only the will to live that kept them moving.

One day, they arrived at a base in the mountain, the Khmer rouge unit who used them, received their break from the mission. They overheard a soldier asked his comrade commander of what they were going to do with the prisoners; and the commander said that they will move out in about a week, and he told the soldiers to chain them to the pig pens for the time being.

The prisoners were so relief that they were going to get some rest after all, but there was only one thing that the Khmer Rouge forgot, was to feed them for the last couple of days ever since they were tied up at the pens. Until a few days later, the prisoners realized that they did not forget because they already tied them to the food source. Most of them ate the pig slob for the first time, were vomited most of it out, because the filthy pigs like to step their dirty feet in the trout; that gave them the flavor of the mud and their crap.

There were a row of more than a few dozen pens along the walkway and each pen was built a few meters apart; they brought the slop buckets on the rolling cart, and they dumped it in the trout along the walkway where they chained the prisoners to the outside corner in between those pens. The surrounding area were planted with all kinds of vegetable, banana and "Kontumtet tree" that it leaves and fruit was known to have the medicinal property that can expel the parasite from human and animal intestinal tract. Many of them adjusted their stomach to the slop all right, but for some the more they ate it the more they vomited it out, so they just contented to eat the plant and leaves that grown at abundant around them and fertilized by their own excrement, it was a kind of recycling arrangement. The slop was made from chopped banana trunk, plant and vegetable, rice kernel and all kinds of leftover and spoiled food.

A supervisor, who ran this pig farm operation, was a middle age cripple man, he was probably a Khmer Rouge soldier who was wounded in battle, and he had a few dozen men and women worked for him in the farm. Comrade 'cripple' was a hardcore communist, and he was furious when the unit that dropped off the prisoners at the pens, left without remove them from there, and he complained that the prisoners ate all the slop that made his pig became skinnier. He walked along the walkway every day carrying a wooden staff and beat up the prisoners at random; he enjoyed beating and shouting at a fat prisoner in particular.

"You are a fat imperialist swine; you steal all the slop that why the pig got just skin and bone, I will kill you" He beat the fat prisoner every day until he died, he order all workers carried a stick to beat any prisoner who reach in the trout while the pig was feeding.

At one of a very hot day, a column of the communist soldier brought their wounded comrades from the front line; a prisoner made a fatal mistake by made his body too visible and looking straight at the column just like he was watching a parade; a vicious communist soldier who was boiling with anger from the frontline, charged straight at the prisoner from across the ditch; Virak sensed danger was eminent, so he crouched down low to the ground below the grass line. All he heard was the sound of coconut shell cracked when hit with hard object, and he knew what it was, it was the prisoner skull cracked when it hit by the AK-47 rifle butt. Some of the workers came out and said.

"What's happen? Why these two dogs laid bleeding here?"

"They were hit by comrade Bophan; they said he was angry because he lost a lot of his soldiers at the front line"

The two prisoners were laid dying in the pool of their blood; they were choking and moaning for five to six hours before they passed away. Their bodies were left lying on the spot for couple days under a hundred degree sun; they started to decompose with millions of insect and maggot devoured the rotten flesh, and the smell became unbearable. The worker untied some prisoners to bury the corps right on the spot in the ditch but the smell was still lingered for days.

Every day gone by that they were chained to the pig pen; the prisoners knew that they were one step closer to the jaw of death. During the day, they sat under the tropical sun and tried in vain to keep the blood sucking flies at bay; they tried to rub mud on the exposed skin and stuff leaves and grass inside their uniform to insulate and protect from weather and insect; in the evening, there were billion of mosquitoes came out and sang the lullaby to put them to sleep, and they will sucked the blood dry from the body of anyone who fall asleep without any protection, and also the rat will try to feed on their open wound, and the farm workers beat them regularly at random just because they could.

All of the Khmer Rouge wore black pajama and cotton krama around their neck at all time throughout the base, and Virak never see any panty line or bra on any woman because he could see their nipples outline pushed up from their pajama top; all the women hair were cut short uniformly, and he never see anyone smiling or joking around at all, and they were look and sound so very serious, and when they sing, the song will be a kind of sickly sad revolutionary tone, for the normal regular love song or traditional song were unheard of; Virak think all these communist are ignorant sick bastard. Beside their women did not wear panties or bras, they were uniformly unattractive except one of them who had sparkle in her eyes; there is not unusual that a girl or a woman has sparkle in their eyes but she was the only one around here that he noticed, the rest of them either men or women, their eyes were emotionally blank like robot.

Sparkle Eye

One afternoon, the monsoon had arrived, it rain very hard, and it was a welcome change and a relief for them because they hadn't have a shower ever since the day they were captured. Virak washed off the mud from his face and hair, pulled grass and leaves out off his uniform so he could wash his whole body. He tried to stand up to drain the dirty water down, but when he saw the slop cart rolled on the walkway, he sat back down real quick in the same dirty puddle of mud and wet grass; when the cart came by he heard a voice.

"Oh, you are just a young man"

Virak looked up at her face and then he recognized that she was Sparkle Eyes in her early twenty; she stood there just a few seconds and then she moved on to the next pen. Virak looked around and saw most of the prisoners had some degree of hair on their face except him; he was astonished with Sparkle Eyes because none of other workers ever acknowledge them or lay their eye on them least of all talk to them, the only time they paid any attention to them was when they beat them up.

A week had passed ever since, the mountain received the initial monsoon rain it rain at irregular interval; Virak was kind of like it when it rain at night because it chased the mosquitoes away, and then he could get himself ready to have a good night sleep. He pulled a stalk of banana leaf to cover his head and faces, leaned back against the pen, stretch his legs, and went to sleep.

The sound of the water flowed in the ditch along the walkway and the raindrop when it hit the banana leaf let his mind drifted to somewhere else in the fog. And then he could hear Strauss's music the Blue Danube softly in the background and the moonlight reflection on the water, then he thought that he was back at the Riverside Garden but it wasn't it, where was he? Was he dead? Was this the dead state felt like? Great! It is better than chained to the pig pen, eating slop, and breathing in the stench smell; Virak's mind flashed through the pleasant vision that made his passion stirred.

He saw Lady S's glorious butt pushed back at his face while she leaned on a gilded window frame, he reached down to unbutton and open his fly to release his now erected penis, and then he thought, wait a minute, why does he still wear this dirty uniform? Oh well, think about it later first thing first. He grabbed Lady S hips to pull her back and plugged his hard shaft through her gap, he trusted hard and deep to try to make every plunge count; then he exploded and felt the sensation of the real heaven, but he was interrupted by something poked on his leg.

When Virak opened his eyes, it's already daylight, and then he looked down at his penis that was still hard and long, and stood proud squirting semen; his dirty pant was down to his knee, and there Sparkle Eyes squatted down at his side.

"What do you think you are doing? If they see this they will kill you with that stick, straight yourself up they are coming"

Virak reacted swiftly, pulled his pant up and rolled himself into a small bundle in the tall grass; he turned to Sparkle Eyes and whispered his thanks to her. From that day on, she acted kind to him and she looked like she got more sparkle in her eyes; and sometime she slipped some food to him wrapped in banana leaf, it was a real treat. Virak appreciated her kindness and thank her profusely; sometime when she stood close he kissed her hand and her knee. At some dark night, she sneaked out from behind the pen and came to have a little chat.

"Why are you ending up here with all these prisoners? You are too young to be a soldier"

"They forced me to join, I am an orphan, I got no family or a place to live, and they gave me food, shelter, uniform and gun at the same time. I don't want to be a soldier in the war. And you, why are you ending up here with the communist?"

"It was happened the same thing to me here, I lived in Phnom Penh, and I went to visit relative in the countryside; and then, the war started, the road was cut off, and I was forced to join them. I have a cousin here as an assistant to the base commander, he pulled me from the combat unit and put me here in this work detail"

"But why do you works in here?"

"He doesn't want anyone to know that we are related, and he told me to keep a low profile"

She had come out quite often, and Virak had asked to find out about her and her life in Phnom Penh. She also asked him about the changing life in the city after the war started. She said she was arranged to be married with the son of a rich merchant; and even though, they just met and she was just get to know him a few months before the war start she said she missed him, and she missed her life in the city and she wish she can be back home with her family and her fiancée.

Virak told her that he wished that he could help her but he was in chain. She said she can help him with the chain if he promised to help her escape back to Phnom Penh, and he agreed with her immediately. So he had her described to him all the information about the base layout, the surrounding area, the troupe strength and their movement; and he also told her to try to get any map and weapon. Virak was still curious about her sneaking out to see him at will, that it might be a communist trick. He asked her about the guard but she said there wasn't any guard here because they don't think the prisoners can escape and survive in this jungle in their present condition. Virak was glad that they were underestimated them.

A couple days later under a dark rainy night, Sparkle Eyes crawled up from behind the pen; it was very unusual for her to come out under the heavy rain like this.

"We got to go now, comrade foreman made a complaint to the base command that you all take too long to die, he want to get ride off all of you by morning, let me see the chain" She used a monkey wrench and a wise grip to lose the nuts and bolts on his wrists and ankles; after all the chain and shackle came off, Virak grabbed the tools and went to free the other prisoners but she stopped him and said.

"No just us two, let's go, they will attract too much attention"

"I got to release them, I can't leave them here, we will have a better chance in number, they are soldiers, and they can help us escape" They release the first prisoner nearby and gave him the tools to free the others; Sparkle Eyes and Virak, went into the work shack to gather any weapon they can find like knives, axes, and long handle machete. Virak hesitated for a moment and thinking about revenge, he want to get his hand on comrade Cripple and comrade Bophan, but his better judgment win, he changed his mind and thinking that he will have his chance when they cross path some other time.

The escapees slipped into the ditch that was filled and flowed with rain water; Sparkle Eyes and Virak; were leading the way followed the current. They were practically swimming; she had a bundle floating in front of her, and Virak swam at her side with one arm around her waist followed by twenty or more escapees in single file. She tried to get his attention and pointed to the shadow of the big tree and the dim lit light of the guard shack below, Virak recognized right away the main guard post that they had come through here many times when they moved the wound and supply; it let him know that they were already free outside of their base, but they were still in danger of being hunt down when they discovered that they were missing.

After the escapees passed the main guard shack the ditch became wider and flowed faster, and at this point it became a river and the water flowed between rocks and boulders, Sparkle Eyes whispered to Virak that she only knew the way up to that point, and the tributary will branched out to many small river that snaked through the mountain and the high plain with many dangerous waterfalls. Virak told her it didn't matter if they know the terrain or not, it's better to float in the river to put some distant between them and the base, they just kept their eyes open for the enemy who might camp out along the river bank, and they should listened for the waterfall ahead.

At sometime before daybreak, they could hear the waterfall roaring around the bend. Virak passed the word and they all scrambled to get on the river bank; he heard someone asked of which side of the bank that they should get on, and a stern voice told them to be quiet and just move on. When they got on the bank Virak saw some of them that just floated pass by; they moved further up the bank and get in the jungle away from the river. The sun rise about the tree top at the east, they stopped by a branch of a small river that had high bank and it flowed between large boulders that they could hide if need be. A stern voice called the escapees to gather at the water edge.

"Is there any officer among us?" Everybody were quiet, there was no reply, for Virak he thought it was better for him to keep his mouth shut because first no one will believe him because he looked too young and second he did not know these soldiers it was hard to tell from friend or foe.

"Is there any senior staff NCO here?" No reply.

"OK, I am staff sergeant so and so, I will be in charge from here on, I will lead us to safety behind our front line, why is she doing here?" He pointed his long handle machete at Sparkle Eye who was squared and took cover behind Virak's back; he used his blade to push SNCO's away and said.

"She is the one who free us last night"

"I want her tie up because I don't trust anyone in this black pajama uniform"

"I don't care what you think, let me tell all of you that she is the one who freed us, you will do no such thing, she is with me and I will take full responsibility" Stern voice stepped forward with both hands gripped the long handle machete, and the blade swung to one side get ready to strike. Virak pushed Sparkle Eyes back into the water, put the blade to the opposite side get ready to defend himself; Stern Voice got into a posture just like a wolf was showing it fang.

"I am in charge……"

Suddenly, they heard voice of people talking from the distant trail over the river bank; Virak quickly dragged Sparkle Eye arm and eased her into the river and he found a spot between the boulders with tree branch and vine covered over their head at the far side bank.

They heard Stern voice commanded the escapees to move between the boulders and floated downstream, Sparkle Eye started to move out but Virak pulled her back, held her body, looked in her eyes, and shook his head. She got the message, stood still in his arm, and laid her head on his shoulder, and Virak could felt her warm and shaky breathing on his neck. There were people talking from the high bank right above them, despite they had tree branch and vine covered over them, her whole body trembled when she heard a man voice.

"I guess most of them probably went down the waterfall, how many dead bodies we found below the fall? Four or five, I think the rest must have floated further downstream, if there are any of them got here as the tracts suggested there might be very few; we need to search down below to find more clue. OH! Look! Over there downstream......Shoot them" She whispered in his ear.

"That voice is comrade Bophan"

The sound of a dozen AK-47 were blasting fully automatic echoed waves after waves the sound of gunfire into the jungle, there were a little pause here and there that suggested the reload of the new magazine; when the sound of gunfire and the Khmer rouge shouting, move further downstream; Virak told her.

"Let's us move upstream, they might return to check this spot because our footprints are all over the water edge"

They tried hard to move upstream as fast as they could along the far side bank, at a few hundred yards from the high bank area, there was a fork of river branched out at forty five degree and flowed very swiftly down slope. They were immediately floated away in the current, on the way; they found a sizable branch that had broken off from somewhere to hang on and camouflaged their head.

Approximately half a day later, the river became very treacherous that they had to climb out on to the bank; first they blend themselves in the forest to observe the surrounding area, they came to a small plain in between mountain peaks, and there was a pristine clearing with a small stream flow through, and it seem like there was no human ever set foot in this area because there were no visible trail anywhere around; and for the Khmer rouge they avoided any high slope in the area under their control it was too difficult to move men and equipments.

And second, Virak had to make some weapon out of the forest, he cut some bamboo, small tree sapling and vine to make a few long spears for their protection from predator animal and some bows and arrows to hunt the prey animal for food. He had to show her how to aim and gave her a moment to practice; the field was teeming with animals they did not have to go far to hunt, in about an hour they killed three rabbits and a six feet long boa constrictor.

And third, he needed to find a spot to build a temporary shelter in order to build a fire for cooking and drying themselves. He chose a high ground spot under the cluster of big trees next to the small river at the clearing edge; They got some bamboo, broad leaves, and vine to build one big panel as the lean to in the middle of a few big trees and a few more panel to protect the fire from the rain and to block the light so it won't be seen from the distant.

And the fourth thing they need to do was easy, they found some firewood and pine sap to build a fire and cook the meat, they haven't had anything to eat since yesterday evening. After the meal, the sky was already dark but they still had one more thing to do was to clean up and dry themselves and their clothes; they waded into the shallow water about waist deep in front of the camp, Virak told her that was necessary for them to strip naked so they could clean and hang their uniform to dry, and she said she had a few dry krama in her bundle that they could wear when finish their clean up.

Virak took off his uniform that was already ripped to thread but he still need it to put it on when he get to the frontline, his skivvy was already falling apart that he had to throw it away; after the bath and the uniforms were already washed. Sparkle Eyes told him to turn his head away, and then she rushed out of the water into the shelter, Virak got out of the water right behind her and his curious eyes saw her surprised round butt smiled at him while she ducked into the shelter.

Virak just stood outside the shelter to let the water dripped off his body and looking into the shelter he could not help but to observe her naked body since he hadn't seen a naked woman for a long time; without the loose black pajama, he was surprised to find that she had a beautiful slender body. She untied her bundle, opened the plastic bag, and pulled out a dry cotton krama to wrap around her body. Then she pulled another identical krama and ducked out from the shelter, she was startled when she saw him stood right outside in the dark stark naked, and sported a stiff erection between his legs; she slowly handed him the krama, and rushed back in the shelter because the rain started to pour down.

Virak wore the krama loin cloth style, and then turn to adjust the two roof panel that leaned together over the fire, and the fourth one to block the light leaned on the other two opposite from their roof shelter; he went in, looked at her red face and then she asked.

"Is that thing has to be like that all the time?"

"What thing?"

"That thing in between your legs"

"Oh, that no, it's just that I haven't seen any beautiful woman body for a long time" She did not say anything after that, and she kept her eye out to the forest edge and pulling the krama down to cover her butt because it was too short to cover from above her breast down to her butt. So Virak suggested for her to wear it just like a sarong that wrap around from the waist down and leave her chest bare. While he turned to get some more broiled meat from the fire, and when he finished with the meat and turned around he saw she had the krama around her waist and her arms covered her breasts.

Virak told her that in this situation, she did not need to be embarrassed because there were only them here, and beside she had beautiful round breasts. Virak was certain that the Khmer rouge never came through this area and the tiger won't sneak up on the camp that has big enough fire burning. he put some more wood on the fire and told her that they both could sleep but she said that he should go to sleep because this was his first nigh sleep in freedom, and she will stay up to tend the fire. Virak was too tired to reason with her, so he lay down to get some sleep, but he noticed that she was shaking and the goose bump on her body; so, he took off the krama from his waist, wrapped over her shoulder, and buried himself under the leaves and he drifted to sleep immediately right after he closed his eyes.

Virak woke up to a dark rainy morning and the windblown so hard that made the air became very chilly, but he was kind of feeling warm and cozy. Virak could feel her naked body wrapped around his and he ran his hand to caress her back down to her bare butt, and then he could feel some sticky stuff on her thighs then he knew that he had a wet dream. Virak believed last night was very cold that she took off the krama to cover both of them and snuggle up to get warm, it was just a simple survival technique that had triggered his wet dream. Virak pulled the krama off his head and saw she was still awake and propped her head up to watch out to the forest edge.

Since the rain was die down a little bit, they got up to throw some wood on the fire and went outside to relief themselves, and then to wash in the river. Virak splashed the water at her thighs to scrub and clean off his sticky mess; she did not say a word and just held on to his shoulder watching his cleaning work. After cleaning themselves, they went back under the shelter, started to eat the roasted rabbit that leftover from last night, and folded the leaf to make a cup for catching rain water that drained off the roof to drink. They seem to lose their inhibition; they sat on the leaves bed bare bottom and wrapped the krama over their shoulder to keep warm.

"I am sorry about last night if I had done anything inappropriate in my sleep, would you please forgive me, it was not my intention at all"

"That's all right; I wonder how do you know all these things since you are still so young?"

"I was taught by a master"

"Really do they have teacher to teach young people for that?"

"It was just for me not the whole country, did you like it?"

There was no answer, she just smile and look down; Virak could see between the krama opening her hard nipples started to pointed out sharp and long just like the tip of the AK-47 bayonet. She saw him looking at her chest, she pulled the krama try to close the opening, but he held her hands and pushed the krama aside to look at both her breasts in full view that they swelled up almost like a cone shape. Virak held both breasts in his hands and rolled the nipple with his fingers. She closed her eyes and lay back on the leaves bed...... His finger rowed in between her slippery gap down to the barrier that made her moaned...... She started to stir fifteen minutes later.

"WE should not do this while we are on the run"

"What did we do? We didn't do anything and you are still a virgin; beside our life is at a moment of uncertainty and there are more reasons to do it so we will not regret later if we don't make it"

"Oh please, don't say like that"

"Whether I say it or not, that is a reality we both know that"

"Oh, you make me feel so afraid"

"I am sorry, I shouldn't say that, but don't worry, we are all right so fare and if we used our head lucks are always on our side; it won't be long we will sit at the central market eating the beef stirred fried noodle in the next few weeks"

They held each other close for comfort and keep warm, covered them with the krama; and they felt asleep. They stayed peacefully at the small and plentiful field by the mountainside. They hunted so they could smoke and preserve the meat for the road ahead; despite her suggestion that they should stay at that spot for a while to let his body recuperated from the captivity, but Virak felt very impatient and he want to be back behind his friendly frontline sooner.

They left that field with all of their weapons and her virginity was still intact. They didn't have any enemy chasing behind them so they took their time and moved cautiously through the mountain and dark forest. It took them more than twenty days to get to the national route. Virak recognized it as the route between Phnom Penh and Kompong Som seaport, but they were not out of danger yet because that area was still in the enemy zone; so they followed the route toward the direction of Kampong Speu province and Phnom Penh.

A few days later they were picked up by a military convoy that pushed an excursion into the enemy zone scavenging for food and firewood, and they were just lucky for being in the right place at the right time. They were sent to headquarter for debriefing and questioning, and Virak had to sing some document to insure her release. At the Kampong Speu province town, Virak thrown away everything that he brought from the jungle, but Sparkle Eyes want to keep the two krama as souvenir.

He went to his battalion headquarter to retrieve some money that he'd stashed away for the needy time like that, and he told them not to tell his family of his return because he want to do it himself. When they arrived in Phnom Penh, Virak asked her for her address so he can drop her off to her family, but then she said that she did not want her family to see her look like that she just came out of the jungle and she asked him to give her some suggestion, so Virak booked them in two separate rooms at a hotel and then he contacted BT and told him to keep his mouth shut and to bring him some gold.

Virak brought her to the central market area where they ate all the comfort food like stirred fried beef noodle that he had promised; he bought some new clothes for himself and a whole new wardrobe for her from silk brocade, high heel to lingerie and jewelry. Next they went to have a medical check up with the doctor who gave them a clean bill of health. Virak brought her to visit places where she wanted to see and some place that he want to show to her.

After they had two week of resting and enjoying life, he thought they had cleansed all the jungle things out of their system by then, but he hadn't heard her mention anything about she want to see her family or the rich merchant's son at all. One evening Virak went to see her in her room; she sat looking out of the window and she was crying.

"What's matter? What's wrong?"

"Nothing, I miss the jungle"

"Wait a minute, do you want to go back there?"

"No, I miss the jungle when we hold each other to go to sleep"

"Ok, that was necessary for our survival and what's now?"

"And now you push me away, we sleep in the separate room, you forgot all the things we had together, you never even remember my name, and here in Phnom Penh I feel like I don't know you anymore"

"Are you finished? And let me explain. I put us in separate room is to give you your own space, your own place and time to think about your life your future, to get yourself ready to face the real world like your family and your fiancée, aren't you going to meet them?"

"I will meet them in time"

"Ok, the things that we had together; were necessary for our survival and it was just at the spur of the moment, it was no way that we could control everything then at that moment of uncertainty. And your name, I did not know your name until I read on the documents at the debriefing, and I never get use to call your name because I already gave you a name the first time I saw you 'Sparkle Eyes'. At the pig pen, every time I saw your beautiful eye, it gave me a great comfort, hope, and a will to live; if I had not met you I probably perish and bury in the ditch by now. You did not know me before and you don't know me now. At the pig pen I was in the fighting for survival mode, and you saw me different from what I am now. Here in Phnom Penh, I have many different lives that I just don't want anyone to know, but for everything I said and the feeling I have about you are true" She got up from the window, walked into his arms, cried some more on his shoulder, kissed his neck and she said.

"Oh darling, thank you, you do have feelings for me, and 'Sparkle Eyes' is a beautiful name that I will cherish the rest of my life along with our krama, but I still want to experience our life at the time in the jungle one more time before I go to face my reality"

Virak did not need to reply, they were just stood there held and kissed each other; Virak checked out from that place and checked in to another hotel that had proper air conditioning. He ordered foods, flowers, and plants to create an ambient that mimic the jungle. Then he adjusted the temperature down to make their room feel chilly in the middle of the hot tropical city before he let her come in the room. She was stunned at the setting in the cold and dark environment; Virak did not give her any time to adjust or scrutinize anything, he just stripped off his and her clothes and eased themselves into a hot bubble bath, they sipped the chilled green coconut drink and took their time slowly to feel each other body in the smooth bubbles. After coming up from the bath, they held their nude body together under the blanket to keep warm for a while until she started to feel restless......There was a little pain for her at the first time when they get rid of her virginity, it's a small price to pay.

They stayed at the penthouse for more than a week to enjoy their moment in time; Virak was certain that he had done his best to satisfy her desire of the jungle fever. He took her to visit the beauty salon, the tailor shop, the jewelry store and some other shops that were necessary for her to get everything she want to transform from a Khmer rouge soldier in black pajama to a stylish well refine beauty. Virak was surprised and at awe to see her dress and act elegantly, he patted himself on the back for his effort and he realized that her desire to be a beautiful woman as she is that instills the confident and show in her manner with good taste, style and class.

One day, she announced her desire and her decision that she wanted to see her family while laying spread eagle on the bed with his hard rod was still lodged deep in between her gap.

"I miss my family I want to go back home, and I thank you for everything you had done for me. I am very grateful that you save my life"

"I am the one who should thank you for everything; you had save my life and I will always cherish the time we had together forever Sparkle Eyes"

Virak was proud to bring her back to her home as a beautiful elegant woman in silk dress and adorned with gold and ruby jewelries. Her family was surprised and find hard to believe that she was just came out from the jungle, they were hardly recognized her. The message was sent immediately to the rich merchant house; the son of the rich merchant came to her house immediately, he was in his late twenty who took over the business from his father. And he was so excited that all he could do was holding her hand, put his face in her palm and cried his heart out.

She just smiled softly with sparkles in her eyes, she looked at Virak and formed her mouth to say thank you. The families had a Fang Sui master to select their married date at some time in the next few weeks. A few days before her married ceremony, she requested to meet Virak at the market, and she told him that she missed her period; and he said to her that she got nothing to worry about because he knew she was a life saver, a life giver and a beautiful person in and out, and she will make a good mother to her child. Virak left a part of him in her and she left a part of her deep in his heart, and he will always remember her as 'Sparkle Eyes' his guardian angel, a Goddess Avatar.

C11-The Turning Point

Virak's family was very happy to see him return home alive, because in most cases when soldiers report capture or missing in action the families will never hear from them again. The elders want to set up a feasting celebration but Virak refused the idea instead he told them to bring food and offering to the temple. He stayed at his house for a few days then he started to feel boring, he wanted to see the Riverside Garden and was craving for some frog rice porridge.

In the evening at the Garden, there were full of party celebrations as usual, the melody of Sinsisamut song humming softly in the air. The moon reflected the golden light on the river and the sweet scents of chompa, jasmine and frangipani mixed with the smell of the promising good food made Virak walked into the back living room by the kitchen. Cousin Kheng saw him first before he went in, he was shocked and surprise to see Virak in the flesh unexpected.

"Oh brother, we were so worried about you but somehow in the back of my mind I always believe that you will come out all right, let's we go inside" And he announced "Hey ladies look who is here!"

When they saw Virak the two women were crying and shouting in unison, and they came up to hug him; Virak noticed that TH did not have her big tummy anymore. And Sovana she was prettier than ever but he did not see any ring on her finger. They asked him so many questions, and he just told them that he was captured and had escaped back.

Later, Sovana did not say a word she just kept on crying on his shoulder, he held her, kissed her forehead, and reassured her that everything will be all right.

TH brought her newborn son to show Virak "Here is your nephew we named him after you" Virak held the baby for a moment and then he started to cry, TH took the baby from him and said it was his feeding time. Virak came to sit at the table with Sovana was still crying on his left arm.

He ate and drank slowly to savor the essence of the tastes that he had missed, while cousin Kheng started to fill him in on what had happened in his absent.

"We were preoccupied with the bad news of your disappearance, and we paid less attention to the business, but we had a good managing staff that made everything ran smoothly, and we still made a good profit.

And Sovana had a lot of marriage proposals but she won't accept anyone; there are a few high ranking functionaries, some high rank military officers, and haft a dozen rich merchants. I don't know what is she looking for? She said she want to hold off for a while because of the bad news, and now that you are back, I hope she will make up her mind soon because good men died like fly in this time of war"

"Ok, give her some time and some room, I will talk to her" And Virak turned to Sovana.

"Can I talk to you? Or you just stay crying all night" She sat up smiling and dapping tear from her eyes, and she took a sip from her glass and said.

"I will decide soon"

Virak went up to the top floor and walked through the flat to see it was clean and devoid of any dust, he thought that Sovana had done a good job at keeping this flat in order.

He took a long leisure shower and walked around naked because he did not want to feel any restriction from clothing or anything else, and then he came to stand in front of the mirror to observe the fresh scars from the jungle all over his body.

He laid a silk krama on the couch by the window, and popped a cassette tape in the magneto phone to play Moonlight Sonata of Beethoven; then he sat back on the couch, looked out of the window over the Mekong river and the reflection of the moonlight.

He thought about the war, the situation of the country, the American sit down to talk with Vietcong in Paris and he wondered why nobody paid any attention or concerned about that this was the turning point of the war for the whole Indochina region.

Virak heard the door at the stair open and close, he immediately could smell the fragrance of jasmine scent from Sovana body before he turn to look at her. She wore a long lotus silk robe carrying a tray in her hands, and when she put it down he saw she brought a couple bowls of frog seafood rice porridge, a plate of roasted duck, bowl of fresh fruit on ice, and a few cold beers.

"I hope you like all these as I remember"

"Oh yes, these are perfect just like you as always"

She smiled let her hair down, untied and dropped the silk robe to the floor; she wore nothing underneath and came to sit on his lap. He held her soft body in his arm; and the feeling of her soft butt on his lap that stirred the fire of his passion.

She fed him a spoonful of rice porridge and a piece of roasted duck, and hand him the chilled glass that he rubbed it on her nipple to toast their first pleasure night together in a long time.

"I don't want you to go to the front line again ever"

"But Sovana, I am a soldier"

"I know you have a sense of duty, you still go even though you have a legitimate reason to stay behind. This last episode is a close call, and it reminded us that war is unpredictable as I am sure you already knew.

Look sweetheart, you have a lot of responsibility for other people life including mine, you are very much need here and just let other do the fighting for now please. I will talk with one officer of the intelligent unit who has a very high connection in the supreme command to get you a post in there Ok"

"Is he the one who want to marry you?"

"Maybe, we'll see"

"Why don't you marry one of them so you can become a supreme lady of the house like my mother and her friend, they do nothing but sit around gossiping among ladies and princesses"

"It's hard to believe that just over a year ago, I sat by the rice field close to the frontline, cooked meager meal for my husband, slept in a makeshift shack with a leaking palm leaves roof when it rain, and listened to gunfire and bomb explosions.

And now I have no husband but I am happy, I feel free, I got everything thank to you, I can become a supreme lady if I want to; you have made me of what I am today, and you make me feel confident, beautiful and satisfy"

"I did not make you, I just bring you here, give you something to do and freedom to choose. You have made everything on your own; and by the way, would you ask your friend the officer for another spot for BT also"

Virak picked a chunk of milk fruit and mangosteen rubbed on her pointed nipple, fed in their mouth and they kissed to savor the essence of these love nectar. She stood up on the couch above him with her gap a few inches from his lips…… She closed her eyes and opened her mouth, moved herself up and down, and moaned with ecstasy…… "Oh my darling, it had been so long……

Virak sat at the corner table on the main floor having his afternoon meal, and there BT with a magazine in his hand and started to spread it out to show Virak some picture.

"Look at the picture here in this French magazine; they said the American talk with Vietcong in Paris"

"This seem like that the American wants to quit the war, the American said they continue to support all three countries to fight against the communist, but I doubt that because what they say now and what they will do later might be different.

The American seem to lost the will to fight this war already, since they just realize that they fight a lost war, and they have no business in sending their men to die in other country by the thousand with no end in sight.

I heard that the American elect their president every four years they say it's democracy it's good for them but it's not good for us because when their new president come into the office their policy always changing they said to follow the will of their people and if the leader won't follow he will not be reelected that's democracy, it's not like our phony democracy here that the leader do whatever he want and crush anyone who criticize his policy.

The American and the Vietcong talk in Paris, is to find a way to quit the war and that mean the American eventually will pull out from Vietnam. I don't think they will send any air support, ammo and supplies, and our country will be overrun by the communist; the American may shout their support but not the material wise.

I think you already know of what the communist will do to us when they come into power, they will shoot us soldiers and all the people in the city who they knew had fight against them; they will hang us that's for sure, and that's the first thing in their agenda; Since we already know it's going to be dooms let get the hell out of here or find the way to prepare to get out just in case…"

A few days later, Sovana introduced BT and Virak to a colonel who was in charge of the intelligent unit, and he brought them to the place that they supposed to report to, their job had a lot of flexibilities and the freedom of movements.

It wasn't long after they got the job in the intelligent unit; the go-betweens came to visit cousin Kheng by the colonel requested for Sovana hand in marriage. They got married a month later. Then, she became Lady Sovana; she still came to her office a couple days a week and kept her flat at the second floor.

Virak went with BT to his family home and gathered everybody into the main hall; first he shown the picture of the American sit down with Vietcong in Paris, and then BT and Virak tried to explain to them about what this mean and what could happen after the American leaving Southeast Asia; and he also explain what they should do ahead of time.

"I think we should move out of the country for the time being, and we should sell all the properties and everything, and move to Thailand or Philippine. It's necessary for a precaution if the communist win and when they come to power nobody will know exactly what happen. For example, if the situation turned bad we will be safe; and at the same token if it turn out to be all right just like everybody want to believe that Prince Sihanouk will come back to restore the monarchy and the country will have peace just like the time before the war; we can always return" An elder answered to his statement.

"Yes, I understand your concern; I also had read that article about the conference in Paris, and that is good for all of us that they are going to find the peaceful solution to stop the war to achieve the lasting peace. I'd talked with the generals in the supreme command, he said the American determine to continue their support for our struggle against the communist, and it doesn't matter what will be the outcome of the conference in Paris we will have nothing to worry about.

As your elder and guardians, we decide against any attempt to sell the properties and to have all of you young kids move to live in the foreign land is unthinkable. We suggest for you to stay close to your brothers and sisters at all time so we can keep an eye on you to make sure that you will not do anything that could harm yourself"

"Just keep your eye on those young one never mind me, if you need to see what I do you know where to find me" Virak left the house with disappointments and frustrations; he went up to BT's place on the top of the club on the river bank tried to devise a plan.

"We know something is going to happen but we don't know when and what will be the outcome, so I suggest we figure out a plan to get out of the country at the time if we need to; don't you think so?"

"Yes and why don't we just fly out to the border and get into Thailand while we can?"

"We will do some traveling to Thailand for sightseeing and gathering of information; and we will come back because I cannot leave them now I hope they change their mind later when things getting tough"

"So what do we need to do now?"

"We will decide to take a route if all hell break loose and we need to get the hell out of here. Whenever the time comes I think we will deal with the Khmer rouge not the Vietcong. We have to think like them and what will they do the day when they come into the city? I think they will kill the high rank officers and the aristocrat, and they will send everybody in the city to live in the countryside like the poor farmer to make the whole society more equal just like China Cultural Revolution; do you like to live like a poor farmer? I don't.

We got to get out of here just before they come in the city, because they will concentrate their force around the city for the final assault if our force resist them; at that time if we are with a small unit outside Phnom Penh they will bypass us and pay their attention to the big installation or come straight into the city, because if they take over the supreme command and the radio and the TV station the whole country will surrender.

We need to make a connection with a small outpost unit near the mine field and the corridor right here that we know the Khmer rouge stopped using it after they secured the surrounding safer area outside the mine field.

We need to persuade the officers to believe our plan by inviting them to the club sometime. We need to learn to speak Thai and English, and I will hook up with some guy in the map storage at the supreme command to get the maps and the information to prepare our route with everything down to logistic you know what I mean let get to work starting tomorrow"

BT did a very good job at gathering the information from the refugee and many other sources. They verified all of the information to make sure that they were accurate; they spotted the coordinate in the map and logged it in a small book with a notation.

They flew to the provincial town near the Thai border area, and also ventured into Thailand to observe the terrain and feature; and they got acquainted with her people to practice the language and learning their similar culture. In the capital of Phnom Penh, Virak talked to all friends and relative about the uncertainty of the outcome of the war after the American withdrawal but there were very few people who share his point of view. For most of the high ranking officers, it was unfathomable to think that the American will abandon all three countries after they had spent millions of dollar and thousands of their soldiers were kill in this war. If the American were going to quit fighting why did they dragged Cambodia into this conflict and then abandon her, it was unthinkable.

The colonel of the intelligent warned Virak personally not to talk about the idea that the American will abandon Cambodia, because the high command had order to control these rumors by detaining anyone who spread the idea. Virak kept his mouth shut after that, and he concentrated on working with his plan and maintaining a good relationship with the officers in a small unit outside the capital.

Princess RD who was Princess Devy's best friend and cousin came to see Virak once in a while, brought news from Devy in Europe. He was very happy to see her; they had become closer after Devy left. They normally sat in the kiosk that was secluded behind the jasmine and yellow bamboo bushes, and they talked about news from Europe, about the school, the war, and the American etc… One morning, RD walked in the kiosk unexpected and it looked like she was in an unhappy mood, and then he asked.

"Good morning RD, what's happen?" She was looking at him with anger in her eyes, and this was the first time he could see her true emotion shown; and this time, we did not start with our formal ritual, and she asked.

"Why did you have to destroy her?"

"Wait a minute RD, what are you talking about?"

"You know what I am talking about, if you don't truly love her by sending her away, why did you rape her?"

"Wait a minute RD; is that Devy we are talking about? Did she say that I rape her?"

"She doesn't have to tell me everything; I have heard from other source that she was pregnant, and her parent force her to have an abortion and arranged for her to get married there"

"Please RD, let me explain Ok, I know Devy never accuse me of raping her even though we had made love, and it was her initiative may be she didn't tell you all the detail, but I never force myself on her; and one more thing, I love her and concern about her well being that's why I was willing to part way so she could live happily and safely in Europe"

"I don't believe you, she was so pure so innocent, you must have forced her since she was just a fragile young woman she could not resist man advance"

"RD you probably forgot that our ages are only a year different, and I will never do anything to harm her, and again I love her I want everything to be the best for her"

"We may be almost the same age but you are a soldier..."

"That's enough, if you won't believe me because I am a soldier; let me show you what raping is all about" Virak stepped quickly toward her and pinned her to a dark corner of the kiosk that covered by thick yellow bamboo bush.

"What are you doing? Leave me alone! Oh no, don't..." Virak tied one end of the krama to cover her mouth and the other end he tied both her wrists behind her back; and then, he pointed a knife at her face to let her see the sharp and pointed metal like a savage beast barred it fang; and he thread her.

"Shut the fuck up Princess! Stay still or I'll kill you, if you please me I might let you live"

He stuck the knife on the pole, roughly yanked her long hair to turn her head to face him, he could see the terrified look in her eyes; then he unbuttoned her white blouse of her school uniform, slid his hand inside her bra to rub her breasts and feel her hard nipples.

And later, he made her stood up, pulled the hem of her blue skirt up to her waist and he slowly push her panty down to her knee, and then he nudged her thighs apart so he could feel below the black patch between her legs. He ran his finger through her soft black fur, moved down to the full lips of her sex, slid his middle finger along her moist slit and rubbed her tamarind seed that made her body squirming like a pussycat.

Virak looked at her face turn pale it was just like she was ready to get into shock; then he thought this was enough to convince her. So he pulled up her panty and let her blue skirt dropped down.

Then he untied the krama from her arms and her mouth; and he used it to wipe the sweat on her face and her neck that just appeared; and he lifted her chin up looking in her eyes.

"This is rape"

Virak let her sit back down on the spot, she slowly buttoned up her blouse, she still looked pale and exhausted from her terrify experience, and she closed her eyes and leaned against the pole. Virak went to sit next to her, put the glass of chilled green coconut to her mouth, wrapped his arm behind her back and urged her to drink.

"Here RD have a sip of this it will make you feel better. I am sorry that I am too rough with you. This is the only way to make you understand the different. It's Ok if you want to cry it out or get mad at me or anything"

She sipped the chilled coconut water, her tear started to roll down her face and she was looking at Virak with disbelief. He gave her a light kiss on her forehead, RD sat on the spot crying until her tear subsided; later she got up, adjusted her clothes, looked at him one last time and she walked away.

Virak went straight to Lady Sovana office, he opened the door, looked at her eyes and he went up to his flat. He stripped all his cloth, wrapped a silk krama and sat on the couch at the back window. Lady Sovana came to stand at the window blocking his view to the river and she looked at him up and down. She grabbed his stiffed pole and asking with an astonished look.

"What's happen? You never want to do before lunch after we had done all night last night" Virak did not answer her, he just let her drop her silk skirt to the floor, pulled her panty down, let her sit on the couch, and spread her legs……

A week after Virak had shown the little episode of rough demonstration, Princess RD unexpectedly came in the kiosk; he was surprised because he didn't expected that she could come back to see him after his roughly handling her here, but he acted normal just like nothing ever happened before, so he got up to greet her with the same ritual of holding and pecking on her cheek.

For some reason he could feel the uneasiness in her manner. She started to tell him that her family will immigrate to Europe next month, and then he gave her a kiss on the cheek to wish her luck with her new life there.

Lady Sovana's unconditional love gave Virak strength to cope with everything that he had to endure and live through life from day to day. The war became more and more intense; there were a lot of his relative from the countryside who fled the communist came to live at his house that they had to feed and built shelter for them.

BT and Virak went to some province towns along the Thai border, and sometime they slipped across the border into Thailand, where they made friend with people at the border who could speak both languages to take them around the area along Thai provinces of Trad and Chanbury. Sometime, they worked at many jobs of menial labor, and at one time they tried their sea leg on the fishing boat.

The Thai fishing industry along the border that hire the Cambodian the most because since there were fewer fishing boat on Cambodian water and it was teeming with fish where on the Thai side the resource was depleting from overfishing by their numerous fleets; beside the fishing industry in Cambodia was dying which was effect by the war.

So in order to get to the new resource the Thai fleets hired the Cambodian fishermen to take their boats to catch fish inside Cambodia all they need to do was to pay the Cambodian navy for protection.

After a few months working on the fishing boat, they returned to Phnom Penh; BT went straight to the front line unit and Virak went to visit his family home and then went to rest at the riverside garden. He felt much better from the hard labor on the fishing boat after a week under the nursing care of Lady Sovana.

Later Virak went to stay at the front line with the company, and he was very impressed and satisfied with everything went smoothly according to their plan. So BT and Virak, moved back and forth between the frontline and the city, they kept an eye on their progress, and had BT brought food and supplies to the front regularly; and in the city they took some English class and learned to speak Thai, then they met an old great uncle who was retired from the French Legionnaire and he told them.

"The language come more easily if you just want to speak, all you have to do is to sleep with the woman, just like I had learned to speak French quickly by sleeping with some French women. I think if you want to speak Chinese all you need to do is to sleep with the Chinese women and the language will come later in no time at all"

BT and Virak were readily agreed with the great uncle idea whole heartedly, but they still read the book and took some class for the time being.

In the early of the year 1974, Virak sat with the officers to discuss and to reevaluate their exit strategy secretly; and then the commander started to describe their present situation.

"We had established a foothold in these few villages around this area thanks to the extra food and supplies that you had provided us, some soldiers who had big family and who do not wish to go along with us, had sent their family to live with the villager and helped keeping an eye on the communist activity.

We advise them not to flee to Phnom Penh when the communist attack around this area. And for the minefield corridor that you had specifically pointed out for us to make the reconnaissance, it appear to be correct that the Khmer rouge had use to move troupes and supplies through it a year ago because it had a good coverage by tall trees and bamboo forest.

Now they don't need to use it anymore because it's dangerous whenever some of their unit took a wrong turn or they were vulnerable and confined when they were under attacked from the air, and so they rather use the safe and direct route in the area that they gain from us.

We haven't tell anyone about this exit route but our recon agree with you that it is a dangerous good hiding place, and after twenty kilometers of slow reconnaissance they haven't reach the end of the corridor yet"

Virak looked in the map and pointed to them.

"According to the terrain feature on the map, the corridor should end at this point where the forest meets the wide open field. From this point on, we will move in Khmer rouge mode always to the border by swinging north toward Posat, and when we get to this point, we will swing west north of the Kirirom and the Cardamom mountain region. It should be less Khmer rouge there because their troop will concentrate around the city and the provincial town.

If everything goes according to our plan and the accuracy of our information we will be in Thailand within a month time" The commander said.

"I try to get some more AK-47 and the farmer black clothing, and we had make crossbow and arrow for everybody but it's hard to find potent venom snake around here. It seem like we get almost everything we need"

"Yes, almost but there is one more thing, I think you need to tell them and make it clear that we don't force anyone to come with us. They can join us when the time comes and we will move toward Thailand, and at anytime anyone wants to partway they can do so at will.

We will tell them when we start out about mission of the defensive posture like evasive, concealment and swift reaction of avoiding the enemy at all cost. I had got all the maps we need so we will not bump into any surprise on the way out.

And if luck is on our side and everything goes well we will be in Thailand within a month or so sitting at the dock having Kha kai yarm and cold beer (Chicken feet and green papaya salad).

At anytime that we may come under attack we must hit them hard and retreat quickly into the forest; for anyone who might became severely wound and unable to move, must understand that we do not have the mean to treat the injury while we will be on the run, so they must think about it and take into consideration before making their own decision.

There is slim chance for a severely injured soldier to escape and catch up with the fast evasive maneuver formation because if the Khmer rouge won't get you the infection will, and this is the fact it will take a miracle for him to stay alive; and again whether you decide to come along or not it's up to you.

If you decide to stay behind you should make yourself look and act like a very poor rice farmer to blend in with the villager and you hope that they will have mercy on you. Either way any of us decide we wish each other luck"

All of the officers were quiet and their mind seem to be in deep thought, Virak hope that he did not bring it out too soon, but he guessed sooner was better than later, because everybody needed to use their own judgment to get ready for the inevitable that will eventually come. And when it come he sensed that it will not going to be pretty, he had a feeling that Cambodia will be painted with blood.

It brought back a chilled memory when he was chained to the pig pen that made the hair on the back of his neck stood up. Then he never again let himself to be in the position to get capture; he would rather die fighting.

Virak asked the commander permission to go along with the recon forward team to see the old Khmer rouge trail in the mine field corridor by his own eye in order to weigh in their survivability during the inevitable.

The recon team spent the last few months surveyed the communist movement and mapped out the edge of the mine field that gave shape to the safe corridor.

The corridor led from a few kilometers from the unit position through thirty five kilometer of forest covered to the edge of the big open field where they set their own mine to deflect the Khmer rouge that had the wide open field in their own territory rather than come to mess with the mine field area.

At about the halfway point the corridor open up from three to five kilometers wide in the thick forest that dotted with old abandon village ponds or bomb craters; Virak asked the recon teams to clear the old village and the surrounding area to make it as their staging point and storage.

Virak had asked the elder guardians at his house once again about moving his family out of the country temporary, but their answer was for better or for worth they will stay put. Virak did not like their idea but there was nothing he could do.

He was very upset and disappointed when those who were close to him did not believe his warning, even cousin Kheng and Lady Sovana; they thought that Virak was overreacted because he had been through hard time in battle.

Virak knew that the American will pull out but he did not know exactly when. The answer came soon enough in the early of 1974, Lady Sovana said most of the functionaries in the diplomatic corps tried to get a post abroad or just took their family to vacation outside of the country.

And there was news from Vietnam that American will pull out next year and the communist start to build up around the city. In Cambodia, they never had any big American force that could give people a clue of the event unfolding; all they could tell that the communist had the upper hand and they came closer and closer to tight the city defense belt.

BT suggested to Virak a while back that they should fly out of the country or to the border town, but then it was unthinkable to leave his family behind. In this situation at that time it was reasonable and easy for just them two flew out of the country to safety, but Virak still had the second thought about leaving the unit at the front line; they lived in the dark, and their lives seemed to depend on him for survival, they had made plan and commitment with him to leave the country to Thailand. They knew many soldiers in the company ever since the war started; they were trained in South Vietnam by the Green Beret and had fought in many battles together against the communist.

They spent their last few days in the city to see people and visit places; it was a kind of nonverbal farewell. Virak spent his last few days with Lady Sovana on his bed in between her sexy legs. He told cousin Kheng that he will resume full control of the Riverside Garden and the Club if Virak did not return, and he should check and provide for his family also.

They went to stay at the front line with the unit in the middle of 1974; Virak suggested to the company commander that it's time to let those who wish to stay behind, moved to blend in with the villager.

After those soldiers who wish to stay behind left to the village, they immediately move two third of the soldier into the corridor, and then they stage an attack on their own empty position by moving the rest of the man out one night, and they fired all of the mortar rounds machine guns and AK-

47 at the position, and then they moved completely into the corridor, wiped all traces of their track, and laid mines and booby traps to seal off their trail.

So now, they were almost completely sealed in the mine field except a small opening at the other end of the corridor that was known to the recon, the commander, Virak and BT.

They hope that no one else outside the corridor know of their where about, because after the night that they staged the attack they had cut off all of their communication with the battalion command, so they will think that the company was annihilated; and the Khmer rouge unit around the area thought that the unit was attacked by somebody and had fallen back to join the parent unit, and for the soldier who stay behind in the village, believed that they were lucky to move out before the attack was taking place.

At the staging area in the old abandon village, the unit started to transform from a company of the government soldier into a Khmer rouge combat unit at the exterior look. They also had to train their mind set from a tactical combat unit into an evasive concealed survival mode of retreat.

They thrown the steel helmet into the bamboo forest and wore the Mao She Tung style green cap, and they changed from their olive drab and tiger stripe uniform to put on the used old farmer black pajama and switched their combat boot with a mismatched pair of a homemade sandal that had made from old rubber wheel cut up tube and tire.

And last but not least, they had a hard time to depart from their M-16 and pick up the old rusted up AK-47 with its old worn blood stain cartridge pouch. They kept the backpack because they had seen the Khmer rouge soldier use it also; Virak hid a loaded Smith & Wesson revolver behind the cartridge pouch.

The unit distributed the dehydrate food, filled up the canteen, and they rubbed mud and dirt on the black pajama to make it look dull and well worn so it won't stand out from the green vegetation background. The recon members were responsible for briefing everybody about the do and don't, and to watch out for danger ahead in the forest.

Virak advised them to find food learn to eat the vegetation and kept the dehydrated food as a last resort; and they must started to set up trap to catch rabbit, bird and snake to preserve them by smoke drying them for adding to their food supply. The company sent all platoons unit to live by the pond inside the bomb crater so they could catch fishes, frogs and snake that dwelled in there; and they could get their bodies acclimatized to the life in the forest.

They started to do the exercise every other day, the exercise was consist of the discipline in movement and the buildup of the endurance; everybody must carried everything that they will take with them on the trip, and they forced march around the forest and at the edge of the mine field for everybody could learn to recognize danger, and they had also staged the case scenario for the swift adaptation in case of under attack, the evasive maneuver, and the concealment to avoid the detection.

A senior staff NCO voiced a complain to the commander that the troop were tired from the nonstop exercised under the hot sun without adequate food and water, and he stated that they haven't had any proper hot rice to eat since last month; Virak immediately interfered and gave the whole company an explanation.

"We all know that everyone of us must feel tired from this exercise, but it is necessary to go through it preparing our mind and body so it could learn to cope with the situation that might become a reality in the very near future. Right now, we only practice every other day to give our body time to adjust, but the time will come, when we step out from this point on it will not be an exercise; while we could we must take what we learn apply to our action and conduct every step of the way twenty four hours a day seven days a week until we reach the Thai border.

Of course, we know that everybody is tired and we know that we don't have enough food and water, but this is just an exercise. When we get out there on the road we will be under this condition twenty four hours a day and there will be no guaranty that we will have enough food and water, and that is why we need to go through this exercise so our mind will not panic under a dire tight spot, and our body should be able to keep up when we need to move fast, if we couldn't that is our death sentence.

We all know that the Khmer rouge will not have mercy on us and they won't take any prisoner; for those of you who had been capture before, we know the deal with this Communist. They may keep some of you alive to serve their purposes either for information or use as beast of burden, but either way they will eliminate you regardless.

For the American prisoners that the Vietcong had captured, that you have heard they keep them alive so they could serve their propaganda, otherwise they will be buried deep underground or disposed off into thin air. And for you as Cambodian government soldier, they will let your corps lay rotten on the spot where they kill you.

That's all I have to say and I want everybody to think about your chance of survival in any situation and case scenario that we do in the exercise, if you cannot keep up now you should think of the other way to survive when the time come and you are on the way out from here"

A senior Staff NCO stepped up and said.

"At this point, as far as I am concern we are no longer a unit of government army, we are on our own and we don't have to listen to this young guy square us about anything; I've been a soldier ever since before many of you were born including you young man. And for the different way to survive I will move out now anyone want to come with me you are welcome to come along, I do have some member of recon with me to show us the way"

Virak was surprised that almost haft of the company joined the senior SNCO, and he was relief that they had some of the recon with them at least; Virak went to stand in front of the senior SNCO to offer him a handshake and to bid him farewell.

"I wish you and your men good luck and good bye go in peace Sergeant"

They shook hand, went to say goodbye to the company commander, and he move his troop out toward the end of the corridor at the open field. Virak looked around and counted all the soldiers who was willing to stay with them, he thought that they were still in good shape even though they were smaller it was more easy for them to maneuver since they were lacked of communication equipments.

They sent their recon ahead of them to warn the forward team to stay out of the break way unit and help them find the way out safely, and also sent a recon team behind them to ensure that they won't do anything out of the ordinary that might jeopardy the exit plan as of now it was hard to tell from friend or foe, so they must be careful to watch their own back.

The recon team reported that the SSNCO group had cross safely out of the mine field and they headed west toward the Kirirom mountain area and according to the map it will put them on the collision path with the Khmer rouge troupe movement corridor, the new made Virak feel chilled down his spine; the commander looked at him and asked.

"What's a matter with you?"

"Sir, if you look in the map they head straight into the Khmer rouge troupe movement area, they have greater chance to collide with them head on; I hope they will move north first before they turn west"

"Yes I certainly hope that they will be all right"

"Sir, I suggest that we should get out of here ASAP, like right now"

"Explain why?"

"Yes sir, the reason that we should move out now because of in case of unforeseen even that some of them might be capture and spill the bean, so we won't stuck in this tight spot"

"Ok that's fair, let's go, it's time guy, get on your feet and move out, and this is not a drill"

So in the late February of 1975, the escape was underway, and the commander sent the recon team ahead to inform the forward team who kept watching the end of the corridor from inside the mine field. It took the unit six hours to go through the many tight spots that at some point were only as wide as their foot print.

The team told them that it was a perfect timing because of the enemy activity in this area and they should leave immediately after night fall; and at the last minute, Virak asked the commander to inform all NCO that in case of separation they should move north to northeast toward the flooded forest below the great lake of Tonle Sap.

They moved in the dark through mostly open field sparse forest and rice field let them know that they were near the villages that need to be avoided because from this point on all the villages were under the Khmer Rouge control ever since the war started and their force were always present there. The escape unit pushed forward through the dark night across the field until they reach the forest again before they could stop to rest.

C12- Exodus

The unit spent their first night of the journey thirty kilometers northeast of Kampong Speu in a forest after they had moved for many hours in the dark night. Virak woke up before sunrise, and he knew that he did not sleep much because his eyelids were still very heavy; he felt his right hand was on the revolver handle and the left was on his knife, then he started to open his eyes slowly to get his bearing, and he turned to look at the other soldiers who lay beside him and he saw they all were awake; they looked at each other and nodded their head to realize that this was it they were on their way, Virak just came to think that everybody feel the same way that they were worry and they could not sleep or relax easily at all.

The officers and the NCOs gathered under a tree while Virak was pointing to them of the spot on the map; they were surprised that they were not too far from Kampong Speu that shown they were considered still in the danger zone; that mean they still had a greater chance to meet the enemy while they were marching forward on the trail, so they decided to move out in that very early morning to put some distant between them and this area.

When they just started to line up their column and ready to take off; suddenly, there were a few Khmer rouge soldiers came out of the forest to greet them.

"Greeting comrade, we knew you had set up camp here last night, but we did not want to disturb while you were resting, we are only a platoon and so we hope that you let us join you marching toward our victory at Phnom Penh"

"Greeting comrade, of course you can join us so we can march toward victory together, we had captured a lot of food supply that we wish to share with you, but may we see the credential order of your mission, it's our unit procedure"

"Oh comrade, didn't you receive the general order from "Brother Number One" at central committee that we don't need any order since this is our combine join force for the final push forward of the revolution march to victory over the imperialist dog sometime next month" The commander looked at us and said.

"Of course, of course, Ok comrade we have almost forgot the small detail like this because our hearts were so excited for us to realize that victory is within our grasp. Ok let lineup your column parallel to us facing Phnom Penh direction so we could march side by side toward victory" The communist unit came out of the forest, and instead of lined up parallel to the escapee they were just merging into the column, and then the commander gave the order.

"That is quite all right if you want to merge with us, and now we become one unit we are honor to receive you into our unit; let us look to the front and we step out NOW!"

They grabbed the Khmer rouge soldier right in front of them and killed him instantly and quietly by stabbing them with their knife or the poison arrow. Within seconds, all Khmer rouge soldiers were lay thrashing in the pool of their blood; they were quickly ordered to turn them on their back and drove the AK-47 bayonet a few times through their hearts to make sure that they were dead.

And then, they were ordered to step out before they could even clean the blood that was still dripping from their bayonet. The unit had three minor injuries, so the medic just treated them while they were on the move. They stepped out in an evasive maneuver from the forest into many directions and then they regrouped at a spot that was hard for them to detect the track, and the unit moved quickly toward the objective. they moved forward day and night with only a few hours rest in between; they tried to make sure that if there was any enemy unit might pursued them they could not and will not catch up with, but they knew that they could have their comrades setting an ambush waiting ahead of them; so it was very important for survival was to make the direction and the timing of the route unpredictable.

The Khmer Rouge might know that any escapees must want to go to Thai border but they did not have a slight idea of which point and when they will pass through at a certain area. Virak hope that the Khmer Rouge won't pay any attention to them, because they have more important thing to do right now was to take over the country, and they were just a few dozen soldiers who tried to survive this Vietnamese and American war.

They marched toward the north and northeast direction that get to the flooded forest south of Tonle Sap in ten days; Virak did not hear anyone complain about the tiredness from the lack of sleep or anything, because everybody knew that they had to pushed themselves beyond their comfort zone; the Omni present of the sight and smell from the enemy bloodstain on their bayonet, kept reminding them about the quick cycle of life and death.

The flooded forest was an unpopulated area because of the high level of rising water from Himalaya every year; right now in March, the forest floor was dry except the occasional old ponds that people dug before the war to catch the fish that trapped after the water receded. Food was plentiful here, there were fishes at abandon in every pond and puddle, and there were track of wild animal all over the forest floor like rabbit, deer, tiger and elephant. In the map it shown no visible landmark except the original lowest water edge where the forest stop growing; the venomous snake were at abandon here, so they took an opportunity to make more potent poison arrow.

They stayed deep in the forest to give the unit some time to rest, and they also hunted wild animal and pulling the fish from the pond to preserve by smoke drying them to add to their food supply. After a week of feeding themselves with fresh cooked fish, deer, rabbit and snake, they became restless because they want to move on but the commander wanted them to stay a little longer so they could stock up some more food.

One afternoon, the rear recon team reported that they saw a unit of company size of Khmer rouge set up camp just five kilometers from their position. They quickly covered up the evident around the area they stayed and erased the track or created a false lead; they moved ten kilometers northwest;

and then turned to southwest for a few days, and then went straight west south of Posat province. They traveled in zigzag and snake pattern and covered up the track as much as they could; they also avoided all open fields but if they couldn't they will cross it by night. The recon team had killed a few of their counterparts with the poison arrow, this killing let them know that the enemy guess of their where about was right, so they changed the direction by turning ninety degrees and stayed on that path for a few days before heading straight west. Every time when they saw sings of the enemy, they quickly turned into any direction that will make their movement unpredictable, and sometime they could not stop to wait for nightfall, so they took off in style across the open field in broad daylight.

One day the enemy had spotted them in an open field about over forty kilometers southwest of Posat, when they were crossing a big wide field; the Khmer rouge fired their eighty two millimeters mortar rounds on them, and then they had to spread out and run quickly toward the closest forest line. They knew that if the enemy could see them, there will be a unit follows right behind and some might wait for them ahead. They got no time to think about anyone that they might leave behind or stop to make a headcount of how many they had lost. They regrouped some distant kilometers away, and then the commander received a report that they had five soldiers missing. They realized that at this time the enemy knew that they were on the run; the enemy will have their recon unit fanned out to many area it will start from the spot that they'd detected them last. From this point on, they had greater chance to walk into an ambush; Virak had voiced his concern to the commander that they should get rid of some non essential idioms to lighten their load so they could move faster, and shorten the formation by folding the column, and turned to their original plan of crossing all open field at night.

In the map there was a bottleneck area between two peaks before an open valley, it looked like a perfect spot to set an ambush. The escapee reacted immediately by breaking the formation into squad column, and moved up the mountain side by side through the thick forest; it took them almost a week to pass that bottleneck area, and then headed down to the flat land on the valley floor so they could move faster. At the time they were kind of relaxing their guard a little bit after a few days though the treacherous terrain on the mountainside. It was not a perfect ambush but it was an ambush just the same; they got the right idea of trying to catch the escapee on the valley floor behind the bottleneck area, but they were not sure where, so they might have split into small ambush and covered a large area, but any way they did a good job at detecting them. When the escapee moved down from the mountainside, they were already a hundred meter pass the ambush kill zone, and the fire power were just squad strength and they were firing on just the last squad column. They lost three soldiers at the ambush; since they had already determine not to engage with them, so they just put their head down and kept moving forward as fast as possible on the edge of the valley floor a little distant, then swung back up the mountainside through the thick forest, and turned to the west slowly for a few weeks to avoid the enemy surprised attack, and so they thought.

The recon team informed the CO that they could sense and smell the montagnards (Mountain tribe people). They all were worry because this was worse news that they ever received; they had just heard their reputation from the recon members who had tangled with them in the battle field before, and now they had to face them in this mountain jungle in their element. They were mountain tribal people who were recruited by the communist as tracker, seek and destroy elite force; they operated by stealth and the lightning speed of elimination. The escapees immediately stopped at a suitable spot, opened up a small concealed defense perimeter, mobilized more recon teams, reinforced everybody poison arrow, and sent them out with a mission of seek and destroy with very extreme prejudice.

At the defense perimeter, they were heavily concealed themselves and made very slow movement and as little as possible; they masked their scent and odor with dirt and moss, buried the waste of the bodily function, strictly enforced their silence, and had the crossbow and poison arrow at the ready mode at all time. They gave the recon three day to accomplish the mission, they must regroup and it did not matter what the outcome will be, because they need to move on to find water. They all agreed that they did not like to have these montagnards follow and hit them while on the move, so they preferred to seek out and eliminate them on their term. They had killed two montagnards at the defense perimeter, and the recon eliminated two teams of four montagnards.

The enemy had killed five soldiers at the perimeter and two recon members; all of this happened within the seventy-two hours time frame. They knew that these montagnards could be killed, but they paid with a very high price, so they decided to move on and will deal with them later at a different terrain outside of their element. They quickly recalled the recon, moved over the top to the other side of the mountain to put themselves out of reach from the enemy in the valley and they were in immediate need to look for the water source three days away according to BT's information, and that will put them closer to the Cardamom mountain area; the area was an unpopulated no man land devoid of civilization according to the map, but in the information log book the refugee had seen the Khmer rouge unit came out from this area, and that the escapees hope that the enemy would be gone from here and move closer to town.

They were avoiding the water source nearby the perimeter since they had considered it's being contaminated by the enemy poison or it may be riddled with mines and booby traps; and that was why they believed it's better for them to get away from this area as soon as possible. And here near the Cardamom mountain area, they found the small spring near the foot of the mountain thank to BT's information log book. The spring was very small that it did not have a name nor shown in the map, but it had a steady stream flowed out from it. They had to wait for a few hours and tried to control their thirst, while the recon made sure the surrounding area was cleared of booby trap, and then they tested the water by force feeding a monkey to make sure it safe to drink. When the monkey did not die four hours later, they let it go, and then started to fill up their canteen. They covered up the trail when moving away from the spring, and then came to rest at a spot six days away at another water source. There was no trace of human present in this pristine jungle; at this place, they were kind of lay down their guard and slept so well that they did not hear when tiger killed one of their soldier in his sleep and dragged the body out from right under their nose. When getting up in the morning, they saw trace of blood and a drag mark on the forest floor, and at the end of the drag mark, they founded the soldier body half eaten by the tiger, was buried under the mount of dead leaves. There was no excuse for the lost, and they did not wait until the second one was taken; they knew they got to move out immediately, because this jungle was too pristine and too wild, and it was infested with too many hungry tigers lurking in the dark forest day and night, that they got to move away from this part of the forest, because they stood in the middle of the tiger domain.

Ten days away from the tiger infested forest, they came to a small clearing by the foot of the mountain with a river flows through it. The field with gentle rolling hill was teeming with deer and rabbits. So they decided that it was safe to stay near the river for a few days to replenish their food supply; they sent out the recon and hunting patrol to sweep through the area to detect any enemy activity, get familiarized with the surrounding terrain, and to hunt for food and medicine in the forest. They had found many kinds of herb and spice to add the flavor to the smoke dry meat in the palm leaves smoke house. When the time comes to start moving on, there were more than twenty soldiers who wish to stay behind, because they were too sick from malaria, parasite, infected wounds from the blood sucking leach bite, and a whole host of other ailments. They were too weak to continue or to keep up with the unit formation; they said that they did not want to slow the unit down, and beside they had found a lot of useful fauna and flora in the area to treat their ailment. The area looked safe and plenty of food, so they decided to stay at the campsite and they thanked the unit for helping them to come out this far safe and alive. They gave them some more supply, map and salt.

More than ten days away from the separate group, the recon detected more and more trace of enemy activities every day while moving forward closer to Thai border. They took the precaution by moving slower, since the border was only forty five kilometers away, and they did not want to make any mistake. At that time, they were between the germ stone town of Pailin to the north and the province town of Koh Kong to the south facing Trad and Chantabury province of Thailand.

One day, they came upon a waste open rice field, they knew that they were closed to some populated area that was not even shown in the map, they believe it got to be some kind of Khmer rouge village that create after the war start, and they got no idea of the village where about. Since there were light rain and fog so the escapees decided to push forward into the open field and hope that rain will conceal them from detection. Yes, it concealed them very well until it stopped raining when they were in the middle of the field, and worst yet that night the moon was started to shine from behind the cloud. They all were kind of hesitated for a moment and wonder of what they should do next? But then it seemed like it was too late, so they were just rushed to cross the field to the other side of the forest edge; it was a beautiful moonlit night, and it made Virak think about all the women that he had share pleasure under many beautiful moonlit nights sky like this one.

Suddenly all hell broke loose, a lone AK-47 fired in automatic mode emptied his magazine to spray the bullets on the escapees and he shouted alarm signal to his comrades. Within a few seconds, it sounded like they were in the ambush kill zone but it wasn't. The sound of a few dozen AK-47 and some machine gun fire, made the unit realized that they stumped upon a platoon of Khmer rouge regular combat unit, because they reacted quickly with discipline fire power; at a normal circumstance Virak think they can take them, but now they got to follow the plan so they just moved away ninety degrees to the left and right, and that made them split into two groups, the group on the left was with the CO and the group on the right was with Virak. They heard the Khmer rouge called to the soldiers who tried to chasse after them; Virak thought that they probably tried to regroup, grabbed their necessary gear and then they will come after them. They moved at fast pace nonstop until daybreak, Virak looked to the front he got two recon members, behind him, He counted twenty-five soldiers, and at some distant behind there was BT with a wound soldier on his back; Virak fell back to talk to him.

"BT, what the hell do you think you are doing? Didn't we agree on the condition before we step out?"

"I know, but I can't leave him because I promised his mother to take him with me to Thailand, you go ahead move on we will follow you"

"BT that is a bad idea, you should not follow them because they create a lot of heavy tracks and with you slow behind they will catch up with you for sure. I suggest that you should move north and then turn west to the border, and if you move at night put North Star on your right shoulder; I will see you at the fishing boat dock in Trad Ok good luck" The wound soldier was just a boy of about thirteen or fourteen years old; the bullet shattered his femur bone and his foot was dangling with just some skin and tissue; his face was so pale from excessive bleeding and his pulse was so weak that Virak hardly feel it. He suggested to BT to cut his foot off, thrown it away and put the tourniquet on the stump so it will temporarily stop bleeding. Virak stopped for a moment in the bush watching BT and the boy soldier disappeared into the forest in the northwest direction, and then he quickly catch up with the group, but all his thought was still with BT, Virak believe he will see BT at the boat dock sometime in the future, but for the boy soldier he doubt it if he will live till the next morning. A recon team member asked Virak for the map of this area; he told him that he did not have any more map with him because the last map of the border region he gave to the CO and now he was with the other group, and Virak told them that they were approximately about thirty-five kilometers from the border opposite from northern Trad province or southern Chanbury.

There were more and more sings of the enemy movement on the trail; the escapees moved very cautiously slow; at some point they hardly made a few kilometers a day, because they advanced blindly without any map to check the terrain and landmark feature ahead of their step. One afternoon, the recon signaled them to stop and motioned Virak to come forward; he moved slowly and quietly under the bush with the recon to a few hundred meters ahead. Virak crouched down next to them and looking through the binocular along the tall and thick bamboo forest edge, there was a line of wilted branches under the bamboo bushes that was out of place and looked unusually different from the green vegetation in the surrounding area. The hairs on the back of his head were standing up, he felt chilled along his spine and his testicle shrunk into his body. They looked at each other and knew that they almost walked into the Khmer rouge ambush kill zone; they retreated to a safe distant, and then head south a few kilometers, and when they turned west along the forest line, they detected another ambush waiting for them. After they had found a few more ambush on the forest line a few kilometers apart; they decided to lay low under the bush and planned to cross the open rice field after nightfall.

They moved out at dust right after the sun slip below the horizon, wading through knee deep water in the rice field avoiding the raised dike and the high ground; they walked in column close behind one another, and dragged their feet close to the bottom to cut down noise from the water splashing and preventing them from stepping on the possible sharp bamboo stick that might be planted under water. They moved around any spot that did not have any rice plant grow out from the water surface, because that was a sign of a possible ditch trap. The front point man had to walk with a long pole to feel the way at every step of the way. After a few kilometer through the field, they felt more confident since they did not encounter any mine or booby trap, so they picked up their pace moving faster across the field to get into the forest.

Three days away from the ambush area, they spotted a group of about six Khmer rouge soldiers who carried some bundles on between the bamboo poles that most of them believe it was food items. Virak suggested to the group that they should avoid them and take other direction, but most men in the group said that they should kill them for the food they carried since they ran out of food about a week ago. Virak disagreed he said they should leave those Khmer rouge alone, and should keep doing what they had done in the past week, that they live of snail, crab, frog and leaves that they picked from the trail and the rice field that kept them alive until now, beside they weren't sure that what the Khmer Rouge soldiers carried were food items or not and that could be a waste of time.

Since Virak could not reason with the majority of the men who determined to kill the Khmer rouge for the items that they carried, he was reluctantly breaking away from the group with three men followed him. They moved quickly away from the group to put some distant between them just in case if anything went wrong and when all hell might break loose so they will have a better chance to live. Now they could move faster since they did not need to wait for any one that could slow them down and did their own reconnaissance along the way.

Approximately a few days later, after they separated from the group, they'd arrived at the Thai border, and then they were prematurely shaking hand to congratulate each other of the mission accomplished. They still concealed themselves in the bushes and observed the terrain in Thailand ahead of them. The three men started to relax because they felt safer to be at the border, but before Virak could warn them of how volatile it could be at the border region; suddenly they heard the intense gunfire and mortar round explosions about less than two kilometers behind them, and it sounded like moving closer by the second. The sound of gunfire anywhere at the border area will attract a lot of attention on both sides, Virak believe they should conceal themselves in the bush to let everything quiet down before they cross the border on their own time.

Before Virak could say anything to them, all three men got up and ran across the border mark into Thai territory; he was just about to follow them but then a line of black uniform men carried M-16 appeared ahead of the three men.

Virak immediately recognized them, they were the Thai frontier police force; he instantly crouched down below the bush and moved away ninety degrees to a different spot, and he looked at the three men were disarmed, tied up and loaded into the cage vehicle. It was happened just like he thought, after a few minutes later, a squad of the frontier police came to check on the old spot where they were if he hadn't moved away he probably get capture too, but up to this point Virak was not in the mood to be capture or tied down, so he moved further away from that gunfire area along the border.

In just a few kilometers away from the old spot, Virak encounter a mine field that made him froze in his track he got no idea how far he was inside the mine field already, but he was sure that he was in a mine field because of the bone and skeleton fragments of men and animals were scattered all over the field, some of them were dead longtime ago that he could see their bone bleached white under the hot sun and the weather, but some were killed recently because he could see their bone were greasy yellow and the spot was still smell like rotten corps, and some bone fragments were still have piece of cloth covered.

And once again, his testicle shrunk into his body that felt chilled allover; Virak turned around to look at the ground around his feet, and he tried to back track his footstep out of the mind field until he could not see any more skeleton fragment in sight, and then he moved back closer to the border mark laying in the bush waiting for the sunset. When the sun slipped under the horizon in the west, Virak prepared himself to cross the border but first he had to discard and dispose of the weapon and everything that he brought with him. He laid his backpack; the AK-47 and its cartridge pouch in the bush, so that if BT or anyone who came out with the company will know that he had reached Thailand.

On the open trail, he stuck all of the poison arrows in the ground and broke the poisonous tip off to show that he no longer intent to use his weapon to hurt anyone from that point on. Virak reached in the backpack to pull out a few personal items that he placed at the bottom but all he could feel was the small picture album and a few inches gashed hole that might be ripped by bullet, and he got no idea where the other plastic bag that he kept his personal Identification card with some gold might be.

Virak slipped into Thailand under dark night sky with a krama wrapped around his waist and the revolver tugged inside his shirt. He knew that he had to move away from the border region as fast as possible. he walked all night and had made a considerable distant from the border, since he had no more fear of stepping on mine or booby trap, and he was just following the easy country road. When the sky in the east started to turn gray he also started to look for a place to rest; he stepped away from the road walking on the rice field dike toward the wooded area, at about a kilometer from the road, he found an abandon small open shack with a bamboo platform under it, he thought that the farmer had used it to rest while they were working in the field, and he didn't think they minded him using it for now because his body felt so tired since there was no any danger around to put any more pressure on him to be on guard so he became relax, sleepy, hungry and lazy all at the same time.

Well first thing first, Virak observed the surrounding area a little bit before laying down to rest on the bamboo platform; he heard the fish jumping in the small lily pond next to the rice field, he started to relax and close his eyes thinking about eating some fish when he get up, and he could hear his gut complaining because he haven't eat anything for a while, but since he hadn't have any good day or night sleep ever since he stepped out from the mine field corridor because he constantly felt the ever present danger. Under the farmer shack, he slept so well that he almost did not have any dream at all, and the only dream he had was swimming and frolicking with some mermaids.

Virak woke up with the smell of wood burning smoke, and then he opened his eyes slowly and sweeping a glance around with his hand on the revolver handle. He saw a man who sat by the terracotta stove stoking the fire and cooking some fishes. Virak started to get up and put his hand up to say greeting when the Thai farmer turned to smile at him and opened his palm to signal Virak to take it easy and not to be alarm; it was a universal language for friendly gesture. Virak smiled back, put his hands together again and trying to say his first sentence in Thai language.

"Sovady krap, phum khortood ma Norn ty NY mai me kwam anu nhat" Virak said good morning, I apologize for sleeping here without any permission. And, he replied.

"Mai pen rail loh" No, it was all right. Virak think the farmer knew that he was a Cambodian who just crossed the border; the farmer was talking about the border, the war, the guard and a lot of thing more that Virak didn't understand at all, but one thing he understood was when he told him to wash and clean himself up so they could eat. Virak nodded his head in agreement; he knew it's about time because he smelled kind of ripe; the farmer pointed to the stream at the next field. After a refreshing bath in the cold stream, the farmer shared his meal with him; they had some rice, broiled catfish, vegetable and hot chili sauce. They ate their meal and tried to communicate in Thai; Virak was surprised that the farmer understood almost everything he said, but he had to correct his speech at every sentence. He told him to spend another night here at the lily pond because it was not safe to go on at night, and beside he will stand out like a sore thumb in the communist black pajama and the old tire sandal. The next morning, the farmer came with his son who was about the same age as Virak; he said his son will take him to the bus station at the district town, and gave him a set of his son cloth completed with a pair of sandal. While Virak was changing from the communist black pajama into the cloth the farmer gave him, he felt very grateful for his generosity, so Virak pulled out the revolver and gave it to the farmer to repay his kindness. The farmer and his son were so surprised they refuse the gift that they could not accepted, because the Smith & Wesson was too expansive; Virak told him that he had to take it because he was no longer need it since he will move on from here, but the farmer and his family were still living here in this border area so he might need it for protection, and then Virak handed the weapon to his son who was very happy and he seemed to appreciate the weapon more than his father. The farmer pulled Virak aside to give him some tip of how to behave like a Thai person, and then he slip a roll of money in his hand and he insisted for Virak to take it so it will be an even trade; Virak nodded his head to accept the money but he pulled out a few hundred pieces and handed him back the roll. Virak bid farewell to the farmer, he could not think of Thai word to say his appreciation for his kindness, so Virak just said his thanks for his tasty food, the sleeping accommodation at the rice field shack and the clothing; he guessed he understood what he mean. On his motorbike, the farmer son took Virak to the bus stop at the district town about forty kilometers away from his village; on the way he kept instructing Virak of how to behave and the do and don't, Virak was very appreciated for his effort to explain to him but he did not think that he understood everything he'd said; so far he made thing look normal like two young Thai men were busy discussing about girl that didn't even bother to stop at the border patrol checkpoint, and the border policemen just waived for them to move forward. At the bus station before Virak got on the bus for Trad province, his new Thai friend gave him a bundle tied in a krama, and he told Virak it was food for the road; they shook hand and said good bye.

    On the bus to Trad, Virak was lost in his thought and the memory of the trip to the northern jungle; and his life at the moment that was drifting toward the unknown. It was already noon; the passengers on the bus were eating their noon meal that made Virak feel hungry also, so he untied the krama bundle, but when he opened it there were the roll of Thai money laid next to the food package that wrapped in the banana leave. Virak ate his meal and accepted that the farmer had his last say; he had some rice, broiled fish, vegetable and hot chili sauce paste that made him had smoke came out of his mouth.

    The bus arrived in Trad main provincial town in late afternoon; from the bus depot, Virak came straight to the fishing boat dock to look for anybody that he used to know or any soldier who might get here ahead of him, but he could not find anyone; beside there were only a few boats left at the dock so most of them must be at sea fishing. Virak went into the coffee shop and convenient store, ordered some pastry, Thai iced tea and a pack of Samit Sibsi cigarette; he smoked the cigarette listening to Thai music from the juke box. There were fishermen and dock workers who came in and out of the coffee shop, and he knew he had to ask some of them for information. Suddenly a fisherman went to the juke box, dropped some coin to play a Cambodian song Sweet Sixteen; Virak noticed who he was and walked out of the coffee shop. Half an hour later when that fisherman came out he followed him to his boat and asked him if he know any Cambodians who just arrive around the dock. The Thai fisherman said there was not many Cambodian refugees came out from the border, but there were a lot of Cambodians working on the fishing boat and right now they were at sea working.

Journey for Wisdom Quest

The Thai fisherman asked Virak if he had a job or a place to stay, Virak told him he got neither so he brought him onto his boat, gave him some food, and then told Virak that his boat need to hire some Cambodian fishermen who willing to risk danger taking their boat to fish in Cambodian water. Virak said he will need a job to do anything but first he want to seek refuge at any Buddhist temple to calm his nerve and to get the bearing of what he want to do with his life in the future. The fisherman said his boat that he work with now was in need of repair, so he decided to go home in the northern province of Thailand to visit his family and his fiancée; and he said that Virak could go with him and he can drop him off at the Buddhist temple that he knew the abbot monk personally, and since the temple was just a few village away by the river and close to the mountain. He boasted that how beautiful the scenery of the temple, the village, the river and the mountain; and he said before Virak ever decided to stay at the temple for good he should visit his village to see their beautiful girls first before he make up his mind. At the Buddhist temple, the fisherman introduced Virak to the abbot monk and asked his permission to stay in the temple to seek spiritual guidance and to ease the suffering of the lost; the fisherman left and he said he will stopping by on his way back to Trad.

First day at the temple, Virak acquired a black loose pant and a long sleeve white pajama shirt, and he put away the colored clothing that the farmer gave him for the time being, because at the temple beside the monk who wore the saffron robe all the laymen and women wear white top black bottom or all white. Virak told the abbot monk that he had worship Lord Wisnu but he was willing to learn the teaching of the Lord Buddha, and the abbot monk replied.

"We did not ask or care of what your belief was or what deity you worship, or what nationality you are. You had come to our Buddhist temple to seek refuge; we will do as much as we can to give you food and shelter out of compassion. We suggested you take time to think thing over, and you can take as much time you want to, or maybe even your whole life time if need be. We suggested that you take a walk in the forest behind the temple that might give you a neutral calm moment and space; we had built some roof grass shelter along the trail. At any time that you need anything from guidance to nourishment you can ask the laymen and women they will be glad to share with you as much as they could, but we should advice you that you should never overindulge yourself on anything. The whole time you stay here you must abide by the temple rules, and the most imported few are.

-There should be no alcohol and drug substance of any kind except those for medicinal purpose.

-Treat all life form with respect even any animal big and small, so you never take live human or animal.

-Refrain from having any ill intention toward others no matter how good, bad, cruel, vicious or murderous they are human, animal or invisible spirit of any form.

All and all you just be nice and relax Ok…live in peace with us here, Oh and let us know if you need any help or anything"

Virak left the abbot monk and went to the market to buy some personal hygiene stuff, and he went to the pharmacy to get some vitamin tablet and the medicine to cleanse the parasite from his body system. And he also got a few clean under wears and a very short haircut.

The first night Virak slept at the temple, there was a long restless night, and when he closed his eyes suddenly the whole world became a demon battle ground. There were demons of all shapes, sizes and colors; and they fought each other everywhere in the air on land and under water. A few demons in particular who were chasing him relentlessly they were the communist demons in black and green pajama with the green smoky hat and they carried AK-47 with fixed bayonet. They were chasing him into the river of blood that was already full of demons hacking each other to pieces. He fought like crazy to keep his head above the bloody water, every time the demon pulled him under the water; he fought so hard for just to get a breath of air, he felt so suffocated that at some point he thought about giving up, because it seemed like a losing battle, there were too many of them, the harder he tried to fight them off with great frustration, the more he felt suffocated and less air he can breathe in; and then, he tried to keep calm but still kept fighting and pushing them away, so he started to feel relax and breathe in and out at ease.

When Virak woke up the sky was already bright, the sun ray shown through the window that made the air felt warm with the smell of smoke from the incent burning. He saw the abbot and a few senior monks; they sat on the chair around his bed chanting the Pali verse. He sat up in bed and wondered what was going on and the abbot monk said.

"We are grateful for the blessing of the Lord Buddha to see you wake up on time for noon meal. Let go to get clean up and come to see us" The monk left for their last meal of the day before noon; Virak got up and went to the water closet, while he was cleaning himself up he could tasted blood in his mouth and some was dripping from his nose, and he also felt strange, his muscle was tight and pained just like after the first day of a hard training exercise. Everybody were kind of avoiding him while he was on his way to the ceremonial hall, and then a novice monk stopped him at the door and told him the abbot monk want to see him in the main pagoda in the middle of the temple ground.

"We see that you'd been through the realm of the spirit between good and evil; we think that you are doing fine because you're still alive. For three days and three nights you are forbidden to come to contact with anyone except monk, the laymen had set up a shelter at the far end of the trail in the forest for you to stay for the duration. It was only for three days Ok, it will be all right, there is nothing can harm you now here is the Katha with the Pali scripture and a special amulet for warrior to go to battle; good luck the Lord Buddha will bless you as always"

Virak went to the far end of the trail, he found a small open shelter covered by peralta grass, and on the bamboo platform they left a reed woven mat, pillow, mosquito net blanket, cooking utensil, some rice and the other food items, and at the other corner there was a stone urn to keep water, a terracotta stove and a pile of firewood; at the center of the roof, they tied a hammock that was a very thoughtful of them. He did not feel hungry at all so he just heat up some water and made himself some tea; he lay in the hammock sipping the hot tea thinking about his life for the past few months he thought it was hell and he was thinking about BT and the other who came out from the mine field corridor together, Virak believed they should be in Thailand already. he think about what the abbot monk said this morning the demon touching and the bleeding, after all he kind of feel fine without any ill effect, so he tried to feel and examine himself all over his body if there was anything was out of place, well he still got all his limps.

At late night, Virak closed his eyes but he could not fall asleep because of the sight and sound and the movement in the forest that made his mind and body reacted to them very sensitively. When he fell asleep eventually, but he could not tell what state of mind he was in, ether he was asleep or awake; it seemed like that there were two persons in his body, one was tired and fell asleep and the other one was staying awake and could see and hear the sight and sound in the forest it was just like a reality dream. In the dark night there were shooting stars crisscrossing the night sky and the gray shadow loomed over his small shelter. Virak felt lonely he wants to cry, but why? And what's for? he'd asked himself, and he tried to reason that there will always be tomorrow, another day, a better day, and everything will be all right and if he want to cry so be it; and finally, he shed some tear anyway, nothing could hold it back in anymore, it burst out like flood water over the dam.

That night he saw a lot of visitor, there were giant fruit bats flapped it wing silently in the night, the vampire bats came to hang itself under the roof, somebody walked all over the roof, and a long black snake came to coil under his bed.

When he opened his eyes, the sky was already bright, he heard a group of the young novice monks called out to him, and they probably tried to make sure that he was still alive; Virak answered them and sat up in the mosquito net. They said something about snake under his bed, he grabbed the bamboo pole that he laid beside the platform and he just nudged it lightly to make it go away.

The snake moved out from under the bed, raised its heads up to look at his face, opened up its hood to let him know that it was a very venomous buffalo cobra, and then it dropped to the ground and moved away into the forest. The novice monks gave Virak some fresh fruit and vegetable and they left. He stepped outside the shelter, munched the fruit and felt the sun ray shown through the thin canopy warming up his face. He felt kind of cheer up a little bit, so he cooked some rice and ate with the food and vegetable that they left for him. After the meal, he started to clean up around the shelter, and then he piled everything up and burned them. When his time was up two days later, he gathered everything that they left for him there, and went to see the abbot monk in the main pagoda.

"We can see that you look fine, you feel better and best of all that you are in good health; and up to this point we don't want to tell you to do anything, after all these thing happen to you here. We suggest that you make your own choice; you can still take your time to think thing over, or if you think that you are already heal you may want to read some book in the library, talk with other senior monk, learn some Thai language, ask the elder layman to help working around the temple with anything you want to do, or if you feel that you are not ready we will understand"

Virak tried to do everything at least once to experience it, so that he could say that at least he'd tried. He went to see the senior monk to learn Thai language and Pali in the manuscript; the novice monks were amused to see a grown man tried to learn Thai at the first grade level, but everybody were surprised to see that Virak could read Pali in the manuscript, and he tried to explain to them that the Pali in the Buddhist manuscript were written in ancient Khmer letter, and any khmer today could still recognized and read them without knowing what it mean in Pali except some word that Khmer and Thai took from the Pali and use in everyday language. And Virak also help working all over the temple to get to know people and to practice his speaking; he worked in the vegetable garden, swept the temple ground, filled up pot hole on the road, fixing the tile roof, and preparing the temple for many Buddhist ceremonies. He started to feel happy, he thought about shaving his head, learned the chanting script and request to become a monk, but the abbot monk told him to wait until after a ceremony called Ngan loy Kratong so he could have some time to think about it.

It was a beautiful ceremony it involved with Buddhist tradition mixed with local custom; it started in the temple during the day, and at night people dressed up to join in the dance, the play and sing song, and good street food. Later during the night, people carried the offering floating basket to the river, and they set up food offering, lighted the candle, burned the incent, wrote a prayer and wished list on a piece of paper they wrote down their different wish and prayer for older people they wished for prosperity, health, wealth, rain or the lottery number, but for the younger single people they wished for love and most likely for the one that they have a feeling for; and then they floated the basket away in the current as an offering to their ancestor spirit; and afterward, people offered each other blessing, wished good luck and shared the good merits that they had received from the temple.

The abbot monk told Virak to go out to enjoy himself with the crown in the festival; so he changed from the black and white layman cloth and put on the old cloth that the farmer gave him. He did not have any plan to do anything with anyone, because he did not know anyone here, he just want to see the people, culture and tasted many different kinds of food but he stopped short from buying beer outside the temple; even though, he felt like to get in the mood into the festival spirit.

Virak bought a small offering float basket that decorated with lotus flower and everything that he need to add on it to make it completed and ready to go; he followed the people to the river. The young men and women, they stood closed together in separated group for support and they glanced at each other smiling at the one that they had a feeling for so they wrote down the name and the wishing love message, light the candle, burned the incent, and they sent the float basket away with the river current to offer to their ancestor spirit.

Virak stood at the river bank alone a little distant from the young crown; he light the candle so he could see what he was doing, and then he burned incent and arranging the items in the basket. He said his prayer in his thought and he wrote down the names of his family and everyone he know from BT to the boy soldier on a piece of paper that had the Buddhist script printed on it, and on another piece of paper he wrote down the person that he had cross path from the one breast Vietcong commander, comrade Bophan, comrade Cripple, the two Vietcong that he had killed at the BM-13 training ground South Vietnam, and anyone that he killed or hurt without his knowledge. He pushed the offering basket off into the current that took it slowly down river, and then he sat down on the river bank; he closed his eyes and cleared away all his thought from his head and his heart.

Suddenly, Virak smelled Chompa flower fragrance from a woman body scent, and he heard a sweet voice from a Thai girl.

"I would like to offer you my best wish and blessing" Virak looked up all he saw was a radiant beautiful angel, she wore a shiny long silk skirt, a long sleeve white laced shirt with a silk krama over one shoulder across her body. When Virak stood up he noticed the Chompa flower adorned her hair, he put his hand together and struggled to offer her his blessing in return with tear welled up in his eyes, and it was rolling down his face. She knew that he was a Cambodian by his accent in his speech, for some reason she was also had tear in her eyes; and then somebody called her name he think.

"Tev let's go, it's time to go home" And then she whispered.

"I must go, good bye for now" Virak could not utter a word because he felt like he had a lump in his throat, and then he just nodded his head with his hand put up together and watching her faded away into the night. After she was gone, Virak sat back at the river bank and wondering why he still had all these emotional feeling and crying in front of a strange woman like a little child. The only explanation was probably the Lord Visnu had seen his miserable life and his loneliness, so that's why he sent a beautiful angel to bless him.

In the next few days, Virak helped clean up the temple after the ceremony, he tried to act normal as usual but there was a struggle in his head and his heart; he kept asking himself if he was ready to live in monkhood the rest of his life, in his head he thought he was ready to leave his ordinary life behind and to become a monk in order to get rid of the cause of suffering. On the other hand he think his suffering was too much for him at his age that it could interfere with his reason and judgment, and beside he was still like the taste of beer and good food, and he still like to listen to beautiful music and his love of woman form; and for the trump card was he had an erection every now and then ever since he saw that beautiful angel at the river bank. He made his decision a few days later; he clean up his space at the temple, washed the layman attire and left it there, and in the morning, he paid his last visit to the abbot monk.

"Your Holiness, I would like to request permission to return to live as a simple life in the society"

"You may go in peace my child, we were reluctant to grant our permission for you to become a monk, and we were right because you are still too young to commit your whole life in monkhood. You may go forth into the world to discover and learn, and you should remember to be tolerated to all and to make a sound judgment. If at any time in life you wish to return the Buddhist temple will welcome you anywhere"

At the boat dock in Trad, his Thai fisherman friend helped him to get a job on his boat; a job on the fishing boat was a good place for single man, drifter and Cambodian refugee, it's a job, a home and an adventure. Now that he got a job he felt just like getting a home or a place to hang his hat; so after he settled in his boat he went to the coffee shop with his friend and they had some beer, the chicken feet with green papaya salad, and this was the first time that he had some beer ever since he came out from Cambodia; they enjoyed the beer, food and cigarette until close to midnight and then they went to sleep on the boat.

When Virak woke up the next morning he could feel the boat was rocking and rolling and he could hear the waves were splashing on the bow, and then he went outside to freshen up at the stern of the boat and could see that they were in the middle of the sea since he could not detect any land at all there were only sky met the sea at the horizon. This was his first day at sea for a long while, and the hangover was one of the bad combination for seasick, he could not eat anything at all for the next couple of days, but after the seasickness was over he gorged on the fresh seafood with a vengeance there were a lot of methods that the fisherman can cook tasty fresh seafood dishes.

One special dish was the fresh dry squid on the boat exhaustion pipe, they cooked it just like the way it sound and it taste very good if you like dried squid. Normally, they cooked the squid right after it was pulled out from the water; they just flatted the squid and pasted it on the clean spot of the exhaustion pipe. And one hour later, they got a piece of delectable hot dry squid served from the hot pipe in the middle of the sea.

C13-A Thai Chompa Angel

A few months later, their struggling old boat needed to go to dry dock for repair again, so the crew must go on land to look for a place to stay for the time being. His Thai friend asked Virak if he had planned to go anywhere or stay at any place, and Virak told him he had neither plan nor place yet, so he said Virak could come along with him to visit his home village. Virak was very happy it was just the right timing, and since he got no plan to do anything at the moment so he just drifted along to the beautiful place that he had seen before.

They took the bus north by way of Bang Kok where they stopped over for a few days so they could go to visit some place around the city, and he could buy some gift for his family and his fiancée. His family and the people in the village, they were so happy to see him because they didn't expect him to be back at that time of the year somebody said that he probably miss his fiancée that why he couldn't stay away from the village for too long. Virak believed the villager were right, at the very next day, his friend put on his best dress and with a bundle of gift under his arm he went to visit his fiancée at the next village twenty-five kilometers away, while Virak stayed back at his home talking to the family and a village elder. Virak told them that they were lucky to live in peace in their beautiful village by the river and the mountain.

"Our village is a nice and peaceful place to live but we lost more and more people to the city and elsewhere because we got no job to offer here, and that trend happened to all villages and towns around here. Our land look beautiful it maybe but is not fertile like the land in the flooded area so we just grow barely enough rice to feed our people"

"Why can't job be created here?"

"It's easy said than done, but how?"

"Well, if the land is not fertile that the crop won't grow well, why not try to raise animal instead like goat and sheep were known that it thrive in desert unfertile soil"

"That is a well put idea, but it's just like I'd said it's easy said than done. Our ancestor were rice farmer for thousands of year and it's hard for us to turn to anything else; and the idea of raising animal in bulk number for slaughter, this is just don't sit right with us as Buddhist. As you may know that we respect all lives even animal life"

"I am sorry Sir, I did not say all these things to offend you at all, that was not my intention I was just said too fast without thinking first. Please forgive me"

"No, No, don't be sorry, you are not the first one that suggest all these ideas and there is nothing wrong at all. I think you are the kind of man we need around here, and why don't you come to settle down here with us since you like our village so much, you can help us to save our land and our way of life"

"I thank you Sir, but this is a big responsibility; and I am too young for the job, I haven't think about settle down yet"

"I think you mature enough even though you may look young, and for settle down that can be arranged, I am the elder and I can speak on your behalf to get you a wife. You wait and see when we have the big ceremony at the temple next week, you will find out how pretty our women are in this part of the country, and don't be shy to let me know if you are interest in any girl Ok"

"Thank you Sir, but I don't think I will need to bother you at all with that matter"

"Well you just keep that in mind, you never know because you haven't seen everything yet" A few days before the big ceremony, his friend was shocked to find out that Virak did not have anything decent to wear except the farmer and the fisherman clothes; Virak told him that he never need any at the boat dock. He said here we were not at the boat dock and he must wear decent modern cloth at the ceremony. So he took Virak to town to get measure at his relative tailor shop. Virak ordered two pants, three shirts, and he was lucky to find a pair of black leather shoes that he like and it fitted properly.

At the day of the big ceremony, the villager prepared elaborated food to bring to the temple; it's an all day affair, and it seemed like a day of picnic and blessing at the temple yard and the ceremonial hall. Everybody wore their best clothes, and now he understood why his friend rushed him to get presentable cloth to wear in order to honor the ceremony and the whole community. A few hours before noon, everything were ready for the main ceremonial session; in the hall right in front of a huge gilded Buddha statue, people filed in to lay their food and the offering in the middle of the hall. A line of monk in saffron robe sat on one side of the hall on the colorful Persian rug, and they were chanting the Pali verse of Buddhist script. People sat to the other side with their feet folded under and their hands up together to receive the merit of blessing.

Virak sat in the rear with group of young men who were kind of restless; they were whispering with their friend and pointing to the front, and when Virak looked up to where they were pointing at he saw a big group of beautiful young women who were in their colorful silk finery with the gold jewelry and some flower on their long shiny black hair; and now he knew the reason why they were restless.

At that time Virak did not have the same interest as most of the young men here; so he just closed his eyes, cleared his thought, and listened to the chanting that made his mind drifted away with the smell of incent burning, the foods, the flowers, and the faint smell of Chompa flower from a woman at the river bank of the other temple that he remembered from a few months ago, and then the scent got his attention.

Virak opened his eyes to look around and tried to find where the scent was coming from; he saw many girls had Chompa flower adorned their hair, and now it was his turn to become restless; his friend looked at him and smiled knowingly that something had hit Virak since he had experience it before. Virak thought to himself that if he could not concentrate to receive merit in this solemn ceremony he should leave the hall; so he excused himself and came to sit outside under a shade tree with some people who were smoking. He light a cigarette and tried to think to find a way of what he want to do in the future since he knew that he couldn't and shouldn't drift away the rest of his life, but the faint scent of Chompa flower from a woman body, had attract all of his attention that he could not think of anything else, but he wondered who was that girl or what was she look like? He was certain that she was in the ceremonial hall because he believed the fainted chompa scent was hers.

In the hall people were divided into small groups of family and friend, and they ate their meal with them under the blessing of the big Buddha statue. Virak followed his friend to the circles of his family and the family of his fiancée, it symbolized a circle of joined families that had become one; Virak remembered the village elder told him about the women in this part of the country, then he thought he was right and he was not exaggerated, there were pretty girls and women everywhere.

The families formed into two circles, the main one were consisted of the parent of both families, his friend and his fiancée, and behind them was the circle of their children and young relatives. After Virak was introduced to her parent and his fiancée by his father, Virak sat folding his legs next to his friend, he ate the spicy Thai food and just kept his eyes on the plates to be polite while he was in the circle with the elders; beside the smell of the burning incent and the Thai spicy food, the Chompa flower fragrance intoxicated his sense.

He could not help but to raise his head and looked around he saw many girls around the circle had Chompa flower on their hair, but he could smelled so strong the scent that he'd smelled at the river bank a few months ago; suddenly, the mother of his friend fiancée called to the next circle of her children.

"Tev would you please bring me some more of that plate"

"Yes, Mother" Now Virak recognized the shape of the face that belong to the beautiful angel at the river bank; she got up, went to get the plate, and she came to kneel beside her mother to hand her the plate that she was asking for, and then she was briefly looking straight at Virak before she went back to sit at her circle right behind her sister. Virak did not know why but the memory at the river bank overwhelmed him, and then he started to feel a lump in his throat and tear started to well up in his eyes; his friend asked him that made everybody in the circle looked at him.

"What's happen man? You still haven't get use to the spicy food yet"

"Oh yes, this one was too spicy for me, would you excuse me please"

Virak took his leave from the circle; from the corner of his eye, he saw the beautiful angel started to have tear in her eyes also; he walked out from the ceremonial hall and went to find a quiet place to sit at the lotus pond in front of the main pagoda, where some young men and women were already there sharing their heart under the shade and between the shrines.

He was thinking about what had just happen in the hall that was almost just like at the river bank during Loy Kratong a few months ago; for him Virak thought he had his reason to cry because of his miserable life, but for the beautiful chompa angel he got no idea why she was crying about, or maybe she could feel his pain, no he did not think so because they didn't talk with each other long enough to get to know one another; what should he do? Should he do something about it? Or he should do nothing about it or maybe he should leave from here for good and pretend like nothing happen at all.

A few days after the ceremony, Virak started to pack his thing and said goodbye to his host to leave with the morning bus for Bang Kok tomorrow; then his friend asked him.

"Before you leave, I have something to ask you about what had happen at the ceremony a few days ago"

"Was it about me crying from the spicy food?"

"Yes about that and it was strange that during the meal you and my fiancée's sister Tev, were crying also; you said you weren't get use to the spicy food, but for her the elders asked her she didn't say anything except crying ever since the ceremony. Is there anything I should know about you two?"

"No there is nothing going on between her and me; and yes, we had met once briefly before during Loy Kratong ceremony at the river bank of the temple where you dropped me off with the abbot monk remember? Then I just came out from Cambodia, and I carried a lot of sorrows were still fresh in my heart. When she was the only person who offered me her blessing, and just like that it made me became emotional and I had tear in my eyes; and what had happened to her I did not know why. And what had happen here at the ceremonial hall, when I knew it was her because of her mother call at the river bank also; it hit me, it was kind of bring back the memory for me, I don't know about her" His friend broke out laughing that brought the attention of his family they came to stand around.

"Ha! Ha! That is beautiful, yes that is fate that have bring you two together again; I could not wait until our village elder hear about this"

"No, no don't bother him man"

"You just sit still; we will take care of everything" He turned to explain everything to his family, and they all smiled at Virak nodding their head; all the men in the family came to shake his hand that he kept asking them what was for?

"Congratulation, Tev is very pretty" Virak was stunt and kind of lost, and did not know what to think, or maybe there was fate or destiny that brought him a drifter to meet this beautiful angel; he did not know and wasn't sure. The village elder walked in the house with a broad smile on his face and he came to hold Virak shoulder.

"This is a beautiful destiny that bring you to us Son, Ok tomorrow we will move in possession to the bride home"

"Wait a minute Sir, why we are so hurry rush into this? Can I have anything to say about this too?"

"No, fate had already decide ever since the big ceremony; Tev is upset crying a lot and she didn't say anything; the family and all of us believe this must be some kind of witchcraft that made her behave like this. And now we know that you are the cause of all this, so you must go there and straight thing out, if you don't show up his wedding will be in jeopardy, because he brought you here"

His friend looked at him pleading, and he felt like he was trapped just because of their believe, and he was mad at himself for crying at the meal circle; he thought that he get over everything, and he was told that through time his pain will heal but when? He tried hard to understand of what had just happen or in the back of his mind he tried to wake himself up and asked was this for real? Well, he tried to reason with himself and look at the bright side, he was always looking for a place to call home, and the boat was kind of a temporary home for drifter, and now he could have a real home and family that he could belong to; and Tev she was beautiful but why did she keep crying for? Was he the cause? And that he will find out soon.

Virak was told that the village elder here, was an older brother of Tev's father and all of the decision making from rice crop to family mater, were involved with the village elder all the time. And now that he is in the picture involved in this family matter; the village elder took this very personal, because Tev is his adopted daughter whom he brought from Bang Kok, and since he did not have family of his own so he let his brother raised Tev in his family; that why she did not have any resemblance to all of her brother and sister. The word was sent immediately to Tev's family and invited guesses to prepare for the involved party with my friend parent who will speak in my behalf.

In the morning, everybody were all dress up and ready to go except Virak; his friend urged him to put on his best tailor cloth, and then they were on their way to Tev's home; he'd heard somebody called it the bride's home already, and for whatever reason he was just resigned to the fate and went along nicely. At Tev's home, they set up a big tent roof just like a big married ceremony that they set up to receive the guess outside the house. From that point on there were all of the village elder performances, he was like a spokesman for all parties involved, and everything were ran according to his guidance. After a lengthy formality according to the custom, Virak was ushered into a room full of all party involved except Tev herself was not present that whom he was impatiently want to see they had him sit in front of the village elder who was in the middle with his back leaned on a pillow against the wall, with his friend and his parent at one side and his fiancée and her parent to the other; then they said.

"The first time that Tev cried for no apparent reason was at the river bank during Loy Kratong, and at the next day she was all right, but at this time when we were at the ceremonial hall, we saw you cried and then she was crying ever since that day of the big ceremony; first we thought that it was the effect of witchcraft, but since our elder had explained to us that you two had met each other at the river bank we have no doubt that fate bring you two together, and for whatever force that bring you here we cannot fight against it, thus you two must get engage to please the force of the spirit, and if you learn to love and wish to live together in matrimony we will be happy to celebrate, but if thing turn to any other way we will accept that must be the will of the divine spirit" Virak tried to reason with them and spoke to the village elder.

"Sir, my friend bring me here the second time to visit his home, and I came with all of my good intentions, and as you know that I am alone all of my family are in Cambodia and I am a drifter I own no wealth; and now that all the elders think what I should do I will follow, but may I speak to Tev I would like to ask her what she think first"

"For us we don't care who you are or whether you are wealthy or not, the divine fate had brought you here so we accept you as you are, we understand for your concern about Tev, yes you can speak to her all you want after the engagement ceremony; let's go, let get it done" So the engagement proceeded according to the village elder plan and everyone was treated to an elaborated feast with a lot of food and drink. The elder warned Virak not to drink any alcohol beverage because this was the time that his character was under scrutiny by all of the relatives and guesses.

When Tev was brought to sit opposite from him at the center of the room, she looked so beautiful and she was like a princess in the silk traditional dress, that he was speechless and he could not take his eye off her; she did not look anything like a girl who had been crying for the last few days. At the gift exchange ceremony, they kneeled facing each other, Virak put a gold necklace around her neck and she gave him a silk krama and an amulet with tear in her eye and a smile on her face. After that the village elder brought Tev and Virak out to introduce to all relatives and guesses, and also they could receive their blessings and gifts.

After the ceremony, all the guesses and relatives had left but Virak must stay at the bride house to work on whatever they decide that he should do in order to gain merit and trust. Virak knew this custom was practice in Cambodia during the last century in the rural countryside at mostly arranged married that most bride and groom may never know or seen each other before; and the groom must work real hard to please the in laws.

He had to share a room with the brother in laws, and they were also his mentors and companions at work on everything he do and the place at everywhere he go. In the last few days, he had seen very little of Tev and he did not have any time to talk to her at all because of the busy work day that kept them apart all day, and he had a chance to see her face only during the evening meal. One evening after the meal, Virak stopped Tev in the hallway and he asked her.

"Tev I want to talk to you, can we sit at the front porch?" She hesitated and answered him in a shy whisper.

"You need to ask permission from my parent first"

"I already did before the ceremony, and they said that I can talk with you all I want after the ceremony" And then she was just looking at him smiling and nodding her head; at the front porch, they sat facing each other at the table with one of her younger brother who tried to pull a chair and sat at the table with them, but Virak stopped him and told him that he needed to talk to his sister alone, and then he protested.

"But Ma and Pa told me to be with you and watch you at all time"

"Yes you can watch us from inside the house" He just nodded his head and went to sit in the house listening to the radio keeping an eye on them. The house was built from brick at the ground floor, and the second floor was made from wood with the front porch, and all were covered by tile roof. Her brother brought out a lit oil lamp and set on the table; Virak took a good look at Tev without her makeup on she looked stunning with her natural beauty under the oil lamp light. She glowed like an angel with her long shiny black hair that adorned with the ever present Chompa flowers and the mesmerizing fragrance that he had remember ever since the first time he met her. This was the first time that they could sit close and took their time looking at each other face to face; she looked so innocent and glowing even under the oil lamp light, and he started,

"Was that you at the river bank?"

"Yes"

"Did you remember my face at the ceremonial hall here?"

"No, I just thought that I had seen you from somewhere, I didn't recognize you not until you started to cry, and you did you remember my face at the ceremonial hall?"

"No, it was too dark at the river bank than, but I remember your scent with the Chompa flower on your hair"

"Is that really?"

"Yes, I knew you were there but I couldn't tell which one that was you until your mother call your name". She smiled at him with her eyes wide open; he could not restrained himself so he grabbed hold of her hands that made her startled and she pulled her hands away quickly just like she just got an electric shock, and she looked around nervously with her face turned red and her eye casted down; and Virak whispered.

"What's wrong?"

"We are not allow to…yet"

"And when?"

"I don't know" Virak reached across the table again to grab her hand and pulled her closer to the table; she looked at him with her mouth gapped open and he could see her emotion flashed through her eyes, their face were only a short distant apart that he could feel her warm short breathing that mixed with her scent and the Chompa fragrance; he felt a little frustrated that they were so close but yet they were separated so far by the custom barrier. He tried to calm himself down by turning his attention away and asked her.

"At the river bank, I cried because I lost my family and my country, and you why did you cry?"

"First when I saw you sat by yourself and sent the offering basket out alone I was kind of feel sorry for you, and I did not know what made me decide to go to you and offered to you my blessing because I normally don't talk to stranger, but when I saw your tear I could feel your sorrow; it was so sudden and so overwhelmed that I could not hold back my tear, and now after we got engaged I feel relief, and right now I'm being close to you my heart feel warm; and you, now tell me how do you feel"

"For me, when I saw you at the river bank I thought that the gods had sent an angel to give me blessing because they feel sorry for me, but when I smell your scent of Chompa at the ceremonial hall I thought my mind was playing trick with me, and when your mother called your name then I knew that was you and the memory at the river brought back the feeling and the pain that I felt when I just came out of Cambodia.

When the village elder, whom I did not know then that he was your father then told me that my fate was sealed; and he brought me here to clear up everything that had happened to you. Then I thought that it was too hasty and I was too young to settle down, but on the other hand I was so happy that I'd found you and to be a part of you and your family. Then I want to talk to you first but I was not permitted, and now I am being near you I know I had developed a love for you that grow stronger every second; after all you are the angel that the gods have sent to me"

They were so preoccupied with each other that they did not pay any attention to the audiences at the window inside the house where the whole family sat quietly listening to the radio and looking at them; Tev was nervous and embarrassed she pulled her hand from his immediately; Virak whispered to her.

"Don't be concerned about what other people think My Love, they have to get use to this after all we are engaged to be married" She did not answer him but she just smiled, looked down on the table and stole a glance at him; her mother call them and suggested that they should turn in for tonight, because the village elder will have some important thing to talk to them tomorrow. Virak woke up early in the morning along with her older brothers and just like every morning when they get up he tried to help them to work the man chores. Tev came to give Virak a set of his cloth and tell him to change without giving any explanation; he guessed there must be something more than ordinary that they had to prepare for. Right before noon, the village elder came to the house with a few district officials, he immediately called everybody to gather in the living room and he had Tev sat in front of him and the officials, and the whole family and Virak stood behind her.

"I am very happy that my only daughter is engaged to be married, and destiny had brought you together, that I could see happiness between you two after only a few days living under one roof; my daughter I give you this track of land as a gift before your wedding, it is not a prime valuable land because it cannot be made into rice field but I hope you and your husband to be will turn it to become a more productive and promising land.

Let sing the document with the officials so it will become legal; ok my brother let bring out the food and the rest of the beer and wine I will have a feast with the official and my soon to be son in law, and set up for us at the front porch please"

The family rushed into the kitchen to bring out the foods and drinks and they set up the table at the front porch for the guesses. The village elder called Virak to join with the guesses at the table and he started to describe about the land.

"This track of land is big but it cannot be made into rice field, because of it sits on the high hilly rocky terrain, so it is considered not valuable, but it has its own many charming characteristics like the bamboo forest along the edge surrounded the entire property that was planted by our ancestors, and they had widened and deepened the low area into a few hectares lake that is connected to the river, so it could store water and enable us to raise the aquatic plants and animals for food naturally. And they had flatten a big area to make a plantation that is full of a few hectares of banana and a hectare of mango and many other kinds of fruit tree, and there is a row of about a hundred coconut trees along the edge of the bamboo fence line. At the rear of the property, there is a small hill mount of about a hundred feet high that has a natural spring flow from it always down to the lake and a rocky field of peralta grass that can be made into roofing material"

At the next morning, Tev walked with Virak to her new land about a few kilometers from her house; when they turned in through the wide gate of the thick bamboo forest along the edge of this big property, he felt happy and relaxed to see this place with the row of the coconut tree, the lake that was full of lotus, lily, water spinach and many other aquatic plants.

A few hundred meters from the gate there was a tall big long roof covered by peralta grass; and there were hundreds of farmer, merchant and workman who were busy trading, loading, unloading and moving their vehicles from the gate always to the roof and the surrounding area, Virak guessed this was a full fledge market, and under the roof there were the village elder's office with dozens of worker at a corner close to the road who oversaw the trading activity.

At the other corner, there were rows of chair and table full of people sat eating their food that they ordered from a small shops and food stalls that had their kitchens connected to the big roof; a grocery store that set next to the office offered varieties of merchandise from clothing cosmetic to foods stuff, condiments, and alcohol beverages; and after the grocery store lined the store of farm equipment, cooking utensil, clothing, dry good, grain, that were across from the stalls of meat, fish, fruit and vegetable. The village elder, who was informed by his worker of their arrival, left the works to his assistant, brought them to a quiet corner table and had them order some food and drink; he looked at Virak and smiled just like he could read his mind and he said.

"You must be surprised to see a thriving market in the middle of nowhere, yes I understand Son, for those who have seen this place for the first time at the beginning from farmers, merchants, tourists and the government officials, and they all were surprised to see a growing market without any town nearby to support it" He paused to look around "Yes, in the beginning I couldn't believe that it grow to become this big; at first I build this big roof for sheltering the workers and the equipments from the sun and rain, since we have hired many workers like the bamboo cutters, the peralta grass harvesters, the roof panel weavers and the cooks.

The merchants and builders only came once in a while when they need to buy bamboo and roofing materials. Later on, I overheard many merchants complained that they had a hard time to fill the order from the big city where people request to buy strictly the organic foods; they want the vegetables from the countryside far away from the big city just likes ours place that grow without using any chemical fertilizer and pesticide, and the animals that raise naturally in the open free range without using any feed that produce from the factory because they are most likely loaded with chemical and substances that can be dangerous to human health.

So I ask all the villagers around here to bring their vegetables and animals to sell to the merchants right here because they were willing to pay the villager's product at a higher price; since then, our reputation grow that make this place evolve to become a busy thriving organic food supply a village market since the last few years, but right now we have been slowing down a lot because of the job shortage so the village lost their population to the city, hence they produce less of the product to supply the city demand, so the merchant had to turn to the other source; and some time our reputation was tainted by people who brought the food product from other place that were not strictly organic and they tried to sell them here.

I like your idea of raising animal and produce organic food from our own organic farm. Later we will go through the property and talk some more about it, but in the mean time just go around and enjoy yourselves; I have to see some merchants from Bang Kok, Tev why don't you show him around I will see you children later around lunch"

They were trying to keep low profile by walking away from the market along the lake shore to another roof shelter about a few hundred meters from the market that the village elder built as a work place and storage area that connected to worker's shelter and kitchen. This roof was almost the same size as the market, it was enormously built, so that gave him the idea that this land possessed materials and space to build many more roof of this size to house a pig farm, a duck farm, a chicken farm to start and with a lots of rooms and materials for expansion.

After the noon meal, the Elder took Tev and Virak on an oxcart that use for transporting bamboo and peralta grass to see all area of the land; they went along the lake and the small creek that flowed from the spring at the mount in the rear of the property, and they went through the banana plantation, the fruit tree plantation, the old grow forest and the rocky field of peralta grass where he think it was a suitable space to raise goat and sheep.

Within a week, Virak had talked with half a dozen whole sale merchants, the farmers, and some agents from the ministry of agriculture. The elder had him talk with Tev's brothers who were trained in animal husbandry and farm management; they drawn and laid out the plan for the building construction. Virak think the elder had a well prepared plan and all the elements that were needed to build and operate an organic raised animal production farm; so at the very next day, the construction workers started to dig holes in the ground and begin to build the farm buildings to house the animals, supplies and materials; a month later, the farm had five buildings; the first one near the farm gate and a few hundred meters from the market, was set for the farm office, the veterinary clinic, and the supply storage.

The building near the lake was for raising duck, the third one for chicken, the fourth one for producing suckling pig, and the fifth one was a barn by the peralta grass field for goat and sheep with some housing for the caretaker.

The elder made Virak's friend and his fiancée as the farm buyer and supplier who went around buying animals, feeds, supplies and materials that were able to start the animal production industry. When the farm was up and running the Elder made Tev eldest brother as the farm manager and the second oldest as the production supervisor, they hired about fifty workers from the farm producers, feeders, cooks, movers, technicians and a full time veterinarian; most of the workers were the Elder's relatives from the surrounding village. The Elder brought his niece who works in a factory office at a distant city to train some young women for the farm office.

It was not long before the farm started to sell fertilized and non fertilized duck eggs every day, and by the time it rolled out the first batch of suckling pig, the farm front office became a mad house and a disorganized wholesale public auction took place where merchants competed among themselves trying to secure an order or an exclusive right over the limit amount of the suckling pig. I had an idea popped in my mind that I immediately asked the Elder to stop this sale for a moment so I could talk to him and his staff in private; the Elder reluctantly stopped the sale for a moment, and we went inside with the farm manager and Tev at my side; and then the Elder said.

"This got to be good, and you got to have legitimate reason to stop this sale because our product is gaining momentum in public demand that's why the auction start to form, and if we make them get upset this might turn them toward our would be competitor"

"Sir the competitor we will have many of them later on down the line; and all we can do are to safeguard the farm image and maintain the consistency of our product quality. The event that happen during this sale of the first batch of the piglet, give me an idea; I think we should reserve the right to sell our product to a few merchants who will supply our piglet to the best prestigious restaurants and rotisserie.

Sir I heard you said that you need letters of recommendation from the client base of consumer in order to apply for a loan from the Royal Committee for the Rural Development, so this is your opportunity to have the merchants that we sell our piglets to, introduce you to their clients whom you may request for the letters of recommendation from.

I think our product should end up at the prestigious restaurants and hotels in Krung Tep where you and the manager should meet with those clients face to face, and you need to make a good first impression by wearing the business attire, showing the picture of the village scenery and the farm etc… I don't think it takes more than a week to gather all those letters, and whenever you think that you have enough and that you are already in Krung Tep, you should bring some imported member of the provincial and local government whom you know to the Royal Committee main office to make a strong case in submitting your application"

The Elder had Virak took a professional photographer around the property to capture the image that he think it should be in the farm photo album. And he want to take the manager, Tev and Virak to get measure for a business suit, but he suggested that since the elder will do his business in Krung Tep that he should wait to buy those business attires when he get to Krung Tep, and Virak told him that he did not need to go since this business talk will involve with the elder and his manager only, but the Elder insisted that Virak should go along or Tev will refuse to go also.

In a very early morning hour, they were boarding an air conditioned bus for Bang Kok; the Elder bought four tickets in a row of two pairs with the aisle in between, he want Virak sit with him so they could talk, but Tev dragged his arm to sit with her and told her father that he need to talk to his farm manager more and because she want to sit next to Virak. This little rebellious episode, was kind of surprise for the Elder, it was unexpected and it was new to him, and this seemed to be her way to show him that she was a grownup woman now and no longer a shy little girl that he get use to look at her any more.

The minute that they were settled into their seat, Tev started to chat with Virak, raised the seat divider and moved closer to him let him feel her warm womanly body, and he could smelled the chompa fragrance from her hair; she leaned back on him and pointed to show him the things and places outside the window while the bus started moving out and the eastern sky was still dark.

The driver turned off the interior light and while the air conditioned unit was flowing in full blasted, Tev reclined their seat, pulled Virak back and laid her head to sleep peacefully on his chest. The Elder and the manager were surprise to see Tev lay on him that way but he acted like there was nothing happen and kept on engaging with the conversation; Virak guessed the engaged couple in the rural countryside were not allowed to get too close and cozy this way at this early stage of courtship. He thinks their generation evolved and set themselves apart from the old tradition at this point in time.

In Bang Kok, they stayed at a home of the Elder's relative on the bank of a canal that they had to take a taxi boat to get in and out from the house to the city street. In the first day, the Elder took them to a big tailor shop at the city center to get them measured for the suit and dress, because they will take a few days to make them, and they went to department store to shop for the other accessories items like tie, shirt, shoe etc…; after they finished picking out the items at the men cloth department, the Elder told Tev to find some dresses for herself beside the business suit and skirt that were already measured; and then she turned to Virak and ask him what else did he think that she should have to wear beside the business suit.

Virak looked around the store, and then something on the wall caught his eye a full length body picture of a princess like in a long Thai traditional silk dress that should look splendid with Tev; he pointed to the picture on the wall and told her.

"I think you should wear something look like that"

"What? Is that princess attire for me?"

"Yes, why not I know that dress will look great on you, you will look ten times better than that"

Tev just smiled with her face turn red and her eye casted down with a demurred manner; other people nearby and the manager were laughing at Virak, and the elder who was just smiling and rolling his eye, but he nodded his head and told them to pick whatever they want.

Virak walked through the aisles helping her choose and pick out three silk dresses, some shoe and others accessories; he also brought her to the cosmetic area to pick out anything she wants, and he want the beauticians advice her about the modern technique in makeup, but they told him not to worry and leave her in their hand all they need was time; so he left her there and instructed the store clerk whose carried all of the items that they picked to wait for her and bring her to the eatery at the ground floor where the Elder and the manager were waiting for us.

At the eatery down stair, Virak told the Elder and the manager to wait at least an hour because modern woman need time, so all they need to do were being patient and wait for her. While they were at the coffee table the Elder reminisced about his life in Bang Kok here when he was a young man in the service of the prince at the royal resident where he had been taking Tev to visit almost every years, and tomorrow he will take her there again so the manager and Virak had to wait at the house or feel free to go around to see Bang Kok.

While they were lost in their thought listening to the Elder talked, they heard a commotion from inside the store that the people turned to look at something that was coming toward the eatery but the Elder seemed to lose his patient in waiting more than an hour for their modern woman, and it's natural that he want Virak to get Tev so they could pay the store and leave, since he wasn't concern about the commotion, but alas, when they looked up there was Tev coming toward them in the full royal regalia follow by throng of people that some were thinking that a royal came to visit the store; the Elder who was beaming with pride and a broad smile on his face said "She is a ..." And then, he paused for a few second to recollect himself, and he went to the cashier counter to pay for the merchandises.

At the next morning, the manager and Virak slept late and planned to go around town for sightseeing later on that afternoon, since they did not need to go anywhere with the Elder and Tev, but the Elder came to get Virak and told them that Tev refused to go without Virak, so he had to jump off the bed, get himself ready in the flash and jump in the water taxi with them right on time. On the way, the Elder was quiet and unusually reserved; Virak turned to Tev and asked her why she refused to go to follow her father wish that may have upset him, and then she replied with her eye fixed on the elder and Virak that exerted her determination.

"I am sorry my Beloved that I make you hurries to catch up with us, and I am sorry father that I don't follow your wish like a good little girl I used to be. From now on my Beloved, I want to go anywhere with you especially this visit to the prince resident, I think we are couple now since we are going to be married, and I don't care what other people think in what stage of courtship that we should be or what we allow to do. Father, it doesn't matter what I become, I am and will always be your good daughter even now that I am grown to become a woman and soon to be a wife"

She grabbed a hold of Virak hand and looked at her father with tear welled up in her eyes, and when she turned to look at Virak and smiled with sweet love in her eyes, Virak raised her hand up and kissed with tenderness that made the people around them include the Elder, were surprised with their show of franked emotion and the physical tenderness that they never seen or they had seen the westerner did in public before. When the Elder recovered from his initial shock, he was contented with a nod and a smile on his face and the realization that the time he did not anticipate had come.

At the prince royal resident, the guard let them in through the Iron Gate to a huge multi level old style villa with a meticulous front lawn and flower garden; a doorman received them and brought them into the main hall that was elaborately decorated where they sat at the gilded chairs waiting for the prince's assistant. Fifteen minutes later, a well dress man came out that Tev whispered to Virak that was the prince's assistant; the man and the Elder, they greeted each other like old friends, and the Elder signaled Virak to wait at the main hall and dragged Tev's hand to follow the assistant into the inner chamber, and Virak could detect Tev displeasure and then he signaled her to just follow them.

After they went inside the inner chamber, Virak sat back in the comfortable gilded chair looking around the room and admiring the decoration like a pair of huge and very long elephant tusks, the many pictures and paintings of the royal extended family from the past to present that hung on the wall around the room.

Suddenly, there was a black and white picture that immediately attracted his attention, because of the face of the woman in the picture had a striking resemblance to Tev excepted the woman in the picture looked older. An assistant came out and called Virak to prepare to go inside to meet the prince, he gave him some instruction to follow the protocol and then he had a guard patted him down to make sure that he did not possess any weapon before they let him crossed the threshold into the chamber.

He crouched down low and came to kneel next to Tev in front of a pair of feet that suppose to be the prince's, and then he ordered them to strait their back and look up at him; he was relief to gaze at a kind face of a middle age man who gave them his blessing and a symbolic touch on their head, and he had invoked the blessing of Buddha for their journey in life.

For a whole week, they visited so many offices and establishments to ask and collect the recommendation letters, first they went from the ministry of commerce, the ministry of agriculture, and many prestigious restaurants, hotel and the few well known rotisseries who received the shipment of their piglet that they were highly praised. The Elder had them put on their newly tailored business suit except Tev that he want her to wear the full princess attire, accessory and make up just like when she came out from the store, and he praised Virak for helping her to choose all those things.

Whether the ministry office or restaurant, all of the people were surprised at their present, Tev's beauty that radiated an air of royalty, and when the Elder pulled out a piece of paper with the gold seal letterhead from the prince office and made the request for the recommendation letter, everyone actually scrambled to produce one for them in a hurry. So a week after, they were ready to pay a visit to the agency for the rural development to submit the loan application; with the manager gave the testimony in every aspect of their farm and the quality of their organic products that were backup by a stack of the recommendation letter from the well known prestigious establishments and offices, and the testimony by the provincial government representative who cited the need of the development in private business, that was enable us to receive the authorization of the initial loan.

After they had achieved the goal that what they came here for; the Elder want to stay in the city for a few more day so they could celebrate their success by visiting Krung Tep landmarks. He insisted on them wearing the business suit and Tev had the silk princess attire on, but the manager and Virak reasoned with him that the suit was too hot for them to wear and walking outside around the city, so he let them wore the long sleeve shirt and slack, but Tev was stuck with the silk princess regalia that she love to have it on. They went to visit all the interesting places around Bang Kok like the Klong Toy market, the palace royal, the Temple of the Emerald Buddha and many more.

At the temple, the Elder suggested that they should kneel to pray and thank Buddha for all the blessing, while they were praying the Elder gave Virak a small box that contained a gold ring with a solitary precious stone in it and he was pointing to Tev who was still had her eye close in deep concentration in her solemn prayer, Virak went to kneel in front of her looking at her angelic face with her hands up together in utmost respect posture.

In the middle of the ceremonial hall when Tev opened her eye with an astonished look on her face and then they were witnessed by the Emerald Buddha, the foreign tourists and everybody else Virak slipped the ring on her finger that surprised Tev with her eyes wide open and they became dampened with her tear of happiness; she leaned forward came in his arms and hid her face in his chest, Virak wrapped his arms around her and turned to whisper his thank to the Elder under the flashing light of the tourist camera.

They were staying embraced on their knees for a few minutes more not to pose for the tourist but they were savored the precious moment that touched their heart and attracted the crowd who form a circle around them in the middle of the ceremonial hall with the Emerald Buddha looked over from above.

They took the overnight bus back to the village; the Elder insisted on them to wear the business suit and tie, because it should complimented Tev dress, so they forced to put it on for the whole trip; Virak could understand that the elder love to see the effect that they had on people it was just like they had seen royalty came into town, it also had the same effect when they got off from the tricycle taxi at the farm. The Elder was beaming with pride; he took off his hat and announced to everybody that the trip to Krung Tep was a fruitfully success and there will be more jobs opening for the villagers.

At the very next day, the Elder ordered the start of the construction of a few more farm roof building and more employees housing, and he told Virak friend to acquire some more brood animals, and he also need to order more supplies and a bigger generator; all of these movements were anticipated the increase of the production volume that fulfilled their goal of expansion. Since the work at the farm was getting busier, Virak cleared a room to sleep near the front office with Tev came to wake him up every morning.

A bank agent and some representative from the agency of the rural development came to visit the farm to evaluate their claim and to finalize the loan authorization; they looked at every building and everything in the farm and they interview some of the production farm workers at random, the manager and the veterinarian. Even though, they knew that they already got the initial phase of the loan, but they said that they had to complete the many forms and stack of paperwork as a formality; Virak guessed the ordinary farmer like them if they submitted the loan application without the intervention from the prince they may never receive the authorization at all, and then he was just about to walk away from this bunch of bureaucrat the Elder told him to wait because Tev was starting to follow right behind him, so they had to wait at the employee cafeteria where the meeting took place.

After their tour around the farm, the bureaucrat came to meet with the Elder and his staff at the farm office; the bank agent looked out on the lake where some workers on small boat cut up the water spinach to make up for the animal feed, and he had a thoughtful look on his face that seemed like he tried to find an appropriate thing to say, Virak felt the atmosphere was so tense and uncomfortable that he could detect the worry look on Tev and the Elder face; and then finally the bank agent turned to look at the Elder and said.

"As far as I am concern this farm is already up and running with a meticulous planning for the operation, but there is only one thing that it is lacking" He paused for a moment and then he looked at Tev up and down and he continued. "I was told this farm was created by some kind of royalty, and now I can see why people said that. A name, your farm does not have a name; I need some kind of name to put on the document. You young lady, you are the owner and mistress of this land give me a name" Tev looked at the Elder and then at Virak, the Elder called Virak to come closer and he said.

"You two need to think of a name for your farm" Virak tried to give some idea what it should be so the Elder and Tev could think of a name in Thai, so Virak suggested that something with royalty meaning with the bamboo around the perimeter that made this farm look like the old ancient fortress, and then he look at the Elder who was smiling, giving a little thought and he said.

"Yes Son, this piece of land was an old fortress in ancient time so this farm should be called 'The Royal Bamboo Fortress' farm from now on" The bank agent got up and shook hand with the Elder and Tev, and then he said.

"Congratulation for your ownership of the Royal Bamboo Fortress farm, we need this size of business to produce wealth in this region, so tomorrow come to our local bank in the provincial town to sign for your initial loan of half a million bath and I suggest you should open an account there also" He looked at Virak and turned to ask the Elder.

"This man doesn't sound like a Thai who is he?"

"No he is not a Thai; he is a refugee from Cambodia"

"Why he is not in the refugee camp at the border, and what is he doing here?"

"He who gave me the idea and the process in creating this farm"

"Good now your farm is created, it is up and running, you don't need his idea anymore, and why don't you send him and all of his kind to the refugee camp at the border. There they are in the process to send them to other country oversea like Europe, America and many other countries" Upon hearing the bank agent word, Tev felt uneasy, she turned pale and stood next to Virak hold onto his arm; and then the Elder said.

"He isn't going anywhere; he is engaged to be married with my daughter"

"But why, we don't want any of his kind come to own any part of Thai soil; this is unthinkable"

"Good day Sir, I'll see you at the bank in town tomorrow" In the next morning, The Elder and the manager went to the city and they came back home with a big happy new that now the farm had half a million baths in the bank account at their disposal to expand the farm operation many time bigger and this was just a smaller initial loan, so they imagined when the farm receive the main bigger loan of millions baths the farm could branch out the operation to many other place and provide jobs to thousands of people in the community. Everybody looked happy except Tev who was quiet and had a worry look on her face.

Tev and Virak walked through the farm together to look at all the aspects of operation and I explained everything that she should know. They walked through the farm hand in hand without any entourage escort anymore because they were working; at one after noon, Tev wants Virak to take her to the barn at the peralta grass field, because they were surprised that the Muslim caretaker there told them that they could begin to sell the young lambs and goat kids. So Virak took a farm newly acquired motor bike and rode with Tev to the barn in the rear of the property along the creek.

Before they got to the barn, Virak stopped the motor bike at the creek bank in the quiet old grow forest with Tev before sunset; she tried to act normal just like nothing was out of the ordinary, but she could not hide her somber mood that hung over her like a dark cloud; Virak parked the bike off the road leaned against a tree and they went to stand silently cool off by the water edge. They became quiet and just stood there looking at each other eye; Virak could not restrain himself anymore so he bent down to kiss her lips softly in the dark quiet old grow forest, he could see his angel closed her eye and drifted away enjoy being kiss with her heart beat faster and her tender body melted in his arms.

The barn was tall like a three story building with wooden plank wall and tin roof, inside it had a high loft for hay and fodder storage and on the ground floor it was divided into many compartments to keep the small kid goats and lambs. There was a long fence to keep the goats and sheep inside this big grass field, and outside the fence near the barn they built a few small houses for the Muslim caretakers who were experienced in goat and sheep husbandry.

They came out to greet them and want to accompany them to the barn, and after they shown them all the lambs and kid goats that they prepared to sell tomorrow Virak told them to go back to their house to rest since they were going to leave soon after they checked on the amount of fodder in the loft that they might need to order some more. Virak told Tev not to become attached emotionally with the adorable little lambs and kid goats that she should just think of them as a part of the production.

The sun was setting in the west and the moon was hanging low close to horizon at the northeastern sky; they climbed up onto the loft and walked around and climbed over the haystack to the big rear window that looked out to the small mount and the grassy field below. They sat on the haystack looking at the boulder on the top of the mountain that casted long shadow by the moonlight, they leaned back on the hay stack with Tev lay her head on his arm, Virak kept looking at her to see how beautiful she was that she was glowing under the moon light, her long shiny black hair that adorned with the ever present chompa flower, her round full breasts that rise and fall follow her breathing and the tight cleavage that pointed to the area beneath her bra, he could feel his erection became stiff poking at her thigh;

Virak reached out to unbutton her shirt so he could see more of her cleavage and feel her breast inside the bra. Suddenly they heard the commotions in the yard below, they stood by the window looking down to the enclosed yard below where the caretaker kept a couple dozen nanny goats those were in estrus with a big stud ram who humped all the nanny goat nonstop one after another. Tev was worry that the big ram might hurt the little nanny goats, but Virak assured her that it was all right he just performed his duty to make the little kid goats. Virak held her from behind, she turned to nestle in his chest and she asked.

"Have you ever been with a woman before?"

"Yes, I have"

"My sister told me that most men will have sex experience with women before they married, but we girls must keep our mind and body pure until we get married"

"That is the old tradition; it is the same as in Cambodia they enforced stricter rule on girls more than on guys"

"Have you ever been with a woman ever since you come out to Thailand?"

"No not yet, do you know that before I met you at the river bank I was considering to become a Buddhist monk and stay in the temple the rest of my life, so I don't have to deal with my suffering, but when I met you at the river I started to change my mind and I went to work on the fishing boat instead, and the little stipend I received on the boat I spent on beer, cigarette and Ka Kay Yam"

"So what's in your mind? What do you think about now?"

"You, I think about you all the time day and night, how about you what do you think?"

"I think about you too and about us. That bank agent words make me worry, I think we should getting married sooner"

Tev stood up, got undress and dropped everything on the haystack, and she was standing there gloriously naked glowing and waiting. Virak fixed his eyes on her slender body and slipped out of his clothes quickly, and suddenly their naked body came together to become one, and they started to kiss and caress that made their body shaken with anticipation of pain and pleasure to come......

"Please my beloved, be gentle with me, I never been with anyone before ever"

"Don't worry Love it's going to be fine" Under the moonlit night sky, she lay back on the hay that was covered by their clothes, and her hand reached out to him with anticipation; Virak took a moment just stood there by her side admiring her naked body that spread on the haystack just like Venus was waiting and longing.

He lay down by her side holding her, and then he slowly kissed from her lips down, Virak want to make that moonlit night to be her first memorable moment in her life. He kissed all over her body that was responding to his every touch and it was spreading open waiting to bloom. He looked down at her face and her doe eyes that looked at him waiting for the ultimatum...... she grabbed hold a handful of hay, and she moaned and sighted under the feeling of pain and pleasure...... For him the pleasure was so great it won't be long that he could feel his crisis was coming and it busted out with a calamity force between good and evil; he felt like the universe was ceased to exist except the sound of the ram that was hissing and grunting while he was still humping those nanny goats, Virak thought the ram got him beaten by a long shot, and he reminded himself to tell the caretaker to feed the stud ram with a triple ration for the appreciation of his hard work day and night. By the time when they got back to the front office, his friend came to ask them with a concern look on his face.

"Where have you two been? Everybody were looking all over for you"

"We went to the barn to check the production and the fodder volume that we should have on hand" His friend looked at them up and down, started to smile and pulled pieces of hay from their clothes and hair.

"Oh yes, of course, you two are working but don't work too hard because you are the owner, that's why we hire all these workers for, and don't forget to clean up all those hay from your hair and your clothes before you go to the house" At the house, with Virak stood speechless next to her, Tev told her parent that they want to get married sooner like next week, and she was going to move in with Virak to the front office right away. Her parents were shocked and speechless like Virak, and then her father started to say something in Thai so fast that Virak couldn't understand a word; her mother started to cry and she said something about ungrateful daughter. But Tev did not listen or let all the commotion that she caused to interfere with her determination in moving out of the house.

At the farm that night, she lay to sleep peacefully in his arms; Virak thought it was best that they just rest to let her body heal properly, but they were couldn't keeping their hand from each other body.

In the morning, the Elder took them to her parent house to ask for their forgiveness and their blessing for their married ceremony that will take place in few weeks. There was another crying session for Tev and her mother, and with Tev and Virak lay at their feet begging for mercy, and after some pleading speeches from them and the Elder her parent gave in, and then they called all of her sibling come to congratulate them.

At the very next day, the Elder started to make all the arrangements necessary to prepare for their married ceremony; for the next two and a half weeks, it was a happiest time for both of them ever since they met at the river bank during Loy Kra Tong, they took his friend advice in letting their job responsibility, and hired two women as Tev's servant.

It was the best decision they had made, and that will leave them free to prepare for their wedding and their pursue of happiness by frequently having picnic in the old grow forest, visiting the goat barn more often than necessary, and making love every chance they got everywhere day and night to make up for lost time.

They had a few blissful weeks day and night together at the farm, and then there were two days away from their big wedding day, her relatives and guests were starting to arrive from the distant places, the big tent was erected and decorated.

In the early morning, Virak sat under their front porch waiting for Tev; he was lost in his thought thinking about the last few weeks that they were together they were inseparable Tev refused to leave his side even for a moment. That morning, Virak felt like something was amiss, the air was at a standstill and the animals did not make a lot of noises like they used to; he felt like something was waiting to happen any moment, and then he got up walking back toward the door to look for Tev because he was kind of missing her to be by his side at all time.

Two government vehicles came swiftly to a screeching halt in front of the porch, a few plain clothes and uniformed law enforcement agents jumped out and rush toward Virak; they ordered him to freeze, snapped handcuff on his wrist and walked him toward the cage van. Virak could recognize the bank agent in the first vehicle even he wore the dark sunglass. Maybe the servants had alert Tev of what was going on outside she was rushing out and shouted.

"Wait! Wait a moment please! That's my husband!"

The agents quickly shoved Virak into the cage, slammed the door, and tried to take off at high speed but they were unable because there were too crowded at the market already in that early morning. Tev ran after the vehicles while they were honking at the crowed and tried to speed away toward the road, she was shouting and screaming from the top of her lung with tear streaming down her face and her long black hair that adorned with chompa flower flown in the wind.

At a hundred yards away from the farm, Virak saw Tev kneeled in the middle of the empty road, she was crying and wailing with her hand holding her chest, and then she laid her head down on the dirt road; that was the last time Virak ever saw the face of his beloved.

They tried to pass Virak through the process in a hurry by dropping all charges, classified him as a refugee, and shipped him out to the distant refugee camp at the Thai-Cambodian border. A month later, his friend found him at the refugee camp and then he brought Virak to meet the Elder at a restaurant in the border town. They sat at the table ordering some food and drink. First they told Virak how happy Tev was when the Elder told her that he will bring Virak back from the refugee camp, and the farm was progressed so fast that their product was highly in demand that they could not fulfill all of the orders on time, so they were forced to increase the production volume. His friend was happy to tell Virak that he is now his brother in law; he got married with

Tev's sister two weeks ago at the farm. The Elder asked Virak.

"So are you ready to come back to the farm now, I will make a petition letter to get you out of here at all cost because you are the love of my daughter and I want to see her happy again" Virak replied.

"Sir, I would love to live with Tev again but not in Thailand; I would like to ask your permission to take Tev to America where we can live free as equal. Here in Thailand, it doesn't matter how long I live here or how well I can speak Thai I will always be treated as another Cambodian, because that's always the way that people think between our two country, and not all Thai that think of me like you do Sir; I could not put into word enough to thank and appreciate your sympathy and generosity that I will never forget. Somebody may have some problem when I married with Tev they believe I will become the owner of the farm, but for me I care less about the farm, all that I want is to be with Tev, so I think it make sense for us to go to live in America Sir"

"Wait a moment son; you already know that Tev is my only daughter, I beg you not to take her away from me and away from Thailand. I don't think that Tev want to go anywhere away from me and the farm. I forbid you from taking Tev away from Thailand. When you want to come back to live with Tev in the farm we will welcome you, but if you want to take Tev away don't even bother to show up or your live will be in danger"

He got up and leave when his friend who was just stepping out from the restroom walked pass Virak and slipped a piece of paper in his hand. Virak sat at the table a few more minutes to think and recollect himself from what had just happened. He noticed an envelope that the Elder had left on the table he was just about to return to him at the bus stop, but when he found a stack of money in it he believe the elder left it there intentionally. Virak took the money to the camp and put it to good use by buying some food for his group. He hired someone to translate his friend note from Thai to Cambodian for him, and what he wrote.

Dear Brother,

I don't have much time to write this note; I think you are right about not want to come back to the farm because the bank agent who brought the police and the immigration to the farm had sent word that he has a mission to protect the loan money and the property from you. He think it will fall in your hand if you get married with Tev, and he wow to do harm if you ever come back to live in the farm. Tev is very miserable and she is pregnant.

I don't know what to say, I guess technically you should take Tev to over sea because you love each other and she is pregnant with your child, but I want you to think about the old man who loves you just as his own flesh and blood.

Tev is his only pride and joy and I think his threat he means every words of it if you decide to come to take her away from him, and even if she is willing to go with you they will not let her leave the country without her father consent.

Whatever you decide to do I wish you luck and you are always being my friend and my brother, and you have brought lots of things to enrich the lives of our community. My married become a reality sooner because of the job you gave me. I don't think Tev should know about your decision because if she decided to come after you I think the outcome will not be good at all because there are a great odd against you both.

I feel very sorry for you two and I pray to Buddha will protect you whatever you decided to do or wherever you decide to go. Oh by the way, my wife and me we want to adopt your child if Tev agree to do so and I will see to it that your baby will grow up to inherit the farm.

So long my brother,

C14-A Goddess Avatar

The refugee camp at the Thai-Cambodian border was a very volatile place, it formed up with many factions and groups of Cambodian; there were the group of the Navy, the Army, the Khmer rouge, the resistant, the Chinese, the Muslim, and many civilian factions that sympathized with some group or the other, and for those small minority factions, they had to band together for safety in numbers. There were many things that the refugee needed to watch out for because they could get kill or they were just disappeared from the camp without a trace. Virak had to keep his identity hidden and blended in with the small minority of young drifter who had knowledge of the situation and used to work on both sides of the border, and they registered at the camp as fishermen with faked name. The refugees were survived by the help of the humanitarian agencies who brought them some food, medical treatment and the comfort to know that other people who lived out there somewhere in the world were still care about them. Some agencies took the opportunity to serve their own agenda like trying to convert the refugee to Christianity. Some of the men in Virak group were willing to receive baptism so they could receive some extra food to help feeding their group, and they knew that once they became Christian they were on the fast track to be petitioned by some church to go to live in other country in Europe or America. For many of them in our group, they tried in vain to apply for the refugee visa to go to any country away from this Thai border camp, but they were rejected because they did not have any identity card and the camp register shown that they were fishermen instead of they claimed that they were soldiers in the application form. They had no choice but to seek help from the other group; some military officers who could speak foreign language, helped to plead their case and to establish their identity with questions and answers and direct interact with the foreign embassy interviewer.

At the end of 1975, some of them were accepted and granted refugee visa to go to the United States; a week before they had to be moved out from the border camp to an American air base in Thailand called OU Ta Pao where they stayed at a processing camp and eventually where they will fly out from. The last day before leaving the refugee camp, Virak wondered alone on the street of the border town, went to say good bye to some fishermen at the boat dock, and then he went to sit at the seaside restaurant and ordered some Mekong beer and Ka Kai Yam.

Virak sat alone sipping cold beer and having a lit cigarette in his hand, looked far out to the sea horizon and reevaluated his decision of leaving this part of the world that he called home behind. Almost all his thought were evolved around Tev and her baby, he tried to think over many times because he was not sure that he made the right decision or if he did the right thing by just flying away leaving Tev here while she was pregnant with his child; and BT where the hell is he? What is he doing? And why does it take him so long? Or did he make a wrong decision by let BT went onto the different trail with that dying boy soldier? Or should he have done thing differently?

Virak's thought went to Sunthary, Soraya, Grandfather and the people at the jungle village, and wondered what have happened to them now? He hope they live in peace and have a better chance there than the people in the lower land; and the city where his terrifying thought drifted to his young siblings, cousin Kheng and his family, Lady Sovana and Sparkle Eye what have become of them now? And then his thinking came back to Tev and her baby, and he pulled out his friend's note and read the translated part over and over many time trying to reanalyze all the meanings and reasons, so just in case if there was anything that he might have miss.

Virak asked himself should he stay in Thailand, go back to the farm and fight so he can be with Tev, but if he do that it will affect the farm and maybe the whole community; it seem like the outcome will not look good for all of them.

Virak felt tired, he did not want to think about fighting anymore, because he had fought so many odds many times in his young life; he had gained some but he also lost a lot of things and people that he hold dear that it seem like all will be gone forever. While listening to the sound of the gentle waves, Virak looked across the sea toward Cambodia under the dark night sky he shed tear for one last time.

Contingent of refugee from Indochina and Virak were boarded a TWA flight for Anchorage Alaska, and they heard that it was a very cold place; the passengers in the whole flight were comprised of the refugee from Cambodia, Laos and Vietnam; many refugees were concerned and wondered what will the American do to them when they get to the freezing place in Alaska, because there were a lot of rumors in the border camp that the American will use the refugees to clear the mine field by let them walk in front of their arm force.

In Virak's group, they knew right away that was just another one of the communist propaganda, while some other refugees were squared to death, most of them in Virak's group were very happy to get out of Thailand; during the interview, they were asked which country that they want to go to? They told the interviewer that they all want to go to the United States because they believed American pulled Cambodia into this Vietnam conflict before leaving Indochina that was why they lost their country and family to the communist.

So they think that America owe them at least a place to live, but for all and all they were glad to be alive and on their way to live their new life in a new country that they know next to nothing about or what their life will be like?

In flight at mealtime, they were served fresh milk that most of them had no idea that they might have problem with the lactose thing in the milk, so they were joyfully ate and drank anything that were put in front of them; half an hour later after the meal, Virak felt his stomach was convulsing and the digestive tract was churning, and then he hurriedly ran to the nearest toilet, but when he got there alas there were long lines on both aisles and they all had the same condition as his, and the more effort that he tried to hold it there was much stronger force that pushing out from within that cause him to lost his battle there thousands feet up in the air. The area around the restroom then smelled terrible that the flight attendants got some spray cans and they sprayed the daylight in the air around them. When Virak's turn to get in the toilet, he pulled his short off and ditched it.

Despite of all the lactose troubles and the turbulences, their plane land safely at Anchorage airport, and from there the refugees took many smaller different connecting flights to their final destinations. Virak's connecting flight landed in the Midwest at Fort Chaffee, Arkansas.

He stepped off the plane set foot in mainland America; he had only a tee shirt on his back, a pair of shower shoe on his feet, and a pair of blue jean without a red penny in his pocket, and he got no family and no English. The American set up the refugee camp in an Army base at Fort Chaffee where the refugee received some clothing, medical and physical checkup, and the government document processing for their resettlement allover United States. The living areas were divided by nationality and circumstance like disease quarantine and the group of military personnel who wished to return back to their country. There was an occasional fight that broke out between the young men from all side; for Virak's group they let other fight, but they were busy making friend with the Vietnamese women since they were friendly and easy to talk with.

There were not many single Cambodian women in the camp, and some of them that attract their attention they were very protective by their family member who watch over them like a hawk. Virak's group activities were very relaxed at their leisure everyday like sleeping in the barrack, eating at the mess hall, learning English language at the library, and hanging around with the Vietnamese women because they had endless supply of beer and cigarette and since they lost both of their two countries to the communist they seek comfort with each other company in friendship and sexual fulfillment.

One day the Cambodian Christian group who were the newly converted firm believers, tried to coerced Virak's group to go to church even though they knew that they were not that much of a disciple, but they needed them to be there that was just helping to show strength in numbers, because they were scrutinized by the Vietnamese and the American that they were not much of as Christian, and then Virak happened to look at the Vietnamese group to see how well they did behave as Christian, he was surprised to see most of the women in their group who were hanged around with him behind the barrack sharing beer, cigarette and sex, and in here they behave just like little angels.

Virak spent most of his time in the library to learn English because he knew how imported to know the language at the country where he's going to live; that had brought back the memory of the great uncle who said if he want to learn to speak French he should sleep with French woman and if he want to learn how to speak Chinese he should sleep with Chinese woman; here in this country they speak English, but Virak think he should wait until he get out of here to live in the real world before he put the great uncle idea into practice, and for now he was just reading the book and listening to the tape that come with it.

All refugee must choose a volunteer agency that help in their resettlement into the American society that fund by the government; the agency received some amount of money for every refugee that they help by sending them to live temporary with an individual sponsor family; the church group preferred helping big family with a lot of children that Virak guess they hope those young one will become a nice church member in the future. For all the single men in his group, it was difficult to get any sponsor, so they were the last group to leave the camp for resettlement process.

Some American group of association or an individual family took advantage of this situation by sponsoring a group of young single man so they could receive compensation from the government, and then they put the refugees to work for their business establishment for a meager wage. Some refugee who received genuine help from their sponsor or the concern American community, they were fare much better than the rest by getting good job with decent pay that enable them to thrive in the society.

Virak belong to the category of the unfortunate few with the restless soul, and he found himself bouncing from place to place that made him feel like he was a drifter all over again, actually he was still a drifter by any definition. A church group in Los Angeles sponsored some group of young single men from Cambodia and Vietnam; they put them to stay in a rundown hotel and had them work to fix the same hotel just to pay for their room and board with no money changing hand at all.

The refugee were unhappy with the situation so they protested; the Vietnamese group moved out of the hotel completely by their community leader, but for the Cambodian they did not have any community organization whatsoever so they just stayed at that hotel and work there to pay for their room and board, and they also kept reminding the sponsor that they want to get a real job. Sometime the sponsor tried to make the refugee go to church on Sunday but most of them refused to go; and most of the time the food that they provided for them was hardly enough.

One day the refugee appointed one of their own as a cook since he claimed that he can cook some Chinese and French food, so then they gave him some money to buy some stuff from the supermarket and wiped up some dishes. He stirs fried some broccoli with some mysterious meat from the can and thrown in some spice and soy sauce; the food was sure smell delicious so they invited a church member who came to visit them to share their meal; after the meal the church member saw the empty can in the trash and then he said.

"Congratulation for your new dog, let me see what kind of dog is that?"

"What did you just say? We don't have any dog"

"Oh really, but I see this empty can of dog food I thought that you all have a dog"

"Oh no is that dog food, we'd just ate that thing the cook had stirs fried with broccoli"

The church member held his mouth and ran to the bathroom and vomited his guts out, since then they had demoted the cook. The church had the decency of sending the refugee to study English couple days a week at a school where there were full of student from many different countries. Then they were fortunate to get acquainted with the lovely women from Latin America and Eastern Europe whom the refugee admired their full and curvy body; almost every one of them was a good cook and some dish like the Arose con pollo, and they were insatiable in bed that we had enjoyed their taco tremendously.

One day, the hotel owner and the church had enough of them so they sent some trouble maker to get some job at the factory of their associate in Las Vegas to replace their cheap labor illegal alien workers who were napped by the immigration. When they got there, Virak knew that they were the legal substitutes but it was all right with them because they were glad to get out of that rundown cheap hotel and came to live at a new place working in a real job. The refugees were put to stay in the illegal alien old apartment; it was fully furnished and it seem like the occupants were leaving in a hurry because their clothes were still in the closet, the bed were not made and dirty dishes were still in the sink. The factory owner told them to throw away anything that they do not want, but the refugees kept all of the illegal immigrant personal belonging in one of the closet just in case they might return to claim them.

After the long day of hard work at the factory, Virak felt tired and bored, so he flipped through the record albums that the alien workers left behind; there were most of Mexican music albums and some of the country music from singer like Willie Nelson, Johnny Cash and Patsy Cline; Virak started to listened to these music and wonder about the people life from the different culture. Suddenly, there was a loud knock at the front door, and when Virak unlocked the door was burst open and a unit of man in uniform rushed pass him into the apartment shouting some word in Spanish with one of them held him to the wall and ask him something in Spanish, and after Virak told him that he did not understand what they said and Virak asked them what was going on, and then the agent shouted to his men that the group don't understand Spanish;

they gathered all of the refugee into the living room and with a group of their neighbor looked at them from the outside, the uniform officers asked where they came from and demanded to see their document. After the refugees shown them the I-94 card that they received from the immigration service at the refugee camp in Fort Chaffee, the agents left their apartment and told their neighbor that they were documented aliens the refugee from Cambodia, but despite the officer explanation their neighbors still shown their displeasure and they said that they do not want these kind of people live among them in their neighborhood. Virak clearly understood what they said but he did not yet had enough English language skill to reply or make any comment back to them, and then he just accepted at the time that he was a refugee an alien who came to live in their home country that these Americans could say to him whatever they like for the time being, because these Americans were ignorance or knew very little of what their government had done, and he believe America still owed him a place to live free because American government was responsible for dragging Cambodia into the Vietnam war, and then they were just quitted fighting, made an exit withdrawal from the war at their convenience, and they abandoned them so call friends and allies to the communist who killed their families and destroyed their home. Yes, that was the reason why he came to the United States of America, he was told that this is a free country and he will stay anywhere he damn please, and if these neighbors did not like that he's being here screw them.

At that time, Virak put everything behind, worked hard at the factory tried to make a living and learned to live peacefully his new life in American society. Then he tried to quit smoking and drinking, and he also had seen the excitement at the casino but he had no interest in gambling or seeing anything at all since at that time he was trying to live right as an example to others people around him, but the loneliness that dawned on him in living without any support structure like trusted family and close friend, he felt like he was lost in the wilderness.

One day, he felt some pain in his stomach and it was getting worst every day. The factory owner sent him back to his sponsor in Los Angeles because he did not have any medical insurance. The doctor told Virak that he got ulcer and the cause of his problem for not dropping the crap regularly and the insufficiency of fluid intake. An old china man told Virak that in his case he need to change the way he live while lacking support from family and friend. So after the doctor prescription did not work effectively, Virak requested to go back to Las Vegas; he sat in the living room listening to Willie Nelson song and trying to figure out what need to be change in his way of living, yes he believed everything in his whole life style that needs to be change ASAP. Virak guessed he tried foolishly to be a good boy by working hard, quit smoking and drinking, and then he realized it did not work because he needed an avenue for the release of the everyday stress. Yes, he need to get back to smoking and drinking and busting his nuts somewhere; his common sense tried to hold him back stopping him from plunging in a hurry by taking one step at a time.

Virak walked a few miles on the desert track along the road to a store to buy some steak, beer, cigarette, fruit, cheese and some other good tasting junk food; on the way back, he was stopped twice by the immigration agent who demand to see his document paper.

And when he got back to the apartment he emptied a beer in the flash, lit a cigarette and cook the steak; and while he was munching the junk food he realized that there were mostly poorly dressed immigrant worker and him who walked along the road in that open desert, and the rest of the world they were driving the vehicles, and then Virak looked at himself in the mirror to see he wore the clothing that were issued to him from the refugee camp in Arkansas ,they were so similar to those of the immigrant workers on the desert track. So he made a mental note that this need to be change.

One Friday evening after receiving his paycheck, Virak took a taxi to the casino with an intention to live an exciting life on the fast lane; he gambled away his paycheck with disregard for winning or losing, and he was indulged with the free foods, drinks and cigarettes. In that exciting night, Virak only remembered that he drank a lot of alcohol, had won some money and made lots of friend who took him to see many places.

They introduced him to some night life, glamorous show and some women. At the next day, Virak woke up in the afternoon with a very bad hangover that he could hardly raise his head off the pillow, and he still wore the clothes that he had on from last night; there were boxes, bags and leather jacket strewn all over the floor in his room. It took Virak a lots of effort to get himself up off his bed, he cursed at himself for not knowing his limitation for drinking too much alcohol beverages in one night, but on the other hand he tried to justify that it was all right to drink, because doctor order that he needed to have a sufficient fluid intake, and then he correct himself that if he drank more of the non alcohol beverage so that he didn't have to be a drunken fool. Virak took a long hot shower, ate some food, and lied down on the couch listening to some Mexican music; it seemed to be an appropriate music for the moment since his head was ringing so it didn't matter if he did not understand anything they sang.

Suddenly, the feeling of ringing was more intense, Virak thought it was probably caused by the wailing in the Mariachi song, so he turned off the music but the ringing was still echoed in his head, and then the ringing sound turned to knocking sound at the front door. When Virak opened the door there stood a strikingly beautiful blond hair lady in her mid twenty, she had a pair of piercing iced blue eye, tied her long blond hair in a knot behind her head, and she wore a long kaki trench coat and a pair of black leather boot; the smell of the French cologne from her body, was kind of helping to clear some cobweb from his head, and he started to ask her.

"Hi, yes Mme may I help you?" She stepped inside with an air of authority, closed the door behind her and then she said.

"How can you help me? You can't even help yourself. Hi, my name is H, and I brought you home last night with a prostitute that you had paid for and then she left when you vomited on the side of the road, remember?"

"No Mme, I did not remember anything from last night nor any name or face; I am sorry, I must have drunk too much alcohol"

"No kidding, I wouldn't surprise at all the way you drank last night. Anyway, I just drop by to see that you are all right and to show you your money that I stashed in your closet" She pulled out a stack of one hundred dollar bills from the closet and she handed it to Virak.

"I did not remember that I win that much money" Without counting the money, Virak split the stack in half, put one haft back in the closet and handed the other half to her, but she refused it and she said.

"The way you played in that drunken state last night, it was unbelievably that you still win and walked away from the casino with that much money and that was why those shady characters roamed around you like flies including that prostitute that you're unashamedly paid for in the middle of the casino. No, I don't want your money just keep it so you can pay the prostitute"

"No Mme, it is not my habit to pay anybody for sex; last night, I did not remember what I have done and I did not expect to win anything at all"

"What do you mean you didn't expect to win? You probably won around ten or twenty thousand dollars at least, despite what you'd spent and gave away to all those people and the prostitute, and you'd bought all these things here"

"No Mme, I seriously did not expect to win anything at all; I have stomach ulcer and I was advised by a china man to change my life style, and so last night was the first time that I ever went to the casino to have a good time and it doesn't matter if I'd gamble away that paycheck. I am grateful for your kindness that you've help to bring me home safely, I hope you accept some of these money I didn't feel like it's entirely mine"

"All right if you insist and if it'll make you feel better, I'll accept it but at any time in the future when you need it you always can come to ask it back from me"

She said goodbye and left; Virak got no idea who she was or where she live but it did not matter he did not intent to get it back it was considered a gift. He went to work regularly and stayed sober during the workdays, but when the weekend started on Friday evening Virak hurriedly freshen up and changed his clothes in the flash like a chameleon, he dressed up in the new clothes that he'd bought like the silk shirt, tie, boots and leather jacket, and then he grabbed a handful of one hundred dollar bill from the stack and went straight to the casino; first Virak had a nice dinner at the food court or one of the restaurants at the casino, and he finished a few beers before started to gamble. Virak did not have much knowledge about all the games that they have there, and for most of the time he like to play the roulette, since it sounded so simple to play that he just put his money on either the red or black areas and numbers, and after he win some money like a few thousand dollars he will move to the next casinos up and down the strip.

In about a month time his winning streak was on the decline, and during that time he won a lots of money that he had almost fill up a shoe box with one hundred dollar bills, Virak did not know how much money in it because he never bother to count them. He had made a lot of friends and met a lot of women who always want some of his money while he was under the influence, then he did not mind to let them have some because those winning money was very easy to come by; and at some point he was contemplated the idea of getting his own place and a car, but when his luck was running out and the shoe box was emptied out down low to the bottom, so did all the friends and the women were disappeared, and the plan for owning a new place and a car was evaporate into thin air; the only thing good came out of this was his stomach ulcer was remarkably healed.

Since then, Virak quitted all of the gambling and partying activities but he still go to the casino on the weekend to eat, drink and enjoy the night live. Now a day, Virak usually walked back home from the casino under the orange street light along the boulevard, since his apartment was just a few miles from the strip.

There were many vehicles of the immigration service agent cruising along the boulevard, because there were many immigrant workers walking along the sidewalk to and fro the casinos even at that hour pass midnight; the vehicles were just slow down and then passing him by, Virak guessed they had recognized him by now since they had stopped him to check his document many time before, or maybe he dressed different from the immigrant workers among the pedestrians, but they were always taking a hard look at them before they moved on; Virak knew that they were just doing their job but they made him feel annoying and frustrating that sometime he turned and just sped away into the dark desert to see how they will react. It was sure enough, the immigration agents turned their vehicles around chasing Virak with the searching strobe lights were pointing on his back, while he stood urinating in the middle of the open desert; after they had verified his document paper they shown their displeasures and then they asked.

"Why were you running for?"

"I exercise my legs"

"You should exercise your legs somewhere else and you better not running in the dark like that next time Boy; that you might get hurt or bitten by rattle snake"

"Thank officer for the warning, but I am all right and beside I will recognize a snake when I see one" An agent came to stand in front of Virak and looked sharply in his eyes, and then the agent said.

"Did you just call me a snake? Boy"

"No, I did not call you a snake and I am not a boy"

"Why do you look at me when you speak?"

"And why not you are looking at me when you speak to me?"

"Because you aliens supposed to keep your eyes on the ground when you are speaking to an officer, do you understand, Boy?"

"This is a free country and certainly not this alien, do you understand Officer?" The agent turned red and sweaty, and then Virak was looking up at a tall white man face but his side vision paid close attention to the agent's shaky hand that held on tight to the pistol grip of his weapon; the other agents held his hand and pulled him away, because there were many people and police squad car were looking on from the boulevard.

After they all left, Virak got back on the boulevard and continued to walk back to his apartment under the desert chilly dark night sky; then he complained silently his grievances to the Gods and Goddesses.

"I pray to all Gods and Goddesses, hear me Oh Lord Visnu, I am tired of cross path with these racist people with one tract mind that full of hatred. Lord what have I done to deserve all these nonsense? I had set up the Bujea offering to all of you Lord, it may not be authentic, since I am thousand miles away from home but at least I try, and if you had done to protect me from harm please accept my thanks and appreciations. And I would like to appeal to Lord Siva, Lord Brahma and Goddess Orma, please let me meet only kind heart people who will bring me peace, happiness and pleasure; can you see that I am miserable and lonely, also drunk and horny"

Suddenly, a vehicle slowed down at Virak's side and blew horn, he thought Oh Lord not again, and when he turned to look at a beautiful face of a blond hair lady that was H who looked at him through the window of her vehicle.

"Hi, what in the world are you doing walk on the street in the middle of the night?"

"Oh Hi… UHH … H, I am going home"

"Hop in, I will drop you off" Virak got in the vehicle, turned to the outside window, smiled at the Goddess Orma, and told her silently in his mind that he will set up a Bujea offering to her when he get home. H said she was just got off work but tonight she did not feel like want to go to her apartment; that was why she turned to that boulevard and then she saw Virak from a distant away.

"Are you still going to the casino and gamble your money away? And after winning now you walk around looking for prostitute?"

"First yes I still go to the casino on the weekend to enjoy the food and the nightlife, and second no I don't gamble anymore because my luck was running out, and third no I am not looking for any prostitute; I walk home just to clear my head since I only live a few miles from here, and what is a prostitute suppose to look like anyway? I heard that prostitution is legal in this state, do they wear a name tag?"

"You are kidding me, you are just joking right?"

"No I am not; I am serious because in South Vietnam when I went to train with the Green Beret, and in town there were those Vietnamese girls who worked in those restaurant-bar, they were called hostess, and it was their job to host at the table and go in the back room with American GI; and in the casino here, I saw waitresses who wear the name tag that said hostess, and I wonder if they do the same job as those hostesses in Vietnam"

H suddenly pulled the vehicle to a screeching halt at the curb, she seemed to be angry at something Virak had just said since she turned to face him that he could see anger in her eye; she shown a name tag on her waitress uniform from under her coat that read Hostess.

"What are you trying to imply Mister? Look here I am a waitress but by no mean that I am a prostitute"

"Wait a minute H; I did not try to imply anything honest! I never think that you are a prostitute, never"

"Never!?, That was why when I dropped you off that night you put your hand all over me after your prostitute friend left"

"Come on H I was drunk and I apologized to you the next day since I did not remember a damn thing from that night. Look here H you are a beautiful woman, and any man see you even if he is drunk or not will always want to put his hand on you or fantasize about doing it regardless; and if any man said otherwise I think he is a liar" I thought I had made my point and made her feel better, because she just smiled and continued to drive; and on the way she was lamenting.

"I guess you are right in a way; I am a dancer by profession, and then a year ago I had an accident that I am unable to dance anymore, that is why I have to work as a waitress to pay my bills and school tuition; and I have this old boyfriend who always tried to persuade me to become a call girl, you know girl who sell themselves for money just like the prostitute, it's the same thing, so I can make a lots of money quicker, but anyway thank for your money that I can avoid that fateful decision for a while, and tonight I don't want to go home because he might come to pressure me again"

"H why don't you stay in my room for a while and I will sleep on the couch, I promise you that neither I nor anyone will bother you"

"No thank you, I owe you a lot already and I don't want to bother you anymore, I think I will just get a room at the motel" In front of Virak's apartment, she just wanted to drop him off and drove on to a motel, but he tried to persuade her that it may not be safe for her to be alone at the motel; after a while, she agreed to stay at his place for that night, so Virak helped bring her big suitcase inside and put it by the bed.

After the shower, Virak grabbed a pillow and a blanket and started to go to the living room, but H held the door close and told him to sleep on his bed, and just for one night she could lay some comforter down and sleep on the floor; and then Virak told her that this is his room and he want her sleep on the bed, and he will sleep on the floor; he told her in Cambodia where he came from he was in the military, and he had slept in the worst possible place that she could imagine, in here for him to sleep on the carpet at the corner of the same room smelling the French cologne from her body, it just like sleeping in the palace.

She sat on the bed in a regal posture with her long splendid legs pointed out from the opening of her robe, she watched Virak set up his Bujea for offering to the Gods, and she told him about her life here in Las Vegas that she had only one more year to graduate and her family home in Northern state where she always feel loved and welcome but she want to make it on her own here in Las Vegas where she could work to pay for her tuition, and then she asked Virak.

"What do you think I should do?"

"I think you should go back to your home to finish your last year in university there where you will live among those who love you, they are your element of support and I understand that you don't have to pay for the room and board there"

"No, I don't have to pay that much like here, but there are not many jobs there, here people spend money, and I can make money easily here"

"Yes, that's right you may make money from your customers very easily here, but most of them want to lay their hand on you; there are a lots of temptation here, and those people around you might persuade and drag you away from your goal your reality to do something that you might not want to do and will regret in the future don't you think?" Virak went to the closet and pulled out the shoebox and gave it to her.

"Here take it, there are maybe six or seven thousand dollars left in that box, it may or may not be enough for your tuition, but take it get out of Las Vegas; I guess at home you probably finish your goal quicker there" H held the box with both hands with her mouth and her eyes wide open, she was speechless and kept looking between the box and Virak, and then she said.

"What is a matter with you? Every time I meet you, you throw money at me, and what do you want from me? "

"No I want nothing from you, ever since I come to this country everybody I'd met, are always want something from me, since you are the only one who don't want anything from me, and you had shown up to help me in time of trouble just like a guardian angel. Please take it; it was just like I've told you before the winning and the money don't mean anything to me; I was just tried to heal myself from ulcer by following an old china man advice"

"And you why don't you go home somewhere to your love one?"

"I cannot go back home to Cambodia now, the communist take away my home, after the American withdrawn from the war in Vietnam there it was just like they handed over those three countries to the communist, and as of now I have no idea where they are or what become of them"

H had tear welled up in her eyes, dropped the box on the bed, came to kneel in front of Virak, held his head, and slowly pulled his face into her bosom. Virak did not know how to react because it was happened so quickly, and then he just tried to breathe normally in between her cleavage.

He was intoxicated by the fragrance of the French cologne and the scent of her womanly body that made him become speechless and sported a raging erection between his legs; the whole surrounding was like a blur, Virak guessed at that moment he felt dizzy because all of his blood rushed down to between his leg and that may cause the oxygen shortage in his brain.

A moment later, she released his head but she still sat on the comforter watching him finish setup his offering. Virak put a metal tray on a cardboard box with a big deep plate in the middle, and then he lit up some candles around the plate and cut some fruits to arrange in the middle of the plate, and then beside the distraction of her French cologne, she asked him to explain everything to her.

"I set up a Bujea is an offering to the Gods and Goddesses"

"What are Gods and Goddesses?"

"The Hindu god"

"I thought that Cambodia main religion is Buddhism"

"Yes but I am a minority few or an almost extinct one of a kind"

"And what are the fruit for?"

"Ok let me explain, the grape in the plate is offer to Lord Visnu the builder God, the banana I had cut part of it so it could stand in the middle of the plate and it represent the Lord Siva Linga his genital, and the half peach here next to the Linga, it represent the Yoni of Goddess her genital.

Ok now let me turn off the light for a minute and the candles around the plate represent the universe in an eggshell around the Gods of creation; here I'd melted a stick of butter that I have on hand, and when I pour it on the Linga with a prayer it flow down through the Yoni of the Goddess; it signify the God and Goddess had achieved their climaxes, the creators had created, and the God and Goddess energy had climaxed in combined forces, and the fruitful pray was answer to the prayer, and when the prayer make the Bujea offering to the God and Goddess, and now the universe have come in full circle; and this is it"

"That is beautiful and what did you pray for?"

"Do I have to tell you everything?"

"Its matter of fact yes, I sleep in your bed and you had feel me up whether you like it or not Mister, I need to know everything"

"Actually, I did not pray I was kind of complain to the Gods and Goddesses"

"And, what did you complain about?"

"Well, I complained about people that God had sent my way were mostly the one tract mind full of hatred in their heart, and that will make the world we live in become an imbalanced evil place that will be unsuitable for decent human habitat; and then, I asked the Goddess Orma to send the kind heart and pleasant angel my way, and then you came by my side a few seconds later"

"Oh, I had read somewhere they call it Pujea, they use a lot of saffron color flower garland and perfume, do you got those too?"

"Yes, I do I got some dandelion flowers from the sidewalk here and the fragrance of your perfume is sufficient"

"Do you really believe in God and Goddess?"

"Actually, I'm not a religious type, and I'm not sure or certain one hundred percent, but there were many inexplicable coincident that had happened to me. For me, I don't really believe in anything that I cannot explain but since I'm alone in this uncertain world I need to talk and confer with something"

"Are you done with the God things, can we eat the fruit?"

"Yes, I think so" H picked up the banana that supposed to be God penis and put it in her mouth, and with her other hand she picked up the half peach that represent the Goddess thing put in his; it was still tasted all right despite it drenched in melted butter, Virak think next time he should use cream instead. And after the Bujea, she was just sitting quietly in deep thought looking at the flickered candle light, and then Virak broke the silent by asking her.

"So, what are you going to do?"

"I think I will take your advice and move back home by next month, but I don't want to go back to my apartment at all"

"You can stay here as long as you want"

"You have done so much for me that I couldn't ever thank you enough"

She put her head down on the pillow laid next to Virak that he did not know what to expect, so he went to get the pillow and blanket from the bed to cover her and lay to sleep by her side. Virak woke up in the morning and he could feel her soft and warm body snuggled up at his side; even before he opened his eye it felt so sublimely comfortable that he did not want to move even though he had an urge to go to the bathroom.

That first day, they were together they went to her place to get the rest of her belonging, and she gave the key to her friend who will move in to take over the place. They went to have their midmorning brunch at the Caesar Palace, and were amazed when they came back to the table from the different direction their plate had almost exactly the same items, they had loch smoked salmon, honeydew, cantaloupe, grape and croissant; and she had a great idea by suggesting that they should wash it down with some champagne. After the meal, they went to a park by a lakeside, and then they submersed in the desert solitude, and listened to the windblown from the mountain.

In the evening, they were talking late into the night telling each other about their life stories; she told him about her life in small town Northern state where she grew up and her life in Vegas as a dancer; Virak told her about his life in Cambodia, about the war and the battles that he had fought, and the profound memory of life in the jungle. It was passed midnight; Virak started to slide down on the comforter and said goodnight to her, she got up and went to the bed, and he thought that night will not be a warm, soft and comfortable night anymore, but he was wrong when he felt her pillow dropped next to his, and then she pulled his arm out, laid her head on it and pulled the blanket to cover them both.

They spent another cozy night on the floor again, and the only thing different was that he felt her sharp hard nipples speared his rib through the thin material of her night gown, that had made him feel restless all night, but he tried painfully hard to restrain himself because he thought that he did not want to take advantage of her.

At the next morning, she got up with a frown on her face. That night before they get ready for bed, she went to sit on the bed with her arms fold in front of her, and she took a hard look at Virak just like she tried to figure him out, and he could see her serious straight face, and her eye swept all over him searching, and then finally, she said.

"I couldn't figure it out why when the first time you saw me you put your hand all over me, and now I sleep in your arm you are so passive that it's just like you don't even see me, why?"

"Maybe because I am not drunk and I don't want you to think that I take advantage of you at your vulnerable time, but I hold your back"

"That is not what I'm talking about, Ok Mister that's enough and be prepared; how about I am going to take advantage of you, just stands by"

Virak could not believe his eyes of what will happen next, he was in a trance and he couldn't take his eye off her. H stood up and shed all her clothes except her black high heel, and after she stood there a moment for him to admire the full length of her naked body, and then she walked slowly toward the comforter, stepped over his chest, and stood tall over him. His eye followed from her high heel up to looked at a pair of her long slender leg of a dancer that was towered over him; the candle light casted an amber ambient at the dimension of the moment.

Virak ran his hands up her smooth legs looking up at the junction triangle, and he saw the mount of two thick lips that formed a vertical pink slit with the head of her pink tamarind seed peaked out at the top and a patch of golden flees that shimmered above. Virak kissed her legs on his way up to the junction for a moment, but she pushed him down on his back and squat down to seat her sex on his lips that all he could see was the blurred image of the golden hue......Virak paused in between her thighs for a moment to admire the artistic form of her body, it was a magnificent sight with those high heels as the icing on the cake. Yes exactly, those high heels should not make for walking since they looked divined when they kicked up in the air just like that, and at that time Virak believed she was an avatar of the Goddess herself...... They kept going on and off until late at night and that he had to call sick for the rest of the week and claimed that his ulcer was relapsed.

In the last three weeks of her stay with him; there was never a day gone by that they did not make love at least twice a day, until she returned to her home. In the last few days before her departure, H took her vehicle to the shop to have it tune up, went shopping for some clothes and gift for her family, and asked Virak to set up a Pujea offering to the Goddess who granted her multiple orgasms that she seldom had before in her life. At night, they lay naked in bed holding each other after they made love; and then she gave him her address and phone number of her home and she told him to keep in touch and come to look for her if he ever needed anything. On the day of her departure, until almost noon that she decided to leave; they hugged, shed some tear, and then she drove away from his life forever.

After her vehicle was disappeared from sight, Virak felt like he had lost a piece of his heart; he searched deep in his soul for a reason and circumstance that they should be together forever but he couldn't. Virak thought it was to the best of her interest for her to finish her education in Northern state first, and then time will tell if they mean to be together again.

In his bedroom, he closed all the window blind to keep it dark, lit up some candles. Under the flickering amber light, Virak looked at the dent spots on the sheetrock wall that H had kicked with her high heel in the moment of her intense orgasm, and he could still strongly smell her body scent mixed with the fragrance of the French cologne that she left a full bottle on the nightstand. And then he prayed "Oh Lord Visnu, I start to miss her so much already, would you please protect her from harms, let her make a safe journey home, and grant her wish of finishing her education".

C15-Global Celestial Nymphs

The Crusader

A friend who lives in New York City asked Virak if he want to move to over there, Virak agreed immediately without any hesitation. He said his farewell to everybody and took a flight to New York City in the middle of winter in 1976.

His friend was sponsor by a church that had members from around the world; Virak enjoyed their friendship and appreciated their generosity and support. During summer, Virak went along with the young missionaries to help them spread the word of God to people around the city, but when it come to a time for him to get baptize he stepped back out because he did not feel right since all they concerned about were aggressively tried to convert his soul to something that he was not sure about; they kept saying that he supposed to believe wholeheartedly with no question ask, and that idea was hard for Virak to agree with since he was trained in anticommunist propaganda and went around Cambodia tried to persuade people in the country of not to believe in anything that they heard or seen that they could not explain with a reasonable fact.

Virak had read books from many different sources and subjects of religions, sciences and philosophies that he could get a hold of, and he had come to a conclusion that all religion teach people by many means of how to become good or better being, to do good deed, to be tolerant and generous to those who are different, to have compassion toward others, to respect the temporary world that they live in etc... But through history, people interpreted religious belief catered to their own need and convenience, and then they labeled others who are different from them as evil.

Virak tried to find a way to live on his own independently, and then a young missionary who was a college student from the upper central state; she was sent to the inner city to serve the church and spread God's word. She had come along with Virak to explore around the city and their long talk on the subway train had made them become a fast close friend. She told him about her beautiful life in the small town USA, her boyfriend's love, her bible college that was nurtured by the grace of God where Virak could come to study to get a college degree with the help of the church if he received God into his heart. Her last sentence was kind of a wakeup call that pulled Virak back to his sense, and in his reality if he was not mistaken this pretty girl with gentle face and sparkle green eye that was full of compassion, was trying to convert him to Christianity; she had done so well that at the beginning he thought it was a genuine friendship that was born out of sympathy and understanding.

Virak told her about his life in Cambodia, the culture and the religious belief, the people and their way of life; she had compared to her life in her bible college where she had study about many different religions, and then Virak told her that what she had learned was just a drop in the bucket and not until she have live through to immerse in the culture of the people who practice the religion then she might come to an understanding and admire what that was all about; and it was just like him that he had live in her culture and understand her religious belief that he become admire and respect, and still he did not want to convert her to become anything else or to believe in anything different, but why should she want to convert him?

Virak think it was the doctrine of her religion that had teach her to look at other religions and believes as unrealistic or false belief that need to be converted and guide to the light of God in order to save their soul from the eternal burning hell. In his case, she firmly believed that he was a lost soul that need to be save and she saw herself as a staunched crusader a God's soldier in shining armor fight all evil in the name of the holy cross.

On a sunny day, The young crusader and Virak took the subway to Manhattan (One of the five borough of New York City) While other missionaries did their other works, she made the saving of his soul to be her final and ultimate task for God crusade before she return back to her home, and present his soul as a trophy in God glory.

It seemed like a great plan in her own mind, but Virak think God worked his mysterious way with his own agenda, and he had other plan in store for them. On the way, they discussed about God (Her God the way she see him) and Christ the savior all the way; they went to visit the statue of liberty on the island and while they were on the ferry Virak told her something about himself. he told her that his name in Pali and Cambodian language mean Live Free, and that's his love of freedom he'll fight to live free from any oppression or restriction in his life and his belief, and he believe this is God intend for him to live free in his glory and if what he believe in or anything he didn't believe in he think God will understand because that was his intention all along.

In another word, God and him they are in good term whatever God might be as long as he know between right and wrong, good and bad, do no harm or have any ill intend toward others physically or mentally, and fight to protect his freedom at all cost. The young crusader told Virak that he sounded like an American; he said "So be it".

In Central Park, they walked along the trail around the lake side watching lovers expressed their feeling toward each other verbally and physically among the flower bushes; the atmosphere of the episodes had made them sensed the rush of a beautiful feeling at the moment in time.

They ceased talking and all of their senses were drawn toward one another, and then while looking at her emerald green eyes, Virak told her that how lovely she look even without any makeup on. For the moment, Virak think that maybe fate or God intention had brought them together; he held her waist, pulled her into his embrace, and then they kissed. he wrapped his arms around her slender body, and with her arms over his shoulder they were lost in their own little world; he sensed that she could feel his erection pressed against the mount between her legs, and then she put her hand on his chest and said that she want to sit down; he could feel and sense her desire, and they went to sit on a bench overlook the lake and then she said.

"We shouldn't do this I promise myself to save my virginity until I get married"

"Of course, I understand completely, and we will not do anything that you don't want to do. We just kiss and I know you feel God gift of pleasure in our existence as human being. This is not sin, its God intend for us to feel love and pleasure"

Inside an apartment that Virak borrowed from a coworker, the young crusader got undressed and lie on a king size bed; Virak held her in his arms and kissed her lips, her cleavage and her mound......

On the subway train back to the church, she was looking kind of worry it shown on her face that Virak had seen many times on the face of the girls who just lose their virginity; he guessed the look shown the guilt that she may have felt that she had done something wrong instead of think of it as a passage of life and time in the universe.

The Missionary Chaperone

For the next few days, they acted normal and Virak was away from her for a while because she got a new assignment somewhere else and he gave her sometime to heal. Then Virak was asked by an older lady who came with the missionary group, she was about in her thirty as an aunt to one of the young missionary and came along as kind of a chaperone, and the church let her stayed in a small room alone in the missionary housing while the rest were segregated by sex and stay in the three to four men rooms; she help to do some work around the church kitchen on the weekend but most of the time she went out to town on her own.

Every way in her manner shown that she was kind of a classy lady with a deeply religious inclined and Virak had seen her teaching the Sunday school classes to young people; Virak had always shown her with respect, but to his wondering eye he could see her curvy body under those loose clothing and detect her sexy smoldering violet eye under her thick rim glass.

Everyone went around the city to spread God word and had an assignment to do some task, but Virak was the only one who did not have any assignment or commit to do anything, so the lady put him to work as her helper because she had to do a lot of shopping for food in bulk for the church kitchen, so Virak had to work with her, moved a lot of heavy food items, and tack along with her all over the city one step behind watching her sexy hip and curvy butt.

Sometime later, she caught his wondering eyes burned the spot on her butt and noticed the bulging erection in his pant, and then she was just smiled, but she seriously warned him to get rid of those evil thought from his head and his heart for Christ sake, and she also kept reminding him that she was a very much older married lady; Virak profusely apologized to her and told her that he never intended to have any evil thought in his head, but he could not help and he promised her that he will try harder in the future.

She accepted his apology and told him to relax since he had a sad face of trying to fight off evil thought with the bulging in his pant was still sticking out, and she said she was flattered that her body still had an effect on young man. After the incident, they forgot of what had happened and what they had talked about, and Virak kept his promise to behave.

A week before her return home, the lady asked Virak to accompany her on an unofficial shopping trip to downtown Manhattan; her unusual provocative attire that shown her deep cleavage and smooth round butt. On their return trip, they were in the middle of the rush hour, so the subway station was jam packed with all the regular commuters who rushed to return home after a hard day work at the office in Manhattan.

Virak leaded the way getting in the crowded subway train car and since there was no seat available he let her stand with her back lean against the far side door with him stood right in front of her. After a few stops at the various stations, there were more and more people getting on than getting off, so the car was packing tighter and the new commuters pressured behind Virak's back made her full breasts cushioned softly on his chest.

Virak turned his eye looking up to the roof of the car to avoid her mesmerizing violet eyes that were starring through his skull only a few inches away, but then his most fear inevitable thing was starting to happen; her warm womanly body that pressed softly on his chest, and her scent that was inexplicably very potent rising from between her cleavage, had made him feel intoxicated with a raging hard on pressing against her loin.

They both tried hard to ignore the effect and they tried to disengage but in this helpless situation they got no room to maneuver, so they were just stood still with Virak suffered silently under the tremendous pressure of a raging erection that tried to stretch out. Virak finally turned to look at her face, shrugged his shoulder.

Followed by the train motion his erection rubbed madly on her heat up loin; and he knew very well the desire passion of the moment that could have an effect on woman body whether she want it or not, but woman is the master of concealment of her emotion just like this lady, he could not tell by just looking at her face, but the steamy heat from her loin and her hard nipples that started to stab on his chest, were not lied about the desire of her passion within.

When the train came to a dark spot where all lights were turned off for a moment, Virak pulled her close and planted a soft kiss on her lips, and when the lights came back on she pulled back and whispered to him with a serious face.

"What do you think you are doing?"

"Kissing you, I am sorry I could not help"

And he did again and again at the next lights out spots until they got back to the church. It was getting dark and the housing was quiet Virak guessed the missionaries were still out preaching. At her door, she unlocked and turned to thank

Virak for helping her, and then she said goodbye and stepped into her room; Virak did not replied, just stepped in right behind her, pushed the door locked, pulled her in his arms and kissed her rapturously.

She acted surprised and tried to push him off by saying that everybody will be in the building any minute, he held her tight, pushed his hand through her top to feel her hard nipples, and told her not to worry that he will leave discreetly by the fire escape outside her window, and when he slid his hand through the waist band of her panty down to her tamarind seed she relaxed and spread open her legs……

For the next few days, she tried to avoid Virak but he insisted that was his assignment to follow her, so in that after noon and every afternoon after that until the day she fly out of New York City, he caught her and pulled her into the church storage room after all the cleanup crew left; he laid her on the bean sack thrown her skirt up, pulled her panty down, and feel up her gap that always wet with anticipation of excitement…… And someday at the same evening, he had a rendezvous with the young crusader to talk and make love until late at night.

On the day of their departure, Virak went along to send them off at JFK airport; on the plane the two ladies probably knew that he was already terribly missed them while on the way back to the church.

The English Teacher

The Italian Sausage and the Heirloom Spaghetti Sauce Recipe

After the two ladies returned to their home, Virak felt boring and lost sense of direction; so he just packed his bag, said his thank and appreciation to the reverend and the church ladies in the kitchen, and then he moved out from the church sanctuary and he just drifted away without a clue or direction of where he supposed to go next. Virak took the subway to down town Manhattan and walked around looking for work and a place to stay; he understood why they won't accept him because with all his belonging in his hand he look just like a homeless, and it darned to him realizing and accepting that he was homeless at that moment.

Virak spent the night in the Port Authority bus station to blend in with stranded passengers that made him feel safe and warm because in late August it started getting very cold at night in New York City; then when he woke up the next day all of his belonging was gone.

Somebody had suggested for him to go to the Welfare office to apply for the public assistant; and the office placed him in a one room apartment equipped with a bed, a small refrigerator and a hot plate for cooking, and he also received some food stamp assistant. Virak went around the city everyday looking for work, and some people advised him to buy a newspaper and looking for job in the employment section, so he started to buy the New York Time to read every morning and beside the employment section he found the news from around the world including bleak news from Cambodia.

A week later, Virak woke up in the morning with a depressing mood, heartburn and a knot in his stomach, and that condition had reminded him of his early day in Las Vegas; and it's a warning sign of the stomach ulcer. So he knew he got to react quickly before it's getting worse, Virak started to drink beer and smoke cigarette again that he haven't been done for a while when he live at the church. In the evening, Virak went out to have some steak dinner and then he went to see a movie and enjoy the night life at Time Square on the forty second street.

Over there, he had met and became friend with some guys from the island of Porto Rico and when he told them that he had a hard time looking for work, they were just laughing and said to him.

"You look like us that is why it's hard for you to find a job, and the job that you can get maybe the one that nobody want, and the pay is at the minimum wage for the job like dishwasher, cleaner etc... and if you don't mind you can come to work with us; the pay is cheap to start with and you get a free decent meal"

Virak agreed to go to work with them without any hesitation; and a few week later, when he receive his first paycheck he reported it to the Public Assistant office to get himself off the welfare system and move out from that one room place; his new friend helped him to get a room near the Spanish Harlem and get him enrolled in the English class.

That English class was a newly formed in the middle of the semester, so there were a mixed bag of student with many different levels of English, and from many different background and nationalities.

The teacher was Miss Y she was about twenty five years old with reddish blond hair, green eyes, medium size breast, small waist and full round lips; Virak was enjoy going to her class almost every day after work. One day in class, he was looking and listening to her in his dreamy state of mind, and he heard she asked the student one by one with the same question.

"What do you want to do when you first come to United States of America?"

Virak heard the student answers like some want to be doctor, lawyer, engineer, nurse or soldier, and some want to eat steak, strawberry or chocolate; suddenly she was in front of him, and she bent down to look in his eye that he could see her tight cleavage and smell the scent from her body that made him gone wild and pulled him out from the dreamy state, and then he just answer her whatever speck of idea that came into his mind.

"What I want to do... Uhhh... Make love to a beautiful woman like you"

Many students in the class did not understand what he'd just said, and for some of them who understood they could not believe what they'd just heard and they want him to repeat; most of the guy, they nodded their head in agreement with him and thought it was the best and honest answer, but all of the ladies were frown at him and thought that he was out of his mind; Virak thought the ladies were right that he was definitely out of his mind and he actually out of the line. Virak looked at Miss Y and apologized to her in whisper.

"I'm sorry"

And he looked down on his desk feeling guilty as hell for the rest of the day. After that, Virak straight up his act, paid attention in his study for the rest of the semester, and hope that everything was forgotten or so he thought: did his English improve? Not much, he thought.

At the end of the semester, Miss Y gave each student a grade card that told each one of them their next level of English class to go to in the next semester. It seemed like that Virak's card was at the bottom of the stack, because everybody received their card and left the room to check the next class. Virak stood in front of her alone while she took her time to give him the card; and then her face change from sweet smiling to a firmly serious look that she was sharply looking at him and said.

"Ok, here is your grade card for the next class level, and since this semester is over as we speak we are no longer student teacher, so let me ask you if you still remember your answer to my question early in the beginning of this semester?"

"Yes Mme, I still do"

"Very well, here is my number, how about you give me a call later; I will have some spaghetti and I want you come to taste my tomato sauce from my grandmother recipe"

She gave him a mischievous smile and left the room before he could say anything to her; Virak was surprised and excited at the same time, and then he wondered what will be in store for him.

Virak asked some guys at his work place to see what they think if they were in his situation, some guy said that he need to dress up nice like a gentleman and bring her some flower like a long stem rose, a box of chocolate, a bottle of vine and maybe something French that will set her mood for romance; but some other guy had a completely different point of view.

"When a woman want you to go up to her place that could mean to get together to talk, to have dinner, to go out somewhere or she just want you to go up there to fuck her"

"And so how will I know?" Virak asked.

"Oh yes you will, it's easy to recognize, when you get there if she is alone and not yet dress up or she just get out of her bathtub, and then you may put your hand on her and fuck her silly right on the spot"

Virak thought he should play it safe by dress up nice the best he could, and went to get a bottle of French wine and some flowers at the store nearby, and then he took the subway to her place followed the address that she gave him. At the building of her apartment complex, he pushed the button of her apartment number near the building front door at the ground floor to announce his arrival, and then while he was just standing there waiting for her reply through the intercom Virak could feel his heartbeat racing faster than usual from the anticipation of what will happen in the next moment; and suddenly her voice was chiming in the intercom to verify who he was and then he pulled the door open when he heard the buzzing signal from her.

Inside the building, Virak walked up the stairwell to a few floors above and then he knocked on her front door. When Miss Y opened her door, Virak realized that one of the guys was right; she was still in her bathrobe with her hair wrapped in a bundle of towel on the top of her head, he could see droplets of water were still on her pink skin and the clean smell of the pure scent from her body that had stirred up all of his senses.

They exchanged formality greeting and then he handed her the rose and the vine; she gracefully accepted the gift with a smile on her face and a comment of appreciation, and then she turned leading him to the kitchen where the sublime aroma of the Italian spice from the pot that simmered on the stove, permeated the air mixed with her body scent.

While following right behind her, his eyes were drawn to the movement of her hip that intensify his sexual feeling and he wondered what will look like under that robe, and then she interrupted his train of thought and said to him.

"I am sorry for not yet get myself ready, and look at you; you look very handsome tonight that I almost couldn't recognize you"

"I dress up for you tonight, and you Mme either way you dress even in that bathrobe you are still look extraordinary divine"

She just smiled with a demurred manner and turned to put the rose in a vase with some water; Virak could feel the warmness at his loin by just looking at her round hip from behind; he could not hold himself any longer, so he went behind her and put his hand to hold her hips, pulled her back to his body, and kissed her neck that made her body jolted with an initial surprise; she quickly turned around, thrown her arm over his shoulder, and they started to kiss passionately.

A moment later, she initiated to undress him by ripping his jacket off and thrown it to the floor, and he was very much obliged to get rid of the rest of his clothes and he reached out to untied the belt of her robe; and while she dropped her arms to her side to give him access, he opened her robe and behold the beautiful sight of the English teacher assets of her naked body underneath that it was just like he had imagined.

Virak put his face at her cleavage that he'd been eying since his first day in her class, and tried to lift her to sit on her kitchen table, but she stopped him and reached to turn off the gas burner under the sauce pot and she hop on the low kitchen table and pulled him over between her open thighs......

It was true what they said that life is a long continuous learning process, and since Virak learned better lying down with Miss Y help his English was improving ten folds; he had committed to learn English and many other languages for a long time to come. And he remembered the great uncle word of wisdom that just had been realized.

At some chilly night in the holiday season, they packed a picnic basket with some wine, cheese, salami, bread etc... and went to the Lincoln Center to sit at the fountain in the middle of the square listening to music came from Every Fisher Hall through underground air duck, that performed by some of the symphony orchestra. She sat between his legs with a wool blanket wrapped around both of them, she leaned back against his chest and he wrapped his arms around her body under her breasts to keep warm.

Latinas Nymphs
Y arroz con pollo

Virak occasionally had to move from place to place around the city to find the affordable and suitable place to live; he'd moved through Manhattan, Bronx, Brooklyn, Queen, Coney Island, and Jersey City.

At some point in time of his life, he was fortunate to meet with many Latinas women, and there was a coincidentally long line of Maria or Jennifer, so he had to assign each one of them a special nickname like Long Hair Maria, Nice Butt Maria, Afro Maria, Afro Jenifer, Long leg Jenifer, Gray Eye Maria, Thick Lower Lips Jenifer etc…

There were two Latinas in particular GE Maria and TLL Jenifer, they were the best of friend since childhood and after they'd graduated from high school Jenifer continued her study at the community college, and Maria got a job at the department store where Virak met her on one of his rare shopping trip.

Virak was attracted to her serene gray eyes and he immediately asked her to go out on a date; they were dating for sometime before she spent the night with him at his place, and then she introduced Virak to her best friend Jenifer and her boyfriend. They were double dating with them from that point on at everything they did and everywhere they went like the movie, disco, private party, family function etc…

The two ladies had almost identical body feature, but Jenifer was more slender and curvier hips that always attracted Virak's attention every time whenever all of them were together; sometime later, Maria had noticed Virak little secret of wandering eye, and one day she confronted him with all kind of questions.

"Your eye seem to glue to Jenifer's butt every time we are together, are you attract to her?"

"No, no Baby, I did not looking at her, it was just happened that she came across my line of sight, and you are the one that I am attract to Baby"

"But I am not the only one"

"Uh well yes, you are the one" He lied, he had a man mentality the same as men everywhere, they are normally attract to and intrigue by almost anything that is unattainable, so the only thing he could do was denied everything that she thrown his way; and from that day on, Virak was very careful to watch his every move every time all of them get together, and later on everything seemed forgotten and returned to normal until the time of Jenifer delivery her baby.

Maria and Virak, they used the calendar as birth control, but some time they forgot to pay attention to detail because of the alcohol and the excitement from the disco, so one day the test shown positive, and Maria announced to her friends and family that she was pregnant that took Virak by surprise; since they were catholic to think about abortion was not an option, and so her family and friend coerced Virak to get engage with Maria, but he tried to reason with them that he was too young and he had not make enough money to support a family yet, they told him that he should not worry about money because she could apply for the public assistant just like most of the family around there.

Since Virak was alone it sound good to have his own family there, so they got engaged and moved in together into an apartment near her family; she quit her job and get on welfare, and they lived happily like husband and wife, while Maria and her family tried to teach Virak how to speak Spanish so she could introduced him to her relative on the island of Porto Rico where they plan to have their married ceremony.

It was true that friend always do everything together; a month later, Jenifer was also announcing her pregnancy and her engagement to her boyfriend as well that had brought all four of them very close. Months later, Maria delivered a healthy bouncing baby boy; he was beautiful and looked equally after both of them like a mixed of Asian and Hispanic.

A month later, Jenifer went to the hospital for her delivery; in the next day, Maria received a phone call from the hospital, and then they left their son with her family and went to visit Jenifer; on the way to the hospital Maria said that she was worry because Jenifer's fiancée sounded upset and need to see both of them at the hospital as soon as possible.

In the hospital room, Jenifer looked tired but she was still smiling when she saw them walk in, Virak could not help stole a look at her full jugs while she lay on the hospital bed laughing at her fiancée who sat at a corner quietly sulking, and then she said.

"He is upset because his son doesn't look like him, and I never mention to you all that one of my great grandmother was part Japanese"

And then all hell broke loose when the nurse rolled the crib into the room so the mother can feed the baby, Virak was so surprise to see Jenifer's son look almost an identical twin to his son; Maria was quickly pulling out their son picture from the hospital and put it next to Jenifer baby face, and then she looked to Virak and Jenifer, started to cry out very loud and ran right out of the hospital; Jenifer's fiancée pointed his finger at her and shout out.

"You are a lying bitch"

And then he turned to Virak with anger in his eyes and he grabbed Virak's neck with both hand trying to choke him.

"I am going to kill you, you are an evil man, and you have destroyed our life"

He was seriously trying to kill him, and Virak had to twist one of his fingers to get himself out of his grip; the hospital security guards came to break them up and thrown both of them out.

When Virak arrived at his place, he saw all of his belonging were piled up on the sidewalk, and her family were trying to kill him, that Virak had to protect himself, grabbed his belonging and moved on to other place for the time being to let thing cool down. Later on he went back to visit his son they won't let him see his baby, and when he tried to explain nobody believe him; Virak went to Jenifer place and it was happened the same way, and so after a few time later Virak stopped go back there altogether since they all told him that Maria and Jenifer had taking their son and moving away and they refused to tell him of their where about.

Over a year later, while Virak was on the subway back from work, he saw a familiar face of a lady who was dress up as an office worker, Virak could not believe it was Jenifer that he hardly recognized her that she looked more prettier with her body was still slender but more curvier.

"Hi Jenifer, how have you been?"

"I am fine thank you, and how about you?"

"I am all right, ever since that day at the hospital I haven't seen anybody, and I was also looking for you but they won't let me know where you were moving to"

"Yes it was happen the same to me too, I try to reach him and Maria through other friend in order to explain and shown my evident, but it seem like no one want to hear me out, and that was why my parent move me away and did not want me to contact any one from there.

Oh I am glad to see you so I can talk all these things out, it seem like we are the only two people that know the truth that our former other half refused to believe. My parent over heard that Maria took your son to the island and she wow not to let you see him again until the day she die. I am sorry that my delivery had cause all these unfortunate events to happen to you"

"No Jen, I don't think it was entirely anybody fault, I am the one should apologize to all of you, because I believe I am the cause to all of these confusion"

"How come you say that? Everything was just find until I deliver a baby that had Asian feature, and that is not anybody fault if they don't believe me"

"It was hard for them to believe your story because neither you nor anyone in your family that have Asian feature; beside Maria had suspected that I attracted to you ever since before you both got pregnant. I had denied everything and I thought it was forgotten until after your delivery"

Jenifer opened her eye wide and tried to make Virak admitted.

"Is that really so! ... Did you really have attracted to me?"

"Yes ..." He admitted to her because it was no use to hide it now, and he was just looking down with a guilty conscience registered on his face, and when Virak sneaked to look at her face she smiled broadly with an amazement look on her face and she said.

"I had suspected that all along myself and now it's confirmed, thank you"

"So how is your son?"

"He is just fine, and he looks and acts a lot like you that's squared me"

"How come, is he that bad?"

"No I mean when he grows up and he still turn out look like you that will make their accusation valid"

"Gee I want to see your son Jen"

"Of course you can come to see him any time; I will get off at the next station if you want to come along"

At the building of her apartment complex, they went to an apartment on the floor below hers to fetch her baby from the neighbor who was babysat for her, and when the neighbor saw Virak she exclaimed.

"So this is the father"

They were just smiled and Jenifer introduced Virak to Mrs. R; they did not deny but just accept the way thing went at the moment. Inside her apartment, Jenifer held her baby next to Virak in front of the mirror; he was amazed at how much the resemblance they had, and he noticed Jenifer had tear rolling down her face, and so he just held her shoulder and said.

"Come on Jen let by gone be by gone, and it seem like it's too late to shed tear anymore"

"How can you say that, we are being accused of the thing that we did not do"

"And now it is not too late Jen, why don't we go ahead and do it if it is ok with you"

And then, she was smiling while she was having tear in her eyes and tuned away looking in a demurred manner.

"Look Jen we are in the same situation and you are an attractive single mother that I ever lay eye on …since …"

She stepped closer to Virak, gave him a quick kiss on his lips, and handed him the baby.

"Let me go to fix us some dinner, here hold your baby"

Virak was glad to accept a father role for the moment. She fixed some food, set up the table for two, and went to freshen up, and when she came out in a house robe, she got the baby, gave him a towel and one of her robe, and told to clean up before dinner.

When Virak came out from the bathroom, she already laid her baby to sleep in the crib in her bedroom, and she lit some candles and turned off all the light in the apartment; Virak walked up to stand behind her, held her waist and pulled her curvy body to his. She turned around, thrown her arms over his shoulder and they kissed for the first time, then for him it was a fantasy had just became a reality; a few minutes later, they stopped and she said.

"Our dinner is getting cold; let us take it slowly ok, we have plenty of time"

Virak pulled the chair out for her, gave her a quick kiss, and went to sit across the table from her; she served saffron rice of the arroz con polo that was the best dish of this kind he ever tasted and once a guy told him that he could gauge how well a woman will be in bed by the taste of her arroz con polo dish. Oh well, he will see if what they said was true with the second part, since her dish tasted exceptionally superb.

After dinner, they sat on the couch talking about their life in the past few years that they had known each other, and that had made her having another bout with tear all over again; Virak wrapped his arms around her to give her comfort, and then they heard the baby was starting to cry.

She brought the baby back to the couch, opened up her robe to reveal a pair of large full breast with nipple pointed straight out, she fed one to the baby mouth and looked up to smile at him. Virak did not wait for an invitation, so he kneeled on the floor in front of her, bent over the baby to kiss her lips down along her neck to her full breast and suck her nipple to taste her life giving warm milk.

She moved the baby to the other side that gave him ample access to her cleavage and below, so he started to untied the belt and open up her robe always, and then she slid her body down and opened her legs wider to present her magnificent gap that puffed up like the back of the small turtle with a slit in the middle it created two thick lips with a small finger size tamarind seed on the top; Virak was at awed by the glorious sight between her legs and intoxicated by her body scent and the fragrance of the island wild flower......

Then she got up with his support to return her baby back to the crib, and after she made sure that he was comfortably sleeping, she kissed him goodnight and she came in his arms. After they kissed for a moment, Virak laid her back on the couch.

He kneeled on the floor in between her wide open thighs and her thick lips gap that seemed to grow bigger and thicker under his touch; she spread her legs out wider and slid her body forward to present her inner pink slit and the red tamarind seed, and it was her best asset that earned her the title Thick Lower Lips Jenifer or Tll Jen from then on......

Virak ended up stay at her place for the weekend and he move in with her later; until a few months later that they agreed to part way, because she knew that his obsession was only to play with her thick lips gap but not to assume the role as a father to her son.

So Virak was reluctantly helping her move to live at the upscale place along Fifth Avenue with a young lawyer who promised to marry her and be a father to her son. Virak offered her his blessing and wished her new family with the best of luck, and then he took the subway back to her old apartment complex.

Mrs. R was in her late twenty, she had slim body a full curvy butt, small waist, and full heavy bust line; she just got a new job a few months ago trying to work herself out of the welfare system, and she claimed that her husband had ran away, but rumor had it that he was locked up in the state prison somewhere for drug trafficking. Virak guessed that why she was in need of a man companion, and she was smart for not running around with any Latino in the neighborhood, because it will ruin her good wife reputation, since in her community rumor move fast like wild fire; and so Virak came in handy when she heard that TLL Jen had move away and he still stayed there to finish the lease of the apartment, Mrs. R discretely volunteered to come up to now his place and feed him some arroz con pollo, and in exchange Virak think she hope that he will make her groan and moan like he did to TLL Jen every night.

At the first night, after TLL Jen had moved out; Virak sat quietly in the living room mesmerizing to the time that they started to live together with her son in this cozy place, and the tragedy of the misunderstanding surround his birth, that had taken his son away from him.

Suddenly, there was a light knock on his door, and when he looked through the peep hole outside he saw Mrs. R stood in front of the door with a pot in her hand. When inside, she said that she thought he must be sad and lonely to be in the place by himself, so she brought some arroz con pollo that Jen had told her that Virak likes so much to cheer him up, and she brought herself to keep him company; she also emphasized that she was willing to act as Jenifer for tonight or whatever it take to make him feel better.

Virak was not surprise when she said that; in the back of his mind, he still kept thinking that nobody can replace TLL Jen, and since she made an offer he think he is game, but he must reluctantly refused of being a good host as a formality.

"But Mrs. R, you are a married woman I cannot let ...!" She cut him off in mid sentence.

"We were not married, we were just living together like you and Jenifer, and one day last year he didn't return; I never think of myself as a married woman, but since everybody looked at us then as a married couple, I was just play along so other men won't bother me"

"I see, so if you are willing to take Jenifer place then go ahead take off your clothes, lie on the couch and open your legs wide; I need to make sure that you can play the role"

"Right now, before diner?"

"Yes, right now, do you have any problem with that?"

Mrs. R was just smiling mischievously; she slowly took her clothes off piece by piece and dropped to the floor, went to sit back on the couch, and opened her legs slowly to reveal her amazing gap like a flower in bloom.

Virak went to kneel on the floor up in front of her for a closer inspection, and he ran his eyes and his hands sweeping all over her body from head to toe; she had a light amber skin tone, long black hair, a pretty face with brown eyes and luscious lips, her slender neck and long limps with manicured nails, and her thick lower lips clean shaved gap that almost matched those of TLL Jen; Virak guessed, she inherited from her complexes varieties of ancestor.

He could smell the scent that radiated from her body, it was unmistakably the fragrance of the island wild flower, and that indicated she had learned her role so meticulously. The next thing he eagerly awaited to see was her performance that will proof her pedigree from the long line of descendant from the Sex Goddess and as a gift to the world. Virak kissed her body that made her squirming and pulling him to between her legs......

Since then, Mrs. R came up to Virak's place almost every night to share her meal and play the role of TLL Jen religiously, until one day she did not show up as usual with her food and her gap, so Virak started to go out to get something to eat, but then he heard a lot of noise from her apartment, and when Virak asked some guys who hanged around on the street they said that Mr. R a respectable rich drug runner was just released from jail because of the overcrowding and his good behavior.

Upon hearing that news, Virak immediately devised a plan to move out keeping his distant from that respectable place, and so did the lease of the place that came to a timely end. At the next day, Mrs. R called Virak from the market somewhere crying through the phone; this time she told the truth that her disappearing boyfriend was involved with the drug smuggling ring, and he was released for jail overcrowded; this time he came home with his prison buddy and as a change man because he did not interest in making love to her at all, but later on in bed he stripped her clothes off and held her legs wide apart at the edge of the bed to let his hairy prison buddy raped her

And after the buddy finished with her, he grabbed her husband and reaming his rear end right in front of her, and she said that it was not only her husband rear end that the buddy reamed, he also forced into hers as well and she was still in pain because he made her virgin rear end bleeding; she told Virak that she will run away soon and advised him to move away also because there will be more drug dealing move into the neighborhood.

Virak took Mrs. R advice to heart and moved away a week later after she disappeared; and as much as he felt sorry for her, Virak could not do anything to help her because they met and developed their tangle web relationship in the middle of a dangerous circumstance that could jeopardize both their life, but they will cherish the memory of the pleasure they shared.

C16-Celestial Nymphs Continue

The Russian Connection

By the time that Virak was looking for an affordable place to live; he met some Russian refugees from the Soviet Union at a demonstration. Then Virak felt sympathy for the fellow refugee from any communist country, so when he heard from a Jewish organization who will hold a demonstration against the imprisonment and torture of the dissidents by the Soviet Union, he volunteered and went to demonstrate there with mostly Russian and Slavic immigrants.

Across the street from the United Nation secretariat building, Virak was giving a sing to hold and walking around in the small park, and then since the space was limited and the demonstrator were numerous, so they were divided into smaller groups and took turn between holding sing walking around and taking a break cheering from the side line. At one of the side line break, Virak sat near a rabbi and his nephew Nicolai, they introduced to one another around and started to talk about the cold war and their struggle for freedom and justice when living under the communist regime, and then they asked Virak for not to be blunt but they want to know what he was doing there with them since he was obviously not Russian. He told them about his sincerity toward fellow refugee from the communist countries, since he himself a refugee from Cambodia that was just fall under the communist control; they told each other about the family and relative that they left behind, and then the rabbi pointed to a lady in black from head to toe who made her speech at the microphone with tear flowing from her eyes in front of the energetic engaging group of audience, and he said that she was his late brother's widow who was not of Jewish faith and her husband apprehended by the KGB and sent to the gulag in Siberia four years ago, and they had never see him ever since; they all had very little hope that they ever see him alive again just like any other prisoners that were sent to gulag.

In the afternoon, after the demonstration had spent its last climax all of the participants were parted to their own separated way; and so was Virak but the rabbi and Nicolai invited him to their home, since they heard that he had no family to celebrate the holiday with. On their way to the subway, Virak was introduced to the sad face lady in black Natasha who was living with the rabbi family in a building a few blocks from the synagogue and a few floors below Nicolai's family. At the building of their resident Virak met with the rabbi and Nicolai big extended family, had a nice kosher Russian dinner, and returned to his place by promising to visit them again next weekend. At his next visit, after he had a little formality greeting with the family, Nicolai who was almost the same age as Virak, took over all of his visiting plans for the whole weekend; they sneaked out of the building with some of his Polish friends, and they went to Coney Island to have some hotdog at Nathan and a few beers and shots of Vodka at the boardwalk looking out to the horizon of the Atlantic ocean.

A few more outings later, Virak became close with Nicolai and his circle of friend, and when he heard that Virak was looking for a place to stay Nicolai asked Virak to share an apartment with one of his polish friend; the idea was for Nicolai to move away from his overcrowded family apartment and the very strict Jewish uncle. A month later, their place became a well known party place and a community center for all of their friends came to hang out, and some teenager sneaked his girlfriend into one of the room to practice playing mama and papa, or they just borrow the room to bust their cherry for the first time. Virak's room was a smallest one at the end of the hallway, and since the other two guys almost always had their girlfriend in their room, so it was the most borrowed; some guy even brought along some loose teenage girl for him but most of the time he refused for he was afraid of the venereal disease.

One day, Virak was surprised to see Natasha in Jordashe designer jean and tee shirt came to have dinner and a few drink with them; Nicolai told them that she decided to get out of her mourning since she receive the news about her husband death in the gulag last year, and now she also tried to get away from the restricted environment in her Jewish brother-in-law house. Natasha looked much younger than when Virak saw her in the black mourning attire, she was about in her late twenty with tall long limbs, blond hair, blue eyes, and a curvy body.

Virak was amazed to see this tall blond hair widow could drink vodka like a lost traveler that was dying from thirst, and found an oasis in the middle of the desert. Since then, she came by to hang around at their place very often and since Nicolai respected her like an aunt and all of them felt sorry for her lost, and then they had to turn most of their friends away who want to come by, so she could have some quiet time; most of the time that she had to stay overnight, Virak always volunteered to vacate the room for her and slept on the couch outside in the living room. Most of the time when they went out somewhere as a group, they always asked Natasha to come along whether they went to the beach or to disco, and everybody usually went in pair with their girlfriend, so that always left Natasha and Virak as two of a kind, and then they always teased them as 'odd couple' that they did not know what to react but were just laughing at it, and then after a while they became getting used to it.

One night, they all came home late from a party; the blizzard dumped very heavily snowstorm; all the streets and vehicles were buried under feet of snow that made any attempt to drive or just walking outside was impossible; so everybody who need to drive further, were stranded and they had to stay at their apartment overnight. Every square foot in the living room were taken by all the stranded couples and the hallway need to keep clear so everyone could used the bathroom that made Virak the last person that got no space to lie down, so he forced to walk back into his room thinking of sleeping on the floor next to the bed.

"Natasha, there is no room for me outside, can I sleep on the floor here if you don't mind?"

"No not at all, but I couldn't let you sleep on the floor, you can sleep up here on the bed if you don't mind I don't mind, and after all this is your room and your bed and it has enough space for two" Virak was just about to decline her offer and reason with her, but he was too tired and too sleepy under the influence of the alcohol, the freezing weather in the blizzard night, and at that unusual circumstance that he could not say another word, and so Virak was just climbing on the bed, slipped in between the sheet with her, closed his eyes, and tried to get some sleep.

An hour later, it was unusually strange that being tired and sleepy as he was but still couldn't fall asleep; Virak was just lay there listening to the howling wind and the icy snow flakes that hit the outside glass of the window, the occasional cracking sound came from the steam pipe of the heating radiator and the warm sublime scent of a woman body that was lying next to him, it made his loin stirring and developing a raging hard on in between his legs, and he guessed that's why he could not fall asleep.

Virak took a deep breathing and had a long exhale that was kind of releasing pressure from his chest and opened his eyes looking at an orange ray of light that shown through the opening of the window drape from the street lamp that casted a strip of reflecting light at the ceiling; and when he turned to look at Natasha, she had her head propped up off the pillow with one hand, and she was looking at him with her eyes wide open; Virak could not help looking at her full breast that was rising and falling under her nightgown, and then he asked her.

"You couldn't fall asleep either?" She was smiling slightly and said.

"I couldn't, and I wonder why… maybe because I had not slept in bed with a man for a long time, or maybe I miss the blizzard night in Russia countryside… Oh God, I am terribly missing my home that I will never see again" Virak could see the reflection of her tear rolling down her face.

"Oh Natasha, it is very hard to be refugee away from home like us, and I understand how you feel, I wish if there is anything that I could make you feel better" Virak reached out to hold her hand, and then he heard an almost inaudible low tone that she whispered.

"Can you hold me, please?" Virak did not say a word and while he was lying on back he stretched one arms out toward her, and then she slid herself closer into his embrace and thrown her left leg over his body hitting his softer shaft that had sprung right back to its rigid state of attention; she looked up to smile at him and she still kept her leg in contact, and said.

"Oh my, I am sorry that I may have caused any of these conditions, can I help?"

Without waiting for any answer, her soft hand crept slowly across his abs down to caress him. They were looking in each other eye knowing the calamity force that had pushed them pass the point of no return and it had made them feel so excited of the inevitable act to follow...... and then their bodies were shaking like they had a high fever. They were drawing toward each other like a magnet. They rushed at each other in a hurry that they felt like want to do everything all at once regardless to the blizzard or the world around them; in the back of Virak's mind, he knew this situation from his experience that he should take thing a little slower, but he also understand that Natasha was in the prime of her life that sexual satisfaction should be a regular part just like nourishment and breathing whether she wants it or not. Virak believed he had given enough thought and consideration to all angles, so he lay her down on her back...... Virak could feel her body shook with a tremendous orgasm that she had to bite her finger stopping herself from shouting out that might disturb the peaceful stormy night.

Virak lay prone drifting away between her legs soaking in sublime ecstasy; they were trying very hard of not making any sound, but they heard all the groaned and moaned noises from the couples in the living room, and there were just like a high fever epidemic spreading in the hens house; they were just looking at each other smiling, and then they snuggled up naked under the down comforter, and went at it again for the second and…….

In the morning, they were the first two people waking up before sunrise, and they went to freshen up; back in the room while Virak was watching Natasha dressing up that made him feel an immediate urge to hold her womanly alluring body, but she begged him to wait until after she finish cooking breakfast for everybody. In the kitchen, Virak was hurriedly helping her cooking, and after they finished their breakfast, they left a big badge of egg, bacon, sausage, and a pot of hot coffee at the table, and then they rushed back into his room to continue what they had left off.

Over two hours later, Virak guessed they had burned up all the calories from the food that was consumed for breakfast that morning, they were sweating so much that the bed sheet beneath them was soaking wet and they could see steam was rising from their body, and their pubic hair and all became matted cake up with frothing sticky mess like a bowl of beating egg white. While Virak was still grinding and pumping in between her legs, they heard the front door bell ringed and a little later the rabbi spoke Russian with Nicolai in an air of intense urgency. Natasha turned pale and rushed to put her cloth on over her sweating body froth and all, and then she kissed Virak and started to speak with tear welling up in her eyes.

"I got to go, rabbi said my husband is still alive and he is in flight on his way here. I am sorry it's my fault… We shouldn't… Anyway please, be understanding, since none of us knew before hand that fate could turn everything upside down into an unexpected difficulty like this. I should be elated and jumping with joy, but this good news seemed to come a little bit too late like twenty four hours. And now what else can I say, I am truly enjoy to be with you so much that I never experience before in my life, and I am deeply appreciated everything you had done for me; please, do not let Nicolai or anyone know about us at all, since I don't know what I am going to decide yet; and would you please get yourself another woman Ok! And this time someone your own age, now smile and wish me luck"

"Yeh right, good luck to you and your husband; go ahead Natasha get yourself ready to receive your husband, and don't worry I will not say a word to anyone; I am very happy for you that you will reunite with your husband"

We kissed for the last time and she hurriedly walked out of the apartment leaving a trail of scented air from the residue of her sexual fulfillment. Virak asked his friends to help him getting a place nearer to his job; everybody did not like to see him leaving.

"Thank you for everything and for helping Natasha copes with her trial difficult time, you help to fill in the gap for her husband; I knew he will appreciate for your good deed"

"My pleasure, don't mention it Nicolai, I'll see you all later"

The Black Beauties
And The Kentucky Fried Chicken

In the Bronx neighborhood, Virak was considered lucky to get a decent one bedroom apartment within a walking distant from the subway station, and it was just around the corner from a Kentucky Fried Chicken restaurant where he had his diner almost every evening, because he did not want to cook after long hours working in the restaurant, the convenience of the location, and his enjoyment of eating fried chicken.

After a long work day, when Virak got up from the underground subway station, he walked a few block to the KFC restaurant, and ordered his usual diner of the Three Pieces Meal that consisted of three pieces of fried chicken with two side orders of coleslaw and mashed potato, a biscuit and a pack of wet napkin. A few months later, all the girls who worked there and went to high school nearby, they knew him by name and his regular routine. The girls used to smoke around the corner by the dumpster behind the restaurant, and sometime on Friday they asked Virak to get them some beer and cigarette in exchange for free fried chicken dinner every evening, and ever since then Virak did not need to go into the restaurant to order his dinner anymore; he just walked around the corner at the back and one of the girls will hand him the meal bag, and he get them some beer and cigarette whenever they ask for it.

One cold day, when Virak got off the train from work he saw one of the young girls which he knew from the restaurant, sat on her valise crying at the subway station platform, and when he asked her she just said "Nothing, I'm Ok" Then Virak gave her a piece of paper with his name and phone number on it, and he tried to talk to her.

"By just looking at you I know you are in some kind of trouble, and if you want too you can come to my place to think it over and do whatever you decide later it will not be too late, but don't need to do anything drastic when you are at your vulnerable time, that may likely get you into deeper trouble. Here take my number, give me a call if you need my help or anything I can do for you. You can stay at my place for a while you know, and you still have your job at the restaurant"

Virak left her there and came to the back of the restaurant to pick up his meal, and went up to his apartment. He took a hot shower, ate the fried chicken that the other girls gave, and lay on a piece of mattress in the living room watching TV and feeling sorry for that poor girl at the train station. And then suddenly, his phone rang, and when he picked it up he heard Sheila she was still crying on the phone and she asked if she could come to stay at his place for tonight. Virak said it was all right and told her to wait for him there; he went to pick her up and brought her back to his apartment, and then he moved all his clothes from the bedroom into the hallway closet and set up his bed to sleep on the mattress in the living room, so he could vacate the bedroom for her to sleep behind close door. When she came in the apartment her eyes were still damped with tear, and then he told her.

"Go ahead set up your stuff to sleep in the bedroom, and if you want to freshen up the bathroom is over there at the end of the hallway, and I still got some fried chicken in the frig if you want to eat, and I will sleep over here in the living room"

Despite the tear in her eyes Sheila laughed at him with a surprising astonished look on her face, and she said.

"Oh Lord, do you still eat fried chicken all these time?"

"Yes, I love eating fried chicken, and you girls give me for free, why not?"

When she came out from the bathroom in her robe, she came to sit on the floor in the living room and started to tell him all about her trouble.

"I want to go somewhere away from around here, I have a lot of problem and I am in a big trouble right now, and nobody seem to care what happen to me at all except you. My boyfriend dumped me the minute I told him that I am pregnant with his child he denied that was his, and he accused me of cheating behind his back. My mother is getting hook on drug and alcohol that she doesn't care about any of us much. My father left home a few years ago, and he never returned after he lost his job we don't know even if he still alive" And then she started to cry again, and he tried to console her.

"Ok I understand, why don't you calm yourself down and go to sleep it off for tonight, and we will talk about it again tomorrow. Keep in mind that there are always some options of solution for any problem big or small, and the best solution is we must learn to recognize all the potential problems and avoid them ahead of time. When there is nobody taking care of you, you got to make yourself responsible enough in order for you to be strong, hard and wise enough to take care for your own self first and for most. Running away may not be the best solution, and you may run into another problem while you are at your weak disadvantage vulnerable time. You can stay here as long as you want, and here is the front door key. Ok we will talk about your problem again tomorrow, Goodnight" The next morning, they had a long talk mainly about her life situation, and when the discussion came down to the subject of abortion that were surrounded by the tug of war between the pro and con, religious belief and freedom of choice; Virak told her all sides of ideology, and then he left the ball in her court so she could learned to be responsible in making her choice and decision. She reluctantly decided to get an abortion, and after that she determined to stay clean, sober and abstinent from sex, and she also wowed to study hard until she could be able to graduate with a diploma.

A few months later, her life was kind of stable and turning around by showing that she had made good progress on many things that she had determined setting out to do. She shown Virak her report card with teachers remarks praising her big improvement, and he haven't seen her running around with the other girls or going out with any boy at all; one of the imported thing was that she stocked the frig full of fried chicken and all kinds of side order, so he did not need to show up behind the restaurant anymore. She also tried to help him paying the bill but Virak refused and made some suggestion that she should use the money to help her family instead. Sometime before Christmas, Sheila bought some presents and went to visit her family. She came back with a serious and sad mood, and when he tried to find out she said that her sibling was fine but her mother was still in the same condition, and that she was careless whether any of her children were coming or going. And then, Virak saw some signs on her face that made him worry from his own experiences, and so he tried to give her some suggestion.

"Sheila, why don't you try out with this idea that it just might help you to clear your mind from stresses?"

"And what idea is that? Let hear it"

"Try to take off on Sunday, and you must clear your mind and your mood from all of your sorrows and angers, dress up kind of sober I guess and go to any church of your choice, pray if you want to, be nice and kind to other people, and help out around the church if they need you. And if you don't want to do any of these things that I just said that is ok with me, but I recommend that you try it out for a few Sunday, and if it doesn't help anything at all you just stop going there if you want to"

"Wow, and now you sounded kind of a spiritual and religious man, why don't you come to the church with me?"

"Don't concern yourself too much about me child, I may sounded a little bit spiritual, but I am certainly not religious; everyone has his or her own way to release stress, and my suggestion is a way for you to try it out that it might help. For me, I am busy doing some demonstration to Mrs. J downstairs of how to achieve calm satisfying bliss quietly, since she is under a lot of stress because she is lonely"

"Is that some kind of Asian Wisdom Quest I heard about? And why don't you show me that? So I don't have to go to find it anywhere else"

"No child, you are still too young to understand it fully. Now go to church or go with God let him show you the way, and that's it, end of discussion"

After Sheila dressed up and left the apartment for work, Virak slipped out to see Mrs. J who was eagerly awaiting his present with her opened arms and opened legs......Virak did not follow up to see whether Sheila took his advice or not, but at some Sunday morning he saw her dressed up with some proper clothing and she left in a calmly manner; then he thought that was a good sign. In the evening, when he got back home from work she didn't say anything or tell him about her day, she just left some food on the table and went into her room to study preparing herself for the exams. A few months later, one Sunday afternoon while Virak was sipping some beer recuperating from a tedious bout of demonstration with Mrs. J, Sheila came to asked him.

"What do you think if a retired couple's asked me to move into their house with them? They are church members"

"This is great news that rarely comes by in a life time, that's good for you, and now it's time for you to learn to make decision that base on facts and knowledge, and I believe that you are mature enough to know the true intention if it is sincere or it's just a trick, but since you ask me I need to meet them before you decide"

"Yes that's right, they are also asked to meet you too. I think they are nice people who retired from teaching and their house is in the suburb outside the city, and they said most of their children were moving out on their own or to college except the two youngest who are still in high school like me and haft of their children were adopted, I think I will fit in the family just fine, but if there is anything wrong I always can hop on the train and come right back here right?"

"Ha ha I don't think it will need to come to that if they are like what you said don't you think?" Virak went with Sheila to meet them at their house in the suburb and they seem to be a nice family, and he think she will be fine living with them. They were surprised when they first saw Virak since as a guardian he was only a few years older than Sheila and he was not a black person. Virak assured them that Sheila was a changed good clean kid despite her trouble young life that'd been through a lot of unfortunate odds, and she will be a good and inspired addition to their family.

On her last day, Virak told Sheila to invite her friends over so they will join in a little celebration for her moving away to her new life with the family. She had some friends from school and most of the girls from the restaurant came over, and Virak get them some pizza, soda and punch, but some girls from the restaurant who used to get some beer from him were not satisfy and they had him get them some beer and cigarette from the neighborhood liquor store. Her party went smoothly without any problem until the appointed time that her adopted family came to pick her up in that evening.

Everybody came to say goodbye to her on the sidewalk next to the family vehicle, and then they all knew that everything will come down to an inevitable end, so Sheila said her farewell to everybody, shed some tear, and she moved away to her new home in style and class on a shiny Cadillac, and all of her friends were also leaving with the rest of the beer and cigarette.

Virak felt great for helping Sheila to survive through her trouble time in life, so he went back upstairs to clean the place up anything that left from the party, got undress and drawn himself a hot bath. Later while he was relaxing quietly in the living room, suddenly there was a knock on the door that astonished him since he did not expect anyone at that time, nevertheless his loin begin to stir immediately that was just because he guessed Mrs. J return home early since she knew he will be alone after Sheila left, and then he put on a robe, swept a glance at the machete behind the door, and looked through the peep hole; Virak was surprised to see one of the girls from the restaurant stood in front of his door with a broad smile on her face, and he believe her name was Cindy maybe she forgot something in his place. When Virak opened the door, she walked in and asked to use the bathroom, so he pointed down the hallway he thinks she already knew where it was. Virak went to lie back on his comfortable mattress at the corner of the living room watching TV. When Cindy asked to use the bathroom, he thought for just a few minutes and she will leave, but after she spent almost haft an hour in there, Virak still heard the water running, and when he looked down the hallway he saw the light shown from inside the bathroom and the door was left ajar, It made him feel concern that something might happen to her in there, so he went to knock on the door and asked.

"Cindy, are you all right in there?"

"Yes, I'm ok, would you please come in here for a second" When Virak pushed the door open he could hardly see anything in there, because it was thick with steam from the hot water that she left running, and when he got closer Virak saw Cindy sat naked on the chair with both feet on the tub edge and she tried to shave the hair in between her legs.

"Would you please help me do this, I can't see because this mirror keep fogging up" Virak sat on the tub edge by her foot and reached back to turn off the hot water, and then he tried to talk to her in a calm tone.

"I think this is not appropriate child, you are too young"

"Oh cut it out, I am over eighteen graduated last year, and what are you worry about that I am under aged or not? You had screwed Sheila and she is not even seventeen yet"

"No I did not, I let her stay here because she needed help, and she stayed in the bedroom while I sleep on the mattress in the living room; she is a changed good kid"

"Do you expect me to believe that you didn't sleep with her? But come to think of it Sheila became a changed person after her accidental pregnancy thing and moving out of her family, I never seen her hook up with any boy or go out partying with anyone at all, so she had been staying here with you all this time you dirty old man, and you had taking care of all her need and want that was why she never hooked up with any boy, and that's why I am here to find out, but it doesn't matter about that now here hold this help me finish shaving"

Virak want to say some more to protest her accusation, but it seemed like it's no use, so he just kept quiet, steadied his hand that held the razor, and concentrated on shaving the hair around her young fat gap. When he finished shaving her, Virak went back to the living room. Then Cindy called him from the bedroom; and in the middle of the bed, she lie on her back, spread her legs wide apart……

"Come on, we're going to make some mess here tonight, it seem like she had taking care of this bedroom very well"

After their first night together, Cindy want to move in with him, but Virak refused and told her she can come to stay there anytime that she want to get together but not to stay permanently. A few months later, Cindy told Virak that a boyfriend want her to move together with him to Alaska to get the job on the pipeline construction, and they tried to build a family there; on their last night together, Virak wish her and her boyfriend the best of luck, while he still lay exhaust in between her leg right after their furious bout and gigantic orgasm, and Virak also advised her to prepare herself body and mind to be busy and to be GENEROUS, because there are fewer women to men ratio up there. On her departure day that they had to fly out from JFK airport, Virak was among her friends and relatives who said goodbye to send her and her boyfriend off to the frozen land.

Few months later, Mrs. J also said her last goodbye to Virak by spending her last night in his bed before she followed her husband who went under some kind of government protection program.

C17-In the United States Marines Corps

One day while he was walking on the street, he saw a Marines Corps poster that said 'The few, the proud, the marine' and it brought him back to the time when he was still in Cambodian Army and was sent to train in South Vietnam with the Green Beret.

While his unit was trained in a maneuver with the marine unit nearby at the Mekong Delta that he admired and want to be one of them.

So Virak decided to walk into a marine recruit station, and he was thinking that now it's time for him to become one of these marine, but to his disappointment the recruiter told him.

"I am sorry at this time man, I cannot take you because right now we are not allow to recruit anyone with green card from these communist countries, not yet"

"But Sergeant, I am a refugee in this country now because I fought against the communist when I was there fighting the Vietcong side by side with the marine, and then my country was not communist yet until the American left those countries, and then I had to shoot my way out. Right now I don't think it's fair to consider that I came from those communist countries"

A few years later, after Virak sworn in to become a citizen of the United States, he went to visit the marine recruit station again. In early1985, he was shipping out with a bunch of raw recruit from the MEP station to the MCRD in San Diego, California.

Starting his boot camp training at almost over the age limit and that made him an oldest recruit in his company, and it was a matter of fact Virak was older than most of his drill instructors; and almost all of them never been baptized in combat.

Virak was in his element to be back in the military, and the training in boot camp was basically the same as the training in South Vietnam by the Green Beret, and the different were the physical training, the doctrine to become a marine, and he had killed a few live Vietcong during field training in South Vietnam.

Virak became a marine with the best shape of physical condition than he ever was in his whole life; on the last day in boot camp was their graduation ceremony, and the MCRD newspaper Chevron printed his picture in camouflage uniform with his M-16 at the shoulder arm, and it read "POW Become Marine" Virak thought it was neat but it might confuse a lot of people.

After they became marines, they were granted a few weeks leave to be with their family, and then they were ordered to report to various different school all over the states to train on the military occupational specialty.

Virak was sent to learn about Bulk Fuel at the military school where many young marines and soldiers became independent for the first time in their live; most marine in Virak's class were not old enough to buy beer or go in the bar, but they were allowed to have a good time at the enlist club.

They enjoyed the beer by the pitcher and danced with the young women marines and soldiers. One evening at the enlist club, a young marine tried to get his attention, pointed to a table, and he said.

"Hear me out, those two army chick at the table there at one o clock, yes those two they come with us tonight, the blond one is mine and she will bring her best friend the brunette if you don't mind"

"No not at all, when the light is out all of them will be just the same"

"Ok, we can switch them lather"

It's not just a job, it's an adventure

That night, when they came out from E club, Virak flagged down the pizza truck that went around the base selling freshly baked pizza and drink, he bought a pizza pie and some cold soft drink, and they went to sit at a small park eating and talking while observing the movement of the military police patrol.

Yes, they must keep a closer look at the present situation and followed the MP patrol movement, because the place that they were going to go to have their fun was off limit; there were a lot of empty barracks at an area in the wood, that Virak got the information from a marine in the last contingent who pointed to him a barrack at the end of the cull de sac that the MP patrol rarely came by, it had an unsecured low window behind the bush.

After they had finished the pizza they still kept on continuing their conversation, since they couldn't move on into their objective, because there were a couple MP patrol vehicles which were still hanging around the area.

All of them felt very impatient to move on, since they had only one common goal in mind, was to screw each other brain out right at the moment, and the two army chicks seemed to be more restless than the two marines; they were shifting their weight squirming on their seat, and if Virak was not mistaken their panties were already soaking wet from their excited anticipation.

Then the window of opportunity arrived, they overheard the MP radio transmitted conversation from the patrol car that a big fight broke out near the E club and the assistant were requested from all units to respond.

After all of the MP patrols left the park area, they looked at each other and knew it's now or never; Virak led them through a dark wooden trail to the barrack with an unsecured window behind the bush.

The two stories long barrack was at the edge of that big ghost town and it sat a few feet off the ground at the end of a cull de sac like that marine had said, and then Virak pushed open the window panel, got himself inside, and pulled the brunette army chick in through that window without any problem despite her large size rack that had to squeeze in; they hurriedly went upstairs and started to get undress, and while Virak was busy tending to the brunette large size rack he heard the young marine called for a helping hand.

Back downstairs, Virak saw the blond chick caught under window panel that was sliding down. Virak told the young marine to pushed her up so he could help her through, the young marine put his shoulder under her butt huffing and puffing, and then Virak pushed the panel up big enough to pull both of her enormous jugs through.

In that dark barrack, Virak paused a moment weighting and admiring her humongous racks that had already popped out of her bra, while she still rested her butt on the young marine shoulder, she smiled at him and knew that he was captivated by her champion material huge breasts, and then she looked at his stiff erection a few inches from her face that made him realized that he didn't have his pant on.

The thrill of that excited moment, made Virak forgot all about the brunette army chick who was waiting upstairs, the young marine who was still huffing and puffing under the weight of the blond chick butt, or the MP patrol car that might come by the area, and then while he was holding tight to her racks his hard shaft mysteriously end up in her waiting mouth that was expertly sucked it in.

A moment later, the young marine was impatiently asking what took Virak so long to pull her through, and he said he saw the headlight of the patrol car came from the distant. So despite Virak reluctant to end that thrilling moment, he had to react immediately by pulling her through, and after they all got in the barrack closed the window panel and led them to where the brunette laid waiting for his return.

She was surprised with embarrassment and she immediately trying to cover herself up, and she complained that why he brought them there since they could stay at the other end in such a big long barrack, but Virak pulled her cloth cover away and dropped himself in between her open legs.

And he told her to have a consideration for all of their comrade in arm at the moment of dire crisis like then when the patrol car was coming, and then he turned to tell the young marine to hit the deck since he was standing next to the rack with the blond chick by his side like he was in a trance looking at the brunette well formed body that lied under Virak with her legs wide open.

He quickly unrolled the mattress at the next bunk bed, they got undress while the brunette and Virak look on, and then the blond chick took initiative following her fellow soldier footstep by laying down on her back with her legs open and pulling the young marine over her. The brunette reached in between Virak's legs to feel his hard shaft and with astonished look she asked.

"Why yours is already soaking wet?"

Virak told her to keep quiet since at that moment the MP were pointing their strobe light through the window, and then he explained to her in a low whisper that it was wet because he was sweating when he was helping their comrade in arm to get in. Virak turned to the side looking at the blond chic who smiled at him knowingly......

On the dark wooden trail, while they walked the two army chicks back to their barrack, Virak remembered that they will have seventy-two hours break at the next holiday weekend, so while the young marine and the blond army chic were walking a little distant up ahead, Virak held the brunette close and whispered in her ear asking her to meet him in town alone next weekend so they can go to spend some time together at Virginia Beach.

She nodded her head in agreement and said that she was excited since she did not have any plan so she will be happy to go with him, and then she thanked him for that exiting night, gave him a kiss and ran into her barrack.

Virak used to go anywhere or do anything with a bunch of marine in his class, but this time he want to be alone with the brunette army chick. So on an early Saturday morning, he went to town alone, rented a car, and went to wait for her at their rendezvous point a little walking distant from the bus stop.

Virak parked the car with the sidewalk from the bus stop in his line of sight through the rear view mirror and waited, but after half an hour pass their appointed time, he started to feel disappoint and believe she had changed her mind and stood him up, and now he was stuck with the rented car and didn't want to go to Virginia Beach alone.

Virak was about to give up and get ready to take off, but he happened to glance at the rear view mirror for one last time checking the sidewalk from the bus stop, and then he saw a blond hair lady in dark sunglass and tight fitted jean came to stand at his rendezvous point and she turned to look around it seemed like that she was waiting for someone, and when Virak saw her gigantic rack then he recognized her immediately from that night at the empty barrack.

Virak blew horn to call her over so that he might find out about her friend, and when she saw him she opened the passenger door and popped herself on the seat that made her humongous orbs jiggled like a bucket of gelatin, and then she turned to look at the back seat and she asked.

"Where is your friend?"

"And where is yours?"

"She could not make it and told me to tell you that she's sorry, because her relative come to pick her up last night, and how about your friend?"

"I'm sorry he couldn't make it also because of his prior engagement at the detachment for the moment; it's too bad that they both couldn't make it. Hey, let's not waste this R and R how about just you and me we go to Virginia Beach?"

"Ok, let's go, oh boy I cannot wait to see the ocean, do you know this is my first time to have a chance to see the ocean, since I live in the land lock state that have no shoreline, and I thank you for asking me"

"I am the one should thank you for saving my day"

At the seaside town, Virak drove around looking for a suitable hotel close to the beach at a walking distant; it took awhile before they found a small hotel outside of the town center that was close enough to the beach. It was already pass thirteen hundred hour in the afternoon by the time they got there, so after they had move all their gear into the hotel room, they went to have lunch at a seafood restaurant in town.

After lunch, they went back to the hotel room and Virak was thinking about having a little siesta before they go down to the beach. While he was laying on the bed, she asked to go to the beach right away, and when Virak turned to look at her she was already put on her bikini and with a beach towel in hand ready to go; and then what got his attention was her huge breasts that almost popped out from her bikini bra; she knew that her gigantic rack attract any man attention, she just smiled with her hand on her hips and she asked him.

"What? What's wrong?"

"Nothing wrong at all, you look terrific, but I thought you looks bigger now than when I pulled you though the window that night" She came to stand closer with her arms on her hips and she asked him again.

"Do you say that I am fat?"

"No, not like that baby, you are as perfect as is then and now, and when we were in the barrack it was dark then, and that's why you looks different then, but let me see" Virak sat on the edge of the bed, pulled her closer in between his legs, and put his hand on her breasts trying to figure the size, and in just a few second of rubbing and weighting, her nipple got hard and pointing through her thin bra; Virak tried to reach behind her to untie her bra strap, but she stopped him smacked his hand and said.

"Cut it out, wait I want to see the ocean first"

"No baby, now please, for marines we dislike the word 'wait' and 'hurry', those two are some of the words that we hear every day and we become sick and tired of them, and whenever we have our R and R we prefer to do many things at once on an impulse, and so this come first allow me please"

Virak stood up, pulled the bra strap off her shoulder, and looked at a pair of huge perfect round breast that still perked up...... Later, they stirred slowly to disengage and got up; she put her hand to plug the flow of their mixed pearly love juice that was oozing out from her gap, and rushed toward the bathroom, but Virak stopped her.

"Wait a second Baby, where are you going?"

"Go to the bathroom to clean up this mess, what?"

"No, there is no need to do that here, we will have our cleansing ceremony in the Atlantic Ocean" Virak let her stepped in the legs and then pulled her bikini up on her leaky gap, and he wiped her hand and thigh with his swim trunk and put it on; he held her hand to step out to go to the beach, but she hesitate to look at the wet spot at the crotch of her bikini bottom soaked with the pearly love juice that was still seeping through.

"I cannot walk out in broad day light looking like this"

"Yes, you can Baby, there is nothing wrong, it is a badge of our pleasure from the Goddess gift, and when the whole world see it they will be at aw and look at you with great esteem of admiration.

Come on, we will have our cleansing ceremony in the ocean, and I know you will enjoy it, don't worry about anything the ocean will disinfect everything"

Virak helped her adjusting her bikini bottom by pull it up to give her wedgies and pressed the material into the slit of her thick lip gap, and then they stepped out of the door.

At a bar on the Beach, they stopped by to have some beer and oyster on the half shell; everybody in the bar enjoyed looking at her luscious orbs and her round butt with the wet crotch bikini bottom that made her squirming restlessly on the bar stool.

On the way out from the bar, they were awestruck watching her swaying hip and the pearly love juice that smeared on her thigh and had left a little puddle on the bar stool seat.

When they were at the door, Virak looked back to see everybody including the bartender, gave him thumb up with cheering, whistling and a round of applause that puzzling her, and then Virak bowed respectfully to accept her nomination while stepping out to the beach.

And while they were walking triumphantly toward the ocean under the gazing glance of admiration from the beachgoer, she asked him with a puzzle look from behind her Rayban sunglass.

"What happened? What was the applause for?"

"It was for you your highness; they had just nominated you to be a 'Divine Sex Goddess' for the moment in time. Be proud my Queen, walk with your head held high"

Virak held her luscious round butt while they were stepping into the waves for her first royal glorious dip to have their cleansing ceremony in the Atlantic Ocean.

Virak held her by her waist and walked her in front of him into the deeper sea water, and when they came to the chest deep level, Virak pulled her bikini bottom down, she raised her knees up and……

She thrown her arms over his shoulder and they kissed for the first time to honor Venus. They stayed and played at the beach all afternoon, and moved around alternately between walking along the beach or laying around on the sand and swimming in the pounding waves.

After the sun went below the horizon, they return to their room to clean up and got dress for the evening; they drove around sightseeing in the seaside town along the beach, and then they went to have dinner at a nice seafood restaurant where Virak introduced to her the deep fried oyster and the big bowl of Bouillabaisse.

After dinner, they walk along the beach under the moonlit night sky, stood at the waves break water edge talking and looking away to the distant horizon with his arm wrapped around her body looking at yonder to a solitary light of a ship was bobbing in the swell of the waves and drifting away to an unknown destination.

They were so exhausted by the time that they had to return to base, and while Virak was driving she dosed off peacefully in the reclined front seat; he glanced at her from time to time and thinking about her easygoing attitude on the way out to the beach that he thought she was just an easy woman with big breasts, but after they had spent some time to get to know one another, Virak realized that she was an intelligent generous good heart person, and she reminded him a lot of H in Las Vegas they were women from a small town USA with a sense of adventure.

Her class had finished a few weeks ahead of his at the different MOS, and on a weekend they spent their last night together at a small motel outside of town before driving her to the airport the next morning.

At the gate of the jet way, they looked at each other and knew that the good time that they had spent together came to an end; they said goodbye and wishing each other luck, and she walked into the plane while Virak stood at the gate watching her plane took off and disappeared into the cloud.

He made a mental note that was another Goddess Avatar floating away from him.

C18-Tour of Duty

Okinawa

After they were graduated from the specialized school, the marines were sent to an assigned unit around the world, and at that time for marines most of their oversea tours were at the embassies, on the Navy ships or to a rock of an island called Okinawa in the middle of the South China Sea about a thousand miles from mainland Japan to the north.

On their way to Okinawa, they had a week layover at camp Pendleton in southern California prepared their document and the orientation about life of the marine in the fleet doctrines.

They were placed to stay in at a wing of a barrack across the street from the PX and next to the wing for the deserter. That had made Virak wonder why did they placed them newbie next to the deserter, and he guessed they want to teach the young marine something before they do anything stupid. All of the deserters wore the civilian clothes.

In front of the barrack, there was a makeshift grave in the flowerbed, it was a shallow grave that shown the tip of a pair of the combat boot with a camouflage cover on the top, decorated with a cross that held the sign it said 'Death before Dishonor'.

That simple shallow grave may had some effect to the young marine way of thinking, because every time that they had their formation for accountability right in front of the grave and made them looked at the deserters with disgust, and they were instructed not to have any interaction with them at all, they were told.

"Marine, you are marines in the fleet now so you must conduct yourself accordingly, do not let yourselves slip down like those worthless men in civilian clothe next door"

And before they know anything or hear any scuttlebutt floating around, their order was cut for oversea deployment to the island of Okinawa. Upon receiving the order, everybody was so excited because for most of them were their first chance to travel to over sea, but for Virak he was excited for the different reason since it will bring him closer to the land he used to live.

On their departure date, they had their reveille earlier in the morning than usual, dressed up smartly in the new Charlie uniform, and ate their last breakfast on CONUS (The continental of the United States) Virak had some biscuit and sausage gravy, a bowl of oatmeal with a few slices of bacon, a glass of chocolate milk from the brown cow (Dispensing box), and an orange from the salad bar, and he avoided the green looking scramble egg as usual.

A few hours later, they were on a jet plane flying over the Pacific Ocean, and their chows were somewhat different from the Marine Corps chow and they were served by some nice flight attendants, they had made the marines thinking and talking about the Mile High Club always to the island.

After a brief stopover at Hawaii, the plane landed on the Okinawa Island at the Kadina Air Force base, and then they were loaded on busses to camp Foster where they stayed for a few days for processing, acclimatization, and the soul searching orientation.

They had to go through an initial orientation immediately right after they got off the bus, and after the whole group went through a joint orientation they separated the women marines to the other room, and since there were all male marine left in the hall an experienced Staff NCO came up, told them to relax, and he gave them a wild precise and unofficial DO and DON'T as followed.

"In most of these bars that catered for the American GI, there are hundreds of those so calls 'Buy Me Drinky Girls' and women or hostesses that they call themselves; they are women were recruited from the Philippines, Thailand and many other places, they are here to work and send money to support their family back home.

And do you know whom do they make their money from?" They all shouted "They make from all of us newbie!"

and he continues "Right, they will make most of their money from all of you newbie unsuspected young punks; they will encourage you to load yourself with alcohol so you will become a drunken wasted, so that it will be easy for them to rip you off.

They might let you grab their ass or rub their teat, and they will ask you to buy them some drink with the price that is four times more than yours and which might only be some fruit punch in a wooden cup that you couldn't tell what's in it.

And one more thing, they might try to marry you handsome devil, it maybe love or not, but you are their ticket to live a good life in the USA, and up there in the states side most married will end up in divorce and you will end up paying for the child support and alimony for the rest of your working life.

Yes marine, you are here on this piece of rock of an island away from home, family, wife and girlfriend, so we understand that you will eventually be horny, and you must keep in mind that there are many strange VDs out there and a new disease call AID that they haven't find any cure for it yet and it spread very fast around the globe like wild fire.

Whatever you are going to do you must prepare to pay when you play if you don't practice SAFE SEX. Some of you may never see your love one again ever that you will go back home in a body bag, so be careful.

On this island, all of us are being away from home that could make us become stressful or a bad case of depression bout; in order to avoid these things most marine will shelter in three things, you might become a PT freak for those who do PT all the time, a religious freak for those who become just like that a religious freak, and last but not least that apply to majority of you will become an alcoholic, because all of the alcohol beverages are cheap at abandon everywhere.

There are the vending machine in the REC. room that sell cold beer at the ready and cheap it cost like a quarter to fifty cents a can, and at the PX a case of Budweiser cost only three dollars and seventy-five cents, but if you buy a can of Bud in the bars out there it will cost you four bucks, so be smart just grab some beer from the machine in the REC. room and get drunk safer near your barrack it will cost less.

There are thousands of male marines on this island, but there are only a few percentages of American women girls and WMs; for the women and girls they are our fellow marines' wives and daughters, and I suggest that these groups are off limit, and this will apply the same courtesy to our sisters branches like the Army The Navy and the Air Force as well.

And when you are out in town you will be careful with the local girls beside those 'Buy Me Drinky Girls' in the bars; some of them may screw with you all night and turn around report to the police in the morning that you rape her.

Many young marines are still in the Japanese jail cell as we speak, and get this in mind marine in the Japanese jail they feed you rice and left over fish head and entrails, and for the American life expectancy in the Japanese jail is only a few years the most; so you should be careful not to get caught in that situation, don't be a foul watch your ass, you must think with your head not with your prick head.

If you are lucky enough to get some poontang to play with, and I suggest that you bust your nuts quietly, keep your mouth shut, and patted yourself on the back to congratulate that you had got some while thousand of marines out here got blue balls.

With these very few women that are available here, you must learn not to be choosy, and you must keep in mind that if she is ugly you tell yourself that she is just plain, and if she is too fat tell yourself that she is not fat she is just healthy, and last but not least if she screw around behind your back or in front of you, don't feel bad, get upset or get mad at all, and all you have to do just forgive her, she is not a slut for she is just GENEROUS, and what do you expect a young healthy American girl deserve more than one… and you just move on to the greener pasture.

By the way there are a lot of ocean waters and beaches around here that you should go out enjoy the scenery around the island, don't just stay in the barrack and beat your meat to death that is not healthy OK all right Good Luck Marine"

After the processing at camp Foster, they were divided and sent to their parent unit around the island; Virak was sent to a unit at camp Hanson in the northern part, and a week later he was end up at Futenma Marines Corps Air station in between camp Foster and downtown Naha in the south.

Virak was one of the lucky few marines that got sent to the Futenma air station in the middle of the civilized world instead of stuck in the back wood at camp Hansen with thousands of blue ball grunt and so few available women around, and those few one were known to be busy pulling the train left and right.

At Futenma air station, it was just like a regular nine to five job with every other weekend three days off. Virak bought a mountain bike to ride on the hilly terrain of Okinawa, and he peddled to work and after work through the small street in town, most of the time he rode across the taro patch on the small wooden bridge to get to the seawall where he like to sit by the wave barrier watching the sunset at the horizon, and on some weekend he rode across town to the other side of the island or to downtown Naha or to the beach in the southern part of the island.

Later Virak acquired a small car from an Air Force Major who was ready to return to the state side, it was an old Toyota Corolla that cost him around seven hundred dollars, it may be an old car but it was still run great, because the Japanese auto inspection was very strict and meticulously done to the last nuts and bolts.

Among the American military personnel, they judged the price of a vehicle by the amount of time it got on the inspection sticker, and that old car had over a year time left on the sticker before it need to be inspect again that cost a couple thousands of dollar, and then he thought it was perfect that at the end of his tour he just sell to the junk yard for a few buck or give it to another marine.

Virak felt that he had a lot more freedom of movement with his newly acquired old car, and that he could venture far and wide around the island.

On the three days weekend Virak like to camp out at the beach or in the mountain, and whenever he had found a nice place he always bring a car load of marine with him to see it, and some time they were at the beach in the middle of a festival that they were just glad to join in celebrate their culture by the sea, and often time they let them tasted their food, their beer, their cigarette and their women.

Virak went fishing at the seawall, trekked through the jungle and mountain to trace the footstep of the marines in the battlefield in World War Two, jumped off the connecting Ike island bridge into the sea snake infested water, and that must be the alcohol made him did it, since they were told that there was no antidote for the sea snake poison.

Virak frequently stopped by the gate two of the Kadina air base to check on the modern electronic, buy the cheap pirate copies of movie tape, eat the special tasty taco at the Jacky Taco Restaurant, have a few beers at the nice dark no name bar, or walk through the Whisper Alley where the professional mature almost at the retirement age whores were still plying their trade catching the desperate drunken GIs.

Virak often dropped off some marines who were in urgent need of some therapy in the Whisper Alley or at the dark no name bar to get the blow job at the dark booth in the rear corner.

In most weekends he went to eat at the Kadina chow hall, because the Air Force knew how to live a good life where the Marines Corps were lacked behind in all aspects.

Japanese Cherry Blossom

One day in early spring, Virak drove north thinking of going camping in the northern part of the island, but he came across a town called Nago during their preparation for the parade that celebrated the Cherry Blossom Festival.

There was a lots of preparation activities of the school children, the American high school band, and the town people on the main street that close to all traffics.

He stood behind a group of people who seem to receive an instruction in Japanese and then they were passing around the bright color baseball caps, and when he was just about to walk away but somebody stopped him, said something in Japanese, and handed him a bright color baseball cap.

Then Virak knew that they gave it to him by mistake that they thought he was with the group, but for the spirit of the festival he popped the hat on his head and walked away from them.

Suddenly at a few hundred yards away from the men, a lady in her mid twenty said something to Virak in Japanese and she was pointing to some bags on the vehicle, and then he was just smiled at her and looking around he saw the men that wore the bright color cap, were carrying something, so he thought that it didn't hurt if he just gave them a hand for the spirit of the festival, so he grabbed the bags, and just followed her group along the parade route.

And when they came to a short break off the main street, the children came to asked Virak for something from the bags, he thought it was a great way to lighten up his load, so he pulled out and gave them anything they want; they had him pulled out almost everything from the bags, and then they laughed when Virak pulled out the wrong thing.

The sound of the children laughing had created a lots of commotions; that made the bossy lady came to investigate and when she saw the children were eating and drinking with everything laid strewn all over the place she was shock and furious, she grabbed the foods and drinks, put them back in the bags, and she shout at Virak in Japanese with all of her furor like the Tsunamis hit the beach.

And the children were amused when they saw him just stood there with all of the bags hung on his shoulder and smiling at the fierce leader that made her became more and more furious, and then Virak thought that he should stop this fun before she passed out with anger and then he said to her in English.

"I am sorry Miss…"

And then he looks at her name tag that was in English and Japanese.

"Miss Hanako I didn't mean to make you upset at all"

She was stunt with her eyes and mouth wide open and then she lowered her voice and her anger, and said.

"I am sorry for shouting at you I thought that you were the festival worker because you wear that cap, how do you get it? And why do you come to carry our bags?"

"Oh no it's my fault and somebody handed this cap to me by mistake that I thought it was for the festival spirit, and I carry your bags because you told me to, isn't that what you had said to me then?"

"Yes that was what I said but I thought you were the festival worker with that cap on"

"It's ok I am glad that I can help you, the children and the festival"

"Thank you very much Mr. …"

"T my name just calls me Virak hi how do you do Miss Hanako?"

"I am fine thank you how do you do?"

"I am happy to meet you and I hope in a better circumstance"

Then the festival official arrived with a few workers, and then he asked Virak for the cap back and had the workers took the bags from his shoulder; the official and Virak, made the profound apology and bowed back and forth for the confusion.

The children and Hanako went back to join the parade possession and he went to sit on the curb with a bunch of marines watching the parade. They started to cheer for the American high school marching band came by, and then Virak sat quietly mesmerizing the face of Hanako smiling and her raging anger.

The parade made numerous pass along Main Street, and when the children saw Virak they waved and smiled at him, and then one of the kids got Hanako's attention and pointed at him, they acknowledged each other with an exchange smile and a wave that made Virak's group of marine gone wild.

"Oh Fuck she waved at you T, man she's gorgeous, let's go T. is she your girl, let introduce us to her friends"

"Ok steady marines; don't get too excited she is not my girl"

"But why did she smile and wave at you?"

"Oh well, we just had a little misunderstanding over there a while ago"

"That's it, that's all you need, and what are you waiting for? An invitation"

"She is a nice lady and maybe the teacher for those children and she had a kind of mean streak"

"Who's the fuck care T. when she open those slender legs wide everything will balance out just fine"

"Shut a fuck up you all, and leave me alone, and watch your fucking mouth because there are a lot of dependants around here"

Yes, Virak knew him also. The Cherry Blossom Festival parade was wrapped up in the afternoon; the Japanese went back to their home, and the American filed in on the bus to return back to their base.

Virak hadn't decide where he want to go next with the nice weather and low humidity and with all the excitements from the festival made him feel hungry, so he stopped by the roadside food stand and ordered a bowl of soba.

After finishing the soba, he just sat there looking to the distant mountain and thinking about what to do and where to go in the next forty-eight hours time off. Suddenly someone came to stand blocking his line of vision, and when he looked up it was Hanako, Virak greeted her and invited her to join him at the table; and then she said.

"Hi again, everybody went home and all of the American busses were all gone, and why are you still here?"

"Hi Miss Hanako, I did not come with the bus, and why are you still here?"

"Oh I am on my way home, but when I see you are sitting here by yourself looking kind of sad, are you still mad at me?"

"No, I am thinking about what to do and where I can go to see since I have this two day free time on my hand?"

"So what is that you normally like to do on your free time?"

"I normally like to camp out at the beach or in the mountain, and visit some nice places"

"Really!, I think if you enjoy camping you will like the forest in the mountain near my grandfather's farm, it's about two hour drive north from Nago here, and do you have a map of Okinawa? I will show you"

"Thank you Miss Hanako it's very nice of you to show me the place, Hanako is a lovely name "

"You are welcome, have a nice camping trip, I got to go see you"

She was just smiled and said goodbye, then it sounded like they will not see each other again for good, and Virak watched her walked away, and then he felt like want to say something to her or ask to see her again, but it did not seem right and word just did not come out from his mouth, and then he thought that if the Goddess want them to be together she will bring them to cross path again at a better circumstance somewhere else.

Virak opened up the trunk of his old Corolla to recheck his food supply one more time to make sure that he got everything he need for two days camping in the wood; he got two cases of beer, a bottle of Hennessey cognac, a cooler full of meats, fruits and eggs, and another cooler full of ice; and the other equipment and supply like charcoal, lighter fluid, paper plate and plastic utensil, some gallon jugs of water, fishing spear and pole, an axe, a machete, and a boom box with some extra battery.

He drove along the main highway north that went around the island along the shoreline, the distant was not too far but the driving took longer time through these hilly terrain and narrow lane in many sharp turns road that he could not drive in higher speed.

Feast with the Men of the Imperial Navy

Virak came to the spot that Hanako had shown him on the map, and when he looked around there was neither farm nor house anywhere in sight; he thought she was right he like this place because it was isolated from any civilization, and there was an old stone temple near a small lake that was surrounded by tall trees and old growth forest in the middle of the mountain.

It was so beautiful and tranquil, that made him feel serene. Virak parked the car near the stone temple, and paused for a moment scanning and observing the surrounding area for anything unusual, wildlife and any unseen danger.

He went in the old temple that covered by tile roof, he could not read the characters on the wall and the column, so he could not tell what the temple was build for or dedicated to any deity? There were signs and artifacts that were left there to let him know that people had come to worship here.

Then Virak setup some fruit and cigarette as an offering, and he burned the candle and incent that were left there in order to ask the spirit that might dwell in the area for permission to use the surrounding area for camping overnight and the permission to build a camp fire.

Virak moved the car to a suitable spot under some big trees near the lake side that was already had an old spot for camp fire with some ring stones; first he pulled out the axe to get some dead firewood in the forest and started to build the fire in the stone ring, and pulled the boom box out and tuned in to the Arm Force radio listening to the classic Rock n Roll.

And then he started to build his cover shelter by tying a poncho to the side of the car and laying some leaves underneath the mat as his bedding, and then he popped a cold beer and poured a few drops down to the ground as an offering to the forest spirit, and sat on a beach chair watching the calm beauty of the surrounding forest and the occasional fish jumping out of the calm clear water of the lake surface.

The sun was just about to go down below the tree top, and the forest became darker and started to get covered by the misty shroud; Virak thrown some more wood on the fire to make the camp fire burn brighter and started to cook steak and some other stuff that he bought from the PX.

After the food was done, Virak fixed a small plate and poured some beer in the plastic cup to make an offering to the forest spirit by placing it under the big tree at the side of the lake, and then he ate the rare steak slowly and washed it down with cold beer.

After dinner, the forest enveloped in deep blue darkness and the stars appeared in the sky about. Virak poured himself some cognac in the plastic cup, and then he laid back in the beach chair, sipping the cognac, smoking a cigar, and looking into the abyss beyond the darkness thinking about Cambodia, the northern jungle, and everybody that he left behind and now he had a chance to get closer, but yet everything was still so far away beyond the sea and it was still under the communist control.

At around midnight, the Arm Force Radio was starting to sign off by playing national anthem the Star Spangle Banner, and then Virak started to get ready for a good night sleep; he dropped some big logs on the fire and hope that it will last for the rest of the night, and he drank a quart of water from the jug to rehydrate his body system, and crawled into the sleeping bag that he'd laid on the mat under the poncho.

Virak was thinking about to turn the radio off before he fall asleep, and he heard the usual thing every night in the radio of the last announcement "Ladies and gentlemen 'KI MI GA YO'" and then they play the Japanese national anthem.

After it was finished, he reached up to turn the box off and zipped up the sleeping bag, and he clear all his thought and closed his eyes, but for some unknown reason Virak still could hear the Japanese music, and he thought that the radio turner was malfunction and he should pull the battery out.

So he got out of the sleeping bag and looked at the radio that all light were out but why he still…... Virak froze for a moment and felt the hair on his neck stood up, and then he was slowly trying to feel for the axe handles and his K-Bar. From the corner of his eyes, he saw a group of men appeared in the gray shadow behind some trees and they moved closer toward the camp fire that made him tighten his grip on the K-bar and the axe handle.

When they came closer to the fire, Virak could see that they all appeared to be Japanese men in uniform and most had blood stain on them. Then by instinct, Virak said his greeting welcoming them to the camp fire, and then put the axe down but kept the K-bar on his hand to show any potential enemy that he determine not to go down without a fight.

The man, who was closest to Virak, seemed to be an officer and the leader of the group, smiled and told him not to be alarm since his group came in peace; Virak did not know what language they spoke but it seemed that they understood each other.

They all appeared to be friendly except a few of them who looked withdrawn, but anyway Virak offered everybody to join him for food and drink, and when he was just about to open the car trunk the leader told him to sit down and not to bother since he will have some of his men cook and serve.

Virak reached in the car to open the trunk and sat next to the leader, few men pulled the cooler from the trunk and started to pass around the cold beer, and put the meat and vegetable on the rack over the fire, and later they passed the meat plate and plastic cup, and a man went around the camp fire pouring cognac for everybody.

After the meal, they still continued with the drinking, smoking and toasting to one another. The whole time, Virak was talking to the leader about the life they had; Virak told him about his life in Cambodia before the war, and the officer told Virak about his life in Osaka before the other war also; while Virak was listening to the description of his life during the peace time that they planned to move to Hawaii, his childhood home in the outskirt of the city, his family and Emperor Hiro Hito whom he revered, and every descriptions that he made had came into Virak mind just like the video stream, and at the end everybody stood up, they had the last toast and the officer said.

"My men and I we thank you for your hospitality and also tell Hanako that we thank her for showing you the way here so that give us an opportunity to have a great time with you, thank you have a good night sleep"

Virak woke up to a bright sunny morning still warm and cozy in the sleeping bag, but he could feel the chilling effect of the mountain air on his face while the camp fire was almost dying out. Virak got up to relief himself while his head and eyelids were still heavy like rock, and then he thrown some logs on the fire, ate some food that left over on the cooking rack, drank a beer and crawled right back into the sleeping bag.

When he woke up the second time it was already afternoon. Around the camp fire, there were plates, cups, beer cans and the food particles lying strewn around on the ground, and this scene had became a puzzle to him because there were around more than a dozen dirty plates on the ground with a lot of food left in them, and Virak remembered that he did not bring that much food with him here when he came out from Futenma, he thought that was strange or maybe they brought some with them to join with his, or they just not a big eater.

Virak started to clean himself up and did a little field day around the camp before leaving the place; he thrown all leftover food particles into the wood as an offering to the lesser spirit in the forest and the wild life, and he bagged all the trash and bring them back to the air station. Virak stayed at the camp to enjoy the forest until late in the afternoon, and then he started to pack, put out the fire, did the final clean up of the area, and moved the car to the stone temple.

Virak took a few minutes, went inside to burn some candle and incent invoking his thank to the spirit for let him used the area, and then he drove off the mountain back to Futenma; on the way, he felt calm and serene, the alcohol effect was gone, his head was clear, and he thought that he was kind of feeling happy and relax and he should do this more often by going back up there to party with those guys, but unfortunately the weather was lousy because it rain most of the time on his next five or six weekends that he couldn't enjoy any outdoor activity at all. So he was just join up with fellow marines had some barbeque and beer on base at the beer garden, went to downtown to have some nice meal, or he just went to sit at the seawall watching the sunset.

On a cold early Sunday morning, Virak walked alone on the sidewalk of downtown Naha looking for a noodle shop that people told him where he could have the best soba of all the noodle shop on the island. Suddenly, a lady who was bundle up in her hooded overcoat, stepped out real fast from a photo shop, and then they collided before he could react to get out of her way, and the bags and packages that she had on her hand were dropped, and spilling the contents onto the sidewalk, while she was stumbling backward.

With his quick reaction, Virak grabbed her arm and pulled her waist to him in order to prevent her from falling; the lady said something real fast in Japanese and Virak was quickly apologize and asked if she was all right, and when the lady looked up from under the hood Virak immediately recognized a familiar face that he had seen over a month ago at the Cherry Blossom Festival in Nago, it was Hanako, and she was surprised for bumping into him and she exclaimed.

"Oh, it's you again, I am sorry that I am not careful ..." Then he cut her short.

"No, it's not yours alone; it's my fault too for being in your path at the wrong time, Hi Hanako"

"Hi, it is still my fault, and what are you doing here so early in the morning?"

"Oh I'm just looking for a particular noodle shop; and you what are you doing here in downtown so early?"

"I came to get some supply for a ceremony"

And then they realized that they were the only two people on the sidewalk that were holding onto each other. Virak invited her to join him in the noodle shop if she knew where it was and that she agreed to join him. Virak released her waist, they looked at her bags and packages that spilled on the sidewalk and started to retrieve them.

Then Virak saw a big black and white portrait photo of a Japanese man in military uniform that he recognized right away, it was the picture of that officer at the night on the mountain who knew Hanako, and then he was just about to say something about him to Hanako but he thought he should wait till later.

Virak helped to carry the big packages for her and they walked to the noodle shop that was just a few blocks away; the restaurant was packed with customers, there were lots of big round tables with big family enjoyed their morning meal, and they were lucky that Hanako managed to get a table for two at a corner. They ordered some soba and a few specialized dishes that she want Virak to try it out, they had their meal at leisure and were so comfortable to be with each other company that it seemed like they did not want to leave too soon until two hours later that they started to walk out from there.

Virak drove her around downtown Naha to pick up all of the things she need, and he thought that he will drive her back to Nago in the north, but she said that she already arrange for her ride back, and so he asked to see her again sometime next weekend, but she said that she will be busy with the ceremony and she promised to go out with him on the weekend after next.

Virak told her that he was so very happy that they will see each other again. Two weeks later, Virak went to pick her up at Nago and they drove around to visit Ikeh Island in the South China Sea on the west side of Okinawa; they visit some resort, had nice lunch at a seafood restaurant, visit temples, and came to sit on the seawall talking and holding each other; and in the evening he brought her back to Nago at sunset.

The Love Motel

On this island, just like many other places in Asia there were places so call 'Love Motel', they were some kind of seclude hotel without any front desk or lobby, they were just kind of row of garage with the rollup electric door that stay open at all time to let patron know that the room was available.

When any client decide to stay in any room all he have to do is pushing the button to close the garage door and the door to the inner room will be unlock, and inside the room was quite a luxury, there will be a nice clean fluffy bed of course, a small refrigerator with all kind of complimentary drink, a clean bathroom with a Jacuzzi tub, a big screen TV.

Patron can order hot food dish on the phone and it will be delivered through a small opening at the back door to ensure the patron privacy that their face will never be seen by anyone; all dealing will be pay by cash only no check, no credit card, no receipt, no name and no witness. When the patron decide to leave all he had to do just pick up the phone, pay the amount require at the back door that will enable the garage door to be open when push the button.

On one weekend, Virak was with Hanako on their third date, and it was raining so hard with strong wind; Hanako said that there was a big storm somewhere in the Pacific Ocean, and then he suggested to Hanako that they should go to some quiet dry place to talk and relax.

He drove to a Love Motel in a quiet seclude area away from town. He got into one of the garage and push the button to close the rolling door, and he walked around to open the door for her and they went inside the room, it was a nice an cozy room; he asked her to order them some hot food, and they were just sat around talking long after they had finish their meal, because Virak did not want to rush thing and beside he did not fully understand how she feel about being in the Love Motel.

Later he suggested that they should try out the Jacuzzi, but after she went into the bathroom to change he had a second thought about being in the water in the middle of typhoon rainstorm that was in full swing outside, but then he ran out of option to get them out of their clothes, since he did not want to get her undress right on the spot that it didn't seem right; while he was lost in his thought for trying to get a woman naked, he got undressed himself, wrapped a towel around, and tried to test the water in the Jacuzzi.

Then Virak sensed that she walked pass behind his back which he could smell a trail of her scent, and when he looked up there next to the bed stood a Goddess Avatar, she was buck naked like a jay bird with only in her high heel, and she was just stood there smiling with an intense look.

Shining light radiated from her body like a divine Goddess herself who came to visit him in that secludes 'Love Motel'. Virak was shocked and awed; He walked slowly toward her or he might say then that her divine power drawn him to her like a magnet.

He stood in front of her looked into her doe eyes and plants a kiss lightly on her lips…… Despite his impatient urge, Virak paused a moment to admire her beautiful form like petal of spring cherry blossom…… While the Pacific typhoon was battering the island outside in full vigor, then she cried out with her body shaking in her own storm. And while Virak was under the tremendous pressure of her squeezing force, he could feel his crisis coming, and as usual his face sheltered at her neck, stretched his legs back and busted out……

A few months later, Hanako was ready to get married with her fiancée, so they spent their last day together in a secluded 'Love Motel', since she knew that after her married ceremony she may never have freedom or another chance to enjoy these wild exciting sexes ever again. They thanked and cherished each other friendship and the most precious time that they had spent together, and she promise to tell her great grandfather about Virak if she ever meet with him later on in any dimension, and then they said their last farewell in each other arms.

Eventually, his oversea tour of duty finally had came to an end, and before Virak left the island, he grabbed a couple cases of beer, a magnum bottle of excellent sake, a few bottles of selected reserved cognac, and some food; and then he drove up north into the mountain to have his last farewell feasting and toasting with the members of the Japanese Imperial Navy, but this time he was honored to have a chance to meet the marines from the old war era who were co existed side by side with their old enemy on this small rock of an island in the Pacific Ocean called Okinawa that Virak hope to see again in the future.

END
Of this story till next dimension
With the next Avatar

www.ingramcontent.com/pod-product-compliance
Lightning Source LLC
Chambersburg PA
CBHW061631040426
42446CB00010B/1358